P9-ELO-193

The Complete Book Of
GREYHOUNDS

Edited by
JULIA BARNES

HOWELL
BOOK HOUSE
NEW YORK

Copyright © 1994 by Ringpress Books Limited.

All rights reserved. No part of this book may be reproduced or transmitted in any form or by any means, electronic or mechanical, including photocopying, recording, or by any information storage and retrieval system, without permission in writing from the Publisher.

HOWELL BOOK HOUSE
A Simon & Schuster Macmillan company,
1633 Broadway, New York, NY 10019.

MACMILLAN is a registered trademark of Macmillan, Inc.

Library of Congress Cataloging-in-Publication data

The Complete book of greyhounds / edited by Julia Barnes.
   1st American edition

    p.   cm.
  ISBN 0-87605-189-1
  1. Greyhounds.   I. Barnes, Julia.
SF429.G67834 1994
636.7'53 – dc20

94-9143
CIP

10 9 8 7 6 5 4
Printed and bound in Singapore

CONTENTS

4

THE CONTRIBUTORS

The *Complete Book of Greyhounds* is written by leading specialists who have unparalleled knowledge of the breed.

CHARLES BLANNING is the Keeper of the English Greyhound Stud Book and Secretary of the National Coursing Club. He writes articles on coursing for *The Field*, *The Sporting Press*, *The Racing Post* and *The Greyhound Star*. He has has co-written a number of books including *The Waterloo Cup: The First 150 Years.* and *The Coursing Year*. In *The Complete Book Of Greyhounds* he writes on the Origins and Early History of the Greyhound (Chapter One), and takes a look at the sport of coursing (Chapter Sixteen).

JOHN KOHNKE BV.Sc (Sydney) RDA is recognised as an international authority on the practical feeding of Greyhounds, and he has vast experience of treating racing injuries. He has written a specialist book, *Veterinary Advice for Greyhound Owners*, and has a regular column in *The Greyhound Star*, Britain's leading Greyhound paper, and the *National Greyhound Review* in America. In this book he writes on the Physiology of the Greyhound (Chapter Two), Feeding and Nutrition (Chapter Three), and Treating Racing Injuries (Chapter Fifteen).

DR MALCOLM B. WILLIS is Senior Lecturer in Animal Breeding and Genetics in the Faculty of Agriculture at the University of Newcastle upon Tyne. He specialises in the study of genetics in relation to dogs, and is known worldwide for his books, magazine articles, seminars and lectures. In this book he turns his attention to the genetic make-up of the Greyhound (Chapter Four).

PATRICK SAWARD is a regular columnist in Britain's daily newspaper, *The Racing Post*. A specialist in breeding and pedigrees, he looks at the international bloodlines shared by racing Greyhounds (Chapter Eight).

Leading journalists **STEVE SMITH** (Britain and Ireland), **TIM HORAN** (USA), **DAVID BRASCH** (Australia), **RON KILPIN** and **J.B. VAN MEEUWEN** (New Zealand) give the lowdown on the sport around the world. **TIM HORAN** also provides profiles of America's sporting superstars (Chapter Seventeen), and **PETER QUILTY** and **PAUL MUNT** write about top dogs in Australia.

The top racing trainers reveal the secrets of their success in Chapter Eight in a series of interviews (conducted by **Errol Blyth**, **Steve Smith**, and **Tim Horan**) with the legendary **GEOFF DE MULDER**, winner of two English Derbies, leading British breeder **NICK SAVVA**, Britain's Champion trainer **LINDA MULLINS**, the great American trainer **HERB 'DUTCH' KOERNER**, who handled the famous Flashy Sir award winner, Dutch Bahama, the highly successful **RON BECKNER**, who has won most of the major American Stakes, **MICHAEL O'SULLIVAN**, winner of the 1992 Irish Derby, and **PAUL WHEELER**, who follows in the footsteps of his father Alan, running one of the top kennels in Australia.

CYNTHIA BRANIGAN, based in America, and **JOHANNA BEUMER**, based in Britain, both devote their lives to caring for ex-racing Greyhounds. They share their vast sum of knowledge and expertise to so that new owners can help their dogs to adapt to a new life as a family companion (Chapter Ten).

IAN BOND has been breeding Greyhounds for the show ring for the last twenty years and he is an International Championship Show judge of the breed. He has bred, owned and handled a Best In Show winner, and he is a regular contributor to the canine press. In *The Complete Book of Greyhounds* he highlights leading show bloodlines (Chapter Six), provides a history of the show Greyhound and the leading kennels (Chapter Eleven), gives his expert analysis of the Breed Standard (Chapter Twelve), and discusses feeding and training methods as he gives an insight into the world of showing Greyhounds (Chapter Thirteen).

Britain's top Greyhound photographer, **STEVE NASH**, has provided the vast majority of the illustrations for this book. Well-known for his superb action photos, Steve has used his skills to provide extensive photographic coverage of schooling, grooming and massage, and handling Greyhounds in the show ring. He is also responsible for the magnificent sequence on Greyhound movement in the first colour section. His extensive library has also been used to provide the most comprehensive pictorial coverage of the Greyhound ever published.

Editor **JULIA BARNES** was the first editor of the Greyhound Star on its launch in 1983. She formerly trained her own Greyhound under the British permit scheme and more recently kept Greyhounds as pets. Her first book *George Curtis: Training Greyhounds* was a huge success and is now in its third edition. She has also edited three editions of Greyhound racing's outstanding reference book, the *Greyhound Fact File*.

Acknowledgements

My thanks to all those who have helped with this project. The many distinguished contributors have not only provided excellent written material, but many have also helped with photographs and other illustrations. John Kohnke has supplied a number of photos, and his tables relating to Feeding and Nutrition and to Treating Racing Injuries are of tremendous value. Thanks are also due to John for helping to source material relating to the racing scene in Australia and New Zealand. Ian Bond has assembed some top-quality photographs of show Greyhounds in Britain, America and Scandinavia. Stanley Petter Jr. (America) has also provided a wonderful selection of his Hewly Greyhounds.

Thanks to Charles Blanning for the loan of his valuable books, and for help with illustrations for the historical and coursing sections. Steve Nash has proved once again that he has no peer in the realm of Greyhound photography.

Finally, this book would not be complete without a special tribute to the Greyhound - the most beautiful of creatures - who has enhanced so many people's lives whether on the racing track, on the coursing field, in the show ring, and perhaps most importantly, as a much-loved member of the family.

JULIA BARNES, MAY 1994.

Chapter One

ORIGINS OF THE BREED

COMPANION OF PRINCES

The Greyhound has always been the prince of dogs and the dog of princes. Its claimed descent from the desert dogs of the pharaohs and the Arabian sheiks has been so enthusiastically documented by all writers on the breed that you begin to wonder, sometimes, whether they are trying to compensate for the less regal image of the Greyhound today. It is almost as if the canine historians feel that the medium of millions of dollars and pounds of betting turnover needs a few smart relations from the past. These ancient dogs of the Egyptians and Arabians were the companions of princes. They rode on his camels, wore his lucky charms and amulets, and, most significantly in a nomadic culture, shared his tent. To this day, the true Romanies never allow their animals inside the caravan.

There is no doubt from archaeological remains that a dog very similar to the Greyhound existed in the Middle East 4,000 years ago. Whether this was definitely the root stock from which sprang the Greyhound, the Saluki and the Afghan Hound would be difficult to establish. We know from nineteenth century paintings of Greyhounds that art can take some dreadful liberties with reality, and the dog on the walls of Egyptian tombs and on Greek vases could well be a dead ringer for a Greyhound – or any other hunting longdog.

The accepted wisdom is that the Greyhound type originated in Egypt, spread through Arabia, and then fanned out through Persia in the East to Russia and India, and through Greece in the West, passing through Imperial Rome on its way to the edges of the Empire in Britain and Ireland. As it travelled, it is argued, Charles Darwin's best-known theory came into play and evolution perfected the long-coated Afghan for the cold winds of the Hindu Kush, and the short-coated Greyhound for the sunny climes of Altcar and Co. Galway. There is something wrong there, surely? If the Greyhound had evolved its own coat in the wilds of Britannia and Hibernia, it would have looked more like an insulated Water Spaniel; and why does the Saluki, the true dog of the desert, have a long coat?

THE SPORTING DOG

Whatever the truth of the matter, we can say with certainty that the Greyhound has changed very little since 500 BC. Coins and other artifacts from Greece show short-coated Greyhounds of a very modern stamp. The reason why the Greyhound breed has remained frozen in time for so long is the nature of its use. The Greyhound, like the dogs of the pharaohs and the Arabian princes, was always a sporting, not a hunting dog, and its quarry was the hare. From earliest times it thrilled its owners with its speed and grace, not its ability to kill. By the first century AD, the coursing of the hare had become well-documented in Roman literature. Ovid wrote in his *Metamorphoses*:

Forerunners of the Greyhound: Mural from an Egyptian tomb of 2200 BC.

A Greyhound coursing a hare on Roman vases, found near Hadrian's Wall.

As when the impatient Greyhound, slipped from far,
Bounds o'er the glade to course the fearful hare
She in her speed does all her safety lie.
And he with double speed pursues his prey,
O'erruns her at the sitting turns; but licks
His chops in vain; yet blows upon the flix,
She seeks the shelter which the neighbouring covert gives,
And gaining it, she doubts if she yet lives.

All the elements of the modern course are here: the "impatient" Greyhound is deliberately held back to give the hare a fair start, and the time-honoured battle between the faster dog and the slower but more agile hare ends when the hare escapes. It is not hunting to a death but the exciting spectacle of the dog and hare in full flight which thrills.

The most complete picture of the Greyhound – and coursing of the time – is given by Flavius Arrianus or Arrian, a Roman citizen of Greek extraction, who lived at the beginning of the second century AD. Arrian was coursing's first apologist, and he wrote in his treatise, which lay undiscovered in the vaults of the Vatican until translated into English in the nineteenth century:

"The true sportsman does not take out his dogs to destroy the hares, but for the sake of the course, and the contest between the dogs and the hares, and is glad if the hare escapes."

Arrian, as did Ovid, refers to the Greyhound as the Celtic Hound, and thought that it originated from Gallia Celtica, or modern-day France. "The more opulent Celts, who live in luxury, course in the following manner. They send out hare finders early in the morning to look over such places as are likely to afford hares in form; and a messenger brings word if they have found any, and what number. They then go out themselves, and having started the hare, slip the dogs after her, and follow on horseback."

Arrian describes the less wealthy coursers "walking-up" hares in a long line, in much the same way as at a small meeting in England today. The importance of giving due law and sportsmanship was emphasised by Arrian: "Whoever courses with Greyhounds, should neither slip them near the hare, nor more than a brace at a time."

ARRIVAL IN BRITAIN

It was, of course, just a step from Gallia Celtica to Britain. The Celtic Hound may have already been popular in Britain before the Roman invasion, but if the Romans did not bring the Greyhound with them, they imported something even more important – the brown hare. The indigenous hare of the British Isles is the blue hare, which lives in high uplands in Britain and everywhere in Ireland. The Romans obviously considered the bigger and faster European or brown hare as a more suitable quarry for their Greyhounds, and it has flourished in the lowlands and downland of Britain ever since. Two twin jars found near Hadrian's Wall show a hare on one and a Greyhound on the other.

In the Dark Ages, after the departure of the Romans, the Greyhound continued to be the prized possession of the rich and noble. A ninth century manuscript shows a Saxon chieftain with his huntsman and a brace of Greyhounds, and in 1014 King Canute set the pattern for the next seven hundred years when he inaugurated the notorious Forest Laws. These reserved vast tracts of the country for hunting for royalty and the nobility, who were the only classes entitled to own Greyhounds. Dogs found in the ownership of lower orders had their feet mutilated to prevent them from hunting.

This may seem harsh in an egalitarian and democratic age, but one thing that it ensured was that the Greyhound breed was carefully nurtured by those privileged to enjoy its ownership. Chaucer's worldly monk in the *Canterbury Tales* spent lavishly on his Greyhounds:

Grehoundes he hadde as swifte as fowel in flight;
Of prikyng and of huntyng for the hare
Was al his lust, for no cost wolde he spare.

Note that in 1350 Chaucer is using the term 'Greyhound' and that its quarry is the hare. Some Greyhound histories have devoted considerable space to speculating on the different form of 'Greyhounds' which may have hunted deer or hare, which may have been rough or smooth-coated. The evidence dates back to the years before Christ, however, that there was already a smooth-coated dog which was used exclusively to course the hare. How the name 'Greyhound' evolved remains lost in the mists of time. The Romans called it a Celtic Hound, while in an exchange of courtesies, some people think that the English term Greyhound evolved from "grek" or "greek" hound, as the Saxons thought the dog had originated in Greece. Another commonly accepted theory is that Greyhound is a corruption of "gazehound", or a dog which hunts by sight only.

IMPROVING THE BREED

The restriction of the ownership of Greyhounds to people of rank, however autocratic it may seem now, ensured that every effort was made to improve the breed. Edmund de Langley, a son of King Edward III, wrote in his *Mayster of Game* in the 1370s:

The Greihound should have a long hede and somedele grete, ymaked in the manner of a luce; a good large mouth and good sessours, the one again the other, so that the nether jaws passe not them above, ne that thei above passe not him neither.
The neck should be grete and longe, and bowed as a swanne's neck.
Her shuldres as a roebuck; the for leggs streght and grete ynow, and nought to hind legges; the feet straught and round as a catte, and great cleas; the boones and the joyntes of the cheyne grete and hard as the chyne of an hert; the thighs great and squarred as an hare; the houghs streight, and not crompyng as of an oxe.
A catte's tayle, making a ring at eend, but not to hie.
Of all manere of Greihoundes there byn both good and evel; Natheless the best hewe is rede falow, with a black moselle.

Not many track people would agree with the last comment that the best colour of a Greyhound is red fawn with a black muzzle, but many coursing owners would agree with de Langley. Even in its early history, therefore, the Greyhound was being bred to conform to an accepted standard of appearance, even to a warning against his "jaws" not being over or undershot. Writing in her *Boke of St Albans* in 1486 Dame Juliana Berners, Abbess of Sopwell Priory at St Albans, summed up de Langley's points in the memorable doggerel:

A Grehound shold be heeded lyke a snake
And neckyd lyke a drake,
Backed lyke a beam,
Syded lyke a bream,
*Foot*ed lyke *a catte,*
Tayllyd lyke a ratte.

De Langley also had some hints on training:
The childe should lede the houndes to scombre twies in the day, in the mornyng and in the evenyng, so that the sonne be up, espaecially in wynter. Then shuld he lat him runne and play longe in a faire medow in the sonne, and then kombe every hounde after other, and wipe him with a grette wisp of straw, and this shall he do every mornyng.

COMPETITIVE COURSING

As far as it is possible to surmise, the ancient coursers ran their dogs merely for the excitement of the course itself, "the contest between the dogs and the Hares", as Arrian writes, not a contest between the dogs themselves. Courses were restricted to a brace of dogs in the interests of sportsmanship, not to try one against the other. Perhaps it took the new thrusting commercial world of the late Tudors to make competition the essential element, a world in which the tournament disappeared and horse racing began, and hunting became a chic spectacle and coursing a form of racing.

What we know for certain is that it was Elizabeth I who instructed the Duke of Norfolk to draw up the rules by which the winners of courses could be judged, which implies that competitive coursing was already popular and needed an accepted code. Shakespeare, who makes various references to coursing and Greyhounds, also provides in *The Merry Wives of Windsor* the first Greyhound owner who would not acknowledge that he was beaten:

Master Slender: "How does your fallow Greyhound? I heard say he was outrun on Cotsale."
Page: "It would not be judged, Sir."

"Fallow", of course, is the modern colour fawn, and "Cotsale" is the Cotswold hills, where there is a coursing club to this day. The rules by which courses are judged have changed since Elizabethan times, but only marginally.

The story of the modern Greyhound really starts in the east of England. This part of the country has been celebrated for its dogs and coursing since the early 1600s when James I journeyed to the obscure village of Fordham on the Suffolk-Cambridge border to try the strength of its legendary hares. The royal party lodged at the *Griffin Inn* in a little country town, a few miles to

Coursing in the reign of James I, from a print dated 1608.

the south, called Newmarket. In time James built a hunting lodge at Newmarket, and as matches between the horses of his followers became as important as those between the king's Greyhounds, Newmarket's march towards becoming the racing capital of the world had begun. In 1619 James ordered his "verderer", Sir Robert Vernon, to turn down a hundred hares and a hundred partridges at Newmarket every year, and the hare has flourished on these chalklands ever since.

THE CREATOR OF MODERN COURSING
The Earl of Orford deserves the title of the creator of modern coursing and therefore of the modern Greyhound, when in 1776 he created the first public coursing club at Swaffham in Norfolk. Previously, coursing matches were private, but the public clubs, running stakes for a number of dogs rather than a succession of individual matches, made the Greyhound and coursing public property. Exactly the same trend took place in horse racing at the same time. Swaffham was followed by Ashdown in 1780, by Malton in 1781, and by Newmarket in 1805.

Lord Orford was a celebrated character in the sporting world of the late 1700s, and liked to drive his own carriage drawn by four stags. Unfortunately on one day when his lordship had almost reached Newmarket in his eccentric conveyance, the Essex hounds picked up his scent – with four stags in the traces they could hardly miss it – and were soon in full cry as Lord Orford careered into Newmarket at full pelt. In the nick of time he sped through the gateway of an inn, and the ostlers slammed the doors shut on the baying pack. Some stories claim that the inn was called *The Ram* after the incident as 'ram' can mean a strong smell. What is certain is that it stood on the site of today's *Rutland Arms*, which was built in 1815 when the old pub was demolished. All this, however, pales in significance compared with his lordship's obsession with Greyhounds.

Warrant wins the Orford Cup in its first year. An historical incident, by Samuel Howett, published in 1807.

Apparently, Orford tried every which way to produce the perfect Greyhound. At one time he had a hundred dogs in his kennels, and is reputed to have tried crosses with Italian Greyhounds, Lurchers, and most notoriously with the Bulldog. The Bulldog cross is one of the hoariest of Greyhound legends. There is no doubt that Orford tried it, as did some others afterwards, but there is no evidence that the blood survived. At least one authority claims that they were useless and Orford gave it up. Oddly enough, one Bulldog-Greyhound cross actually ran in the mid 1800s and packed it in after 400 hundred yards, although the theory was that the cross would give the Greyhound more grit. Another old legend blames the prejudice against the colour brindle on the Bulldog-cross, while yet another does the same for light fawn!

The well-known breeders Captain Ellis and Mr Dunn managed to slip some odd creatures into the Stud Book at the beginning of this century. These were crosses between Mr Dunn's Afghan, Baz, and Captain Ellis's Greyhound bitches. They turned out to be useless, and only one, Woodcar Buzzer, ever ran at a public meeting in 1914 when it was promptly beaten. Edward Dent, the breeder and trainer of Fullerton, saw Dunn at a meeting with one of his Afghans and told him: "All you want is an organ to make you complete."

The Rules of the Swaffham Society would have hardly encouraged much experiment with Lurchers, as Rule XIV stated: "No rough-haired dog to be deemed a Greyhound." This would seem at odds with the claims of some writers on the origin of the Greyhound, who cheerfully write about all forms of hunting hounds – Wolfhounds, Deerhounds, and all – from Saxon times to the eighteenth century as if they were all Greyhounds. The thesis seems to be that in the late eighteenth century the modern Greyhound derived from this polyglot selection, whereas, as we have seen, the smooth-coated Greyhound which coursed the hare was in existence before Christ.

Richard Blome's engraving of coursing in 1608, in the reign of James I, shows the timeless elements of coursing: two smooth-coated Greyhounds, beaters, and the hare. Writing some thirty years earlier, Markham saw long-coated dogs as "held most proper for vermin, or wild beasts", while the smooth-coated Greyhound "are of all dogs whatsoever the most noble and princely, strong, nimble, swift and valiant; and though of slender, and very fine proportions, yet so well knit and coupled together, and so seconded with spirit and mettle, that they are master of all other dogs whatsoever." Lord Orford was not so popular with his family as with the sporting public. He had inherited the title from his father, son of the famous politician Sir Robert Walpole, 1st Earl of

Orford, who had built Houghton Hall. Orford's expenditure on Greyhounds was enormous and eventually he was forced to sell the family's splendid collection of paintings to Catherine the Great of Russia. They hang in the Hermitage Museum in St Petersburg to this day. In fact Orford had inherited huge debts from his father and grandfather for the building of Houghton Hall, and his reputation as the black sheep of the family (no portrait of him hangs in the house even now) is somewhat unfair. The standard treatment in the eighteenth century for eccentrics was to lock them up out of the public gaze, and this fate eventually befell his lordship. The legend goes that on the day his bitch, Czarina, was to run a match on Newmarket Heath, Orford escaped from his prison. The old man, without a topcoat on a freezing winter's day, and clad only in his customary black suit and tricorn hat, watched Czarina defeat Maria, raised his hat to his bitch, and fell back off his pony stone dead. The course is said to have taken place on Chippenham Field, which in those days stretched from Chippenham Park across to the Limekilns gallops on the Bury Road where the noble lord expired. As Czarina is reckoned to have been whelped in 1781, she would have been ten at the time and won 47 matches without loss.

COLONEL THOMAS THORNTON

Orford's Greyhounds came under the hammer at Tattersall's, many of them, including Czarina, being knocked down to the Yorkshireman, Colonel Thornton. Thomas Thornton was born in 1757, the son of a very wealthy Yorkshire squire, and, soon after coming of age, he bought the estate of Allerton Mauleverer for £110,000 from the Duke of York, reputedly with money won from the Duke and his friends in gaming. With typical arrogance, Thornton renamed it Thornville Royal. Thornton was a considerable athlete, once covering four miles in thirty-two minutes and jumping 5ft 9ins, his own height, to land bets. Mainly, however, he devoted his life to breeding everything from racehorses to Pointers, and to killing animals. When he moved from Thornville Royal to an estate in Bedfordshire he took his Greyhounds, wearing coats embroidered with the details of their successes, a wagon loaded with guns, fishing-rods, and other hunting hardware, plus a menagerie of wild animals which he used to turn loose and hunt.

After Thornton had bought Czarina at the dispersal sale, she whelped her first litter at the advanced age of thirteen, which included Claret. He was the sire of the legendary litter out of Phyllis, which included Snowball and Major. Snowball, who despite his name was a black dog, is remembered in legend for the course on Flixton Brow, a few miles west of where the Sherburn

Czarina and Maria in the celebrated match which ended with the death of Lord Orford.

The legendary Snowball, immortalised in verse by Sir Walter Scott.

Farmers meeting takes place to this day. Snowball, his sister, and a sapling twelve months old found a hare near Flixton and coursed it down the steepest part of the Wold. The hare then turned back and took them up and down the hill at least twice, until only Snowball was left in pursuit. After a course of over four miles Snowball drove the hare into Flixton village where he pulled it down in the middle of the street.

Fairytale apart, Snowball was undoubtedly a great Greyhound, winning four cups and over thirty matches. Goodlake records that he won the Malton Cup for his owner Major Topham, Thornton's close friend, in 1798 and 1800. It was left to Sir Walter Scott to immortalise him in verse:

'Twas when fleet Snowball's head was waxen grey,
A luckless lev'ret met him on his way;
Who knows not Snowball? He whose race renowned
Is still victorious on each coursing ground.
Swaffham, Newmarket, and the Roman Camp
Have seen them victors o'er each meaner stamp.
In vain the youngling sought with doubling wile
The hedge, the hill, the thicket or the stile,
Experience sage the lack of speed supplied,
And in the gap he sought, – the victim died.

Who knows not Snowball? Absolutely no one by the time Thornton and Topham had finished shouting about him. When he was retired, Topham inserted a notice in the press reading: "Snowball, the property of Major Topham of Wold Cottage, Yorkshire, and who was supposed to be the best Greyhound that ever was, won four cups and above thirty matches, does not run any more." A Mr Durand, sick to death of Snowball mania, offered to run his Bellissima against any dog by Snowball or related to him for a thousand guineas to put a stop once and for all time to the "pompous and repeated puffings of the Flixton Wolds", as one letter in the press called them. Thornton answered the challenge with Snowball's brother, Major, and the match was due to be run on Sutton Heights near Carshalton in Surrey. On the great day a huge crowd gathered to see Major led out wearing a coat with Thornton's coat of arms on one side and the motto embroidered in gold on the other "Major aut ne plus ultra", or "Nothing can be greater than Major." The old brindle, now eleven years old, stripped for action and Mr Durand was so overwhelmed by Major's looks and the Thornton showmanship, he declared he had no chance against such a dog and handed over the pot without bothering to run. On behalf of the throng he begged Thornton to let Major run alone. A boxed hare was released and, according to one account, Major leapt upon it "in one bound" and killed it. Thornton died in exile in France whence he had fled in 1817 to escape his creditors. His last refuge in London had been a house in the Edgware Road with a mantrap beneath each window, a loaded punt gun in the hall trained on the front door, and two boarhounds running loose to back it up.

KING COB

Major Topham seems to have been more level-headed than his friend, and was one of the first people to keep proper pedigrees of his dogs and to support the notion of public sires. Snowball's status as a popular hero and public sire was a measure of how the importance of coursing and the Greyhound grew nationally in the early 1800s. To begin with, successful breeders as far as possible used their own stock, and some would prefer a dog to be put down rather than be bred from by someone who might run against them in the future.

   Captain Daintree, who had a private kennel of over a hundred dogs in the 1830s, was one of the first to advertise a public stud dog. His King Cob, winner of the Newmarket Cup and the St Leger,

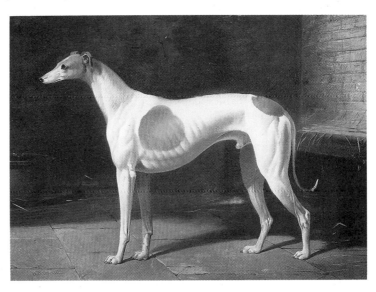

Captain Daintree's King Cob (Ion – Kate), the first influential public stud dog. Whelped in 1838, he won the Newmarket Cup in 1840 and the St Leger at Barton-on-Humber in 1841.

was just as successful at stud as on the field. John Jardine, a member of the famous Dumfriesshire sporting family which continues to this day as the Buchanan-Jardines of Castlemilk, journeyed all the way from Scotland to East Anglia to mate a bitch to King Cob, as Captain Ellis later described "by coach, and by waggon, and on foot...into Cambridgeshire; in part of this journey, the floods being out, he had to swim the Wash, with greater success than King John." The effect on the breed of the general use of recognised stud dogs like King Cob and Beacon was dramatic. One Scotsman went all the way to London to buy a King Cob bitch, Queen Of The May, but was rewarded by breeding from her the 1851 Waterloo Cup winner, Hughie Graham.

THE VICTORIAN ERA

All sorts of factors combined in the 1840s and 1850s to make coursing and all sports more popular. The wealth of the manufacturing classes provided the resources for leisure, and the trains which they built made it easier to get to coursing meetings. Crowds and the number of owners grew, and with it the rivalry and the quest to own and breed the best Greyhounds. The Victorian obsession with sport helped to perfect the Greyhound in the same way as the racehorse to such an extent that even the decadence of the twentieth century has failed to ruin the breed totally.

The demands made on the runners at coursing meetings in the mid-nineteenth century were extreme. The downland meetings at Ashdown and Amesbury were recognised as the ultimate, while Altcar, home of the Waterloo Cup, was not considered testing enough. If you walk the huge, rolling fields at Ashdown near Lambourn today, you can imagine the enormous courses which were run here. The hares were driven out of scrubland like Compton Bottom on to the downs where they raced away from the dogs, sometimes for three miles before leaving the dogs behind exhausted. The majority of the crowd would have been mounted and rode after the dogs to watch every twist and turn. "The Ashdown Cavalry are there," wrote the racing journalist Henry Hall Dixon of a meeting in 1860, "at least 400 strong; and when a hare does take the hill, and they all sit down in their saddles and catch hold of their horses' heads, the very ground seems to start and tremble under them." Others would follow on foot or watch from carriages drawn up on the hill above the coursing grounds. At Amesbury they met at Stonehenge, and for the October Champion meeting of 1864 there were 208 dogs on the card, including 122 in the bitch puppy stake and 86 dog puppies. On the second day of the meeting the judge, George Warwick, estimated that he rode 130 miles and exhausted four horses.

Vast sums were expended on the breeding, rearing and training of the dogs. Most of the puppies were reared on "walks" in the remote hills, especially in Cumberland and on the Scottish borders, where they could enjoy complete freedom. It was a practice which remained until the 1950s when the increase in traffic made it impossible, even in the remotest areas.

TRADITIONAL REARING

It would be difficult to contest that the Greyhound has taken a nose-dive in quality since the traditional method of rearing disappeared. Until the Second War, when at last all British farmers were guaranteed at least a subsistence income, rearing a Greyhound puppy at half a crown a week on the farm's own skim-milk made the difference between survival and ruin for many hill farmers. Rotten Row, winner of the Waterloo Cup in 1937 and runner-up in 1936 and 1938, was reared by Jos Waugh at Low Tod Hills near Roadhead. When Rotten Row won the Waterloo, the owner, Rowland Rank, sent Waugh a hundred pounds. With it he bought ten heifers, which laid the basis of some prosperity on the little hill farm. The Waughs swore that from that moment there would always be a Greyhound at Low Tod Hills, and there is one to this day.

"Reared with full liberty" was not just an empty phrase in those days. The puppies were let loose to run the whole day on the fells, chasing everything that came their way up and down the hills. In the evening they returned to the farm to get their teeth into whatever carcass was pulled from the boiler and to shelter in the barns. The hard weather made hard dogs. Henry Thompson bred and reared some famous Greyhounds at Cleugh Brae Farm, near Otterburn, including the Waterloo winners Thoughtless Beauty and Texture, a divider Troughend, and the 1901 runner-up which was named after his farm. Round the walls of the kitchen, wooden boxes packed with straw were suspended from the ceiling on ropes, and on winter nights the puppies would come in at dark and jump into their draught-free beds to enjoy the warmth of the burning range. The famous trainer, Tom Wright, regularly made trips back to his native Cumberland to check on the progress of his master's saplings. If the puppies were ever found fastened up, they were immediately taken away and the walk never used again. In their second spring the puppies would either go into training for their puppy season, or be sent to the sales in London.

THE GREYHOUND STUD BOOK

With all the resources which were lavished on the breeding of Greyhounds throughout the nineteenth century, it seems ludicrous now that it took until 1882 before the National Coursing Club introduced compulsory registration of dogs for coursing. Ever since Thomas Goodlake's first attempt in 1828, informal attempts had been made by people like Thomas Thacker and Robert Welch to keep public records of breeding, but the nearest the NCC, in its early days, could come to controlling breeding was to allow objections to the age of your opponent in puppy stakes. When Coomassie won the first of her two Waterloos in 1877 as a puppy, a Carlisle breeder swore that her breeding was falsified and that she was an all-age bitch from a litter of his own.

A number of people have been credited with being the driving force behind the setting up of the Stud Book, including Captain Ellis and Mr Dunn, but it was a Scotsman, Robert Paterson, that proposed it to the National Coursing Club and, more importantly, another Scotsman, David Brown, who undertook the thankless task of running it. David Brown of Dalry in Ayrshire had been a journalist for years, contributing to *Thacker* in the 1850s under the superb penname of 'Spunkie', and then covering the Scottish meetings for *Bell's Life* and *The Field* as 'Maida'. In 1882 the entries for the first volume were on a voluntary basis, while for the following season all running dogs would have to be registered. The antagonism towards the idea of a stud book is obvious from the absence of any registrations from Lord Sefton and other prominent members of the NCC in that first volume.

David Brown published the Stud Book from Dalry for ten years until ill-health forced him to give it up. It was then taken over by another journalist, W.F. Lamonby, 'Skiddaw' of the *Coursing Calendar*, who published it from the offices of *The Field* magazine until 1914. Graham had organised the entries in a cumbersome alphabetical list of names with their breeding following, as Thacker and Welch had done forty years before. It was Lamonby who introduced the modern format of entering dogs beneath their sire and dam, each one having the number of the volume in which it was originally registered following its name. This has been followed ever since by the Irish, American and Australian stud books. In recognition of its status as the original stud book, the British book continues to be called simply *The Greyhound Stud Book*.

THE NEW SPORT

Some people would argue that the slow death of the Greyhound breed began on December 14th 1876 – or was it 7.30 in the evening of July 24th 1926? On the former, King's Delight won the first course ever run at an 'enclosed' or 'park' coursing meeting, at Plumpton in Sussex. On the latter occasion, Mistley won the first modern Greyhound race in England at Belle Vue Stadium, Manchester. The 'park coursing' meetings, as they came to be known, put a premium on speed, as the grounds were never more than 800 yards long compared with the three-mile courses of the old downland meetings. Even when enclosed coursing fell out of favour in England, the 'open' grounds were contrived to produce much shorter courses, and in Ireland 'park' meetings have reigned supreme for over a hundred years. Significantly, when track racing began, the favoured sires were dogs which had shown brilliant pace but little stamina or control on the field, such as Mutton Cutlet and Melksham Tom.Lord Tweedsmouth commented at a meeting of the NCC's Standing Committee in 1928: "Some of the creatures we see here now are most awful, and must have awful progeny." Certainly, park coursing and track racing have had a marked effect on the physical as well as the psychological nature of the Greyhound. The modern coursing dog is twenty per cent heavier than he was only thirty years ago, and some track dogs are so flat-sided that a puff of wind would blow them over. Both would probably expire from agoraphobia or shock if slipped on a hare on the Wiltshire Downs with some of their ancestors which perfected the breed.

Chapter Two

PHYSIOLOGY OF THE GREYHOUND

The Greyhound is truly a remarkable athlete. The modern Greyhound is trained for races ranging from 280 to over 700 metres to utilise its natural sprint ability. Greyhounds also compete in longer distance endurance and hurdle racing, coursing, and even marathon racing in excess of 1000 metres lasting about 60 seconds. Over the past 150 years Greyhounds have been selected and bred for lure racing and coursing, with refinement in the breed for sprinting ability. However, not only does the Greyhound have to possess the genetic and physical requirements that include strength, stamina and speed, it also has to have the mental attitude of a highly competitive athlete.

GENERAL PHYSIQUE

In many ways, the general structure of the racing Greyhound and the racing horse have many similarities. However, the racing Greyhound has a much higher power to weight ratio than the horse, with faster acceleration and speed over a sprint distance. With a high power to weight ratio and speed bred into the Greyhound, the high acceleration and stress loads carried by muscles increases the risk of upper limb muscle injuries, and lower limb tendon, joint and toe injuries.

In contrast to the racing horse, the Greyhound has a multi-toed foot, which whilst providing traction, is prone to injury during acceleration and cornering on tracks with shifting surfaces, inadequate banking or a change in surface. The physical strength of the racing Greyhound can be maximised by a combination of careful training programmes and a well-balanced diet. Generally, well-fed, fit Greyhounds are usually faster and less prone to injury than Greyhounds that are not well cared for or not prepared for the distance to be raced. The fact that an animal is born a Greyhound, does not necessarily ensure that it will be a winner on the race track. A Greyhound may have the physical strength, biomechanical stride length and stamina to race, but lack the keenness and mental approach required to be a successful winner. Good training skills are required to bring out the maximum ability of an individual Greyhound on the racetrack. Many Greyhounds, however, are not fully trained or at their physical peak until after their first two or three races.

ENERGY SYSTEMS

Rapidly contracting muscles use large amounts of stored energy during high-speed exercise. However, a Greyhound only expends about four per cent of its total daily energy needed during an average thirty second race. A Greyhound utilises two different types of energy-producing pathways, depending on the rate of muscular contraction. At slower speeds up to 30-40 kms an hour (20-25mph), oxygen carried to the muscles by the blood is used by 'aerobic' metabolic pathways to produce energy for contraction. However, at normal racing speeds of up to 70km an hour (30-40mph), the supply of oxygen becomes limited, and energy is produced, with a decreased dependence on oxygen, by what is termed "anaerobic" energy production. The anaerobic fast speed pathway uses up energy stores twelve times faster than the slower aerobic oxygen pathway.

Greyhounds cannot run at maximum speed for long distances. Both systems are conditioned by galloping at full speed. The Greyhound uses its energy stores about two to three times faster to accelerate from the start than it does for galloping at full speed. In fact, during the first 7 1/2 seconds of a race, when its maximum power to weight ratio is used for acceleration, almost half the total energy expended during a race is consumed. In the final 22 1/2 seconds of a thirty second race, the racing Greyhound uses about the same amount of energy, to complete the remainder of a race, as it does jumping from the traps and accelerating to the first bend on a normal circle track.

TYPES OF ENERGY PRODUCTION

Dr. Ross Staaden, an Australian veterinarian, has carried out extensive treadmill and race track studies to help our understanding of Greyhound exercise physiology. The Greyhound can utilise different types of energy stores in its muscle, depending on the stage and distance of a race. These include high energy phosphates, glycogen, sugars and, to some extent, fat. However, using glycogen aerobically gives ten per cent more high phosphate muscle energy than using fat in the same way. High energy compounds called phosphogens, supply the energy source for contracting muscle cells.

In the first 7 1/2 seconds of a race the Greyhound metabolises energy without the need for oxygen, using limited stores of these high energy sources. In a short race, lasting up to thirty seconds, the muscles generate up to seventy-five to eighty per cent of their power from anaerobic energy production. The high energy phosphate compounds are the immediate energy source for acceleration. These provide a high level of energy, without the build-up of metabolic by-products, such as lactic acid. However, after this time, the energy production pathway switches to using carbohydrates or glycogen stored in the muscles.

Glycogen, a carbohydrate-type compound, is accumulated in the muscles as stored energy during training. Proper conditioning and an adequate dietary balance of carbohydrates, protein and fat will maximise glycogen storage in muscles during training. During the mid to final stages of a race, the fast muscular contractions cannot obtain enough oxygen for efficient aerobic power, and only about half the stored glycogen reserves are metabolised using oxygen. Over a typical thirty second sprint gallop, the Greyhound produces only about one quarter of its total energy using oxygen. However, if glycogen is broken down in the muscles where the oxygen supply is limited, the muscles use the less efficient anaerobic energy pathway. This results in the build-up of metabolites, such as lactic acid, in the muscles that limit further energy use and cause typical muscular fatigue.

In a longer race over forty-five seconds or so, about eighty per cent of the total energy in the final run to the post is produced using oxygen. The biggest limiting factor in Greyhounds that are excitable or not properly conditioned or unfit for the distance and speed of the race, is the rapid accumulation of lactic acid as a by-product of glycogen breakdown, early in the race. The presence of lactic acid in the muscles results in fatigue, suppresses further metabolic activity and slows the animal.

Lactic acid trapped in the muscles results in stiffness and soreness in the back and hindlimb propulsion muscles, particularly in the recovery period after a race. In Greyhounds unfit for the distance or speed, the accumulation of excess lactic acid in the back and hindlimb muscles leads to swelling due to acidosis, or lowering of pH, which results in symptoms described as 'blowing up' along the back and upper hindlimb. This is because the accumulated acid attracts water into the muscle cells, which then swell up within a few minutes after a race. However, when a Greyhound

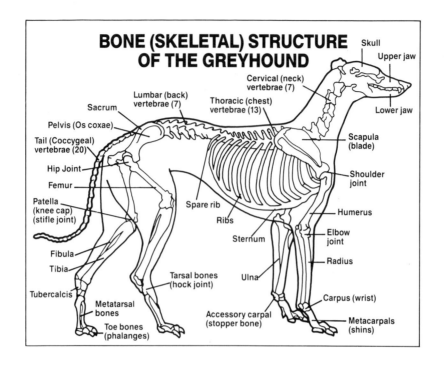

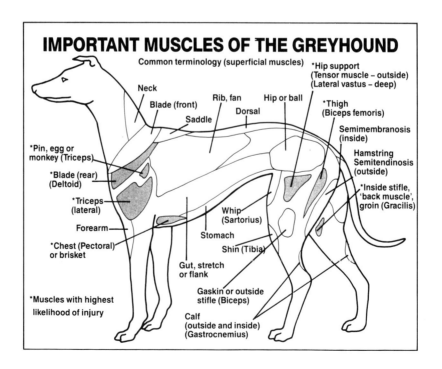

is properly conditioned by a careful training programme to reduce the mid race reliance on anaerobic pathways, this reduces the suppressive effects of lactic acid. Moreover, training increases the muscle cells' tolerance to build-up of lactic acid, and reduces the risk of fatigue in properly conditioned muscles. With conditioning, the 'sprint economy' is increased, with changes in rate of blood delivery, and muscle fibre efficiency. This can only be done by handslips and trials, as walking does not improve fast twitch fibre efficiency.

The majority of Greyhounds are trained for flat races, taking from fifteen to forty seconds to gallop. The lengths of the individual stadium and trial tracks influence the distance over which the Greyhound should be conditioned. Greyhounds galloping on shorter training tracks or over shorter distances are not conditioned for longer race distances. Although they may be able to lead the field up to the halfway mark or so, they may not have sufficient energy reserves to maintain speed to the finish. Unfit Greyhounds are more likely to suffer muscle injuries or cramp in a race. Therefore, preferably, the animal should be trained and trialled over the distance selected for its race. However, as an animal ages and gains strength and experience, it may become more adapted to longer distance races. Training to condition the animal to gallop over a set distance has a direct effect on the muscle fibres themselves.

MUSCLE FIBRE TYPES

Generally, during training the muscles themselves increase in size in response to the effect of increasing exercise speed and load as the Greyhound is allowed to gallop over increasingly longer distances. In fact, researchers have shown that some muscle fibres actually split to increase their size as they respond to training.

The muscles themselves contain various types of fibres. Greyhounds are born with the distribution of each type of fibre, depending on the genetic make-up and performance ability. There are basically two main types of muscle fibres present in the muscles of a racing Greyhound. These are known as slow twitch and fast twitch fibres. Studies have shown that racing Greyhounds have a larger number of fast twitch fibres, average 96.9 per cent in their semitendinosis muscles (the propulsion muscles running down the rear of the back legs) compared with 87.4 per cent in other breeds of dogs.

SLOW TWITCH FIBRES

There are two forms of slow contracting or slow twitch fibres that are able to sustain muscle tension for a long period without fatigue. True slow twitch or (tonic fibres) are not used for galloping. They only have a role in aiding a Greyhound to stand and support its weight. The other type of slow twitch fibre, known as slow basic fibres, are slowly contracting fibres that are also resistant to fatigue. They utilise fat for energy by aerobic metabolism, with some glycogen at faster speeds. Fat is the lightest form of energy to store in the body, weighing only about twelve per cent as an equivalent energy store to glycogen. However, the Greyhound runs more on glycogen stores due to its fast, all-stops-out galloping speed. They have a lower rate of energy usage, requiring between thirty to seventy per cent as much energy to do the same amount of work as fast twitch fibres. These fibres are brought into action to propel the Greyhound at the walk to economise on energy use.

FAST TWITCH FIBRES

True fast twitch fibres are also divided into two separate groups for simplicity. The first type, or the fast twitch glycolytic or white fibres, can metabolise energy without the need for oxygen. These are used for high speed galloping, particularly where oxygen supply to the muscles is limited at peak speed. The other type of fast twitch fibres are called oxidative or pink fibres. The Greyhound has a higher proportion of fast twitch oxidative fibres than other dogs, and most other animal athletes. These have a high level of enzymes that utilise oxygen in metabolising glycogen as energy for muscle contraction. These fibres are fairly resistant to fatigue, and are used during the middle and later stages of a race. As the tension and speed is increased in the muscles, the fast twitch fibres are recruited and developed in preference to the slower twitch fibres.

The Greyhound uses all types of muscle fibres for acceleration from the start of a race. The fast twitch fibres are then recruited during rapid muscle activity to give rapid, powerful contractions to propel the Greyhound during a race. Muscle development and increase in power of contraction is related to the amount of tension developed in the muscle during training. Muscles become stronger by gradually increasing the speed and distance galloped during training. The ability to increase the speed of muscle contraction, as well as the strength and power, is conditioned by regular galloping during training.

Walking a Greyhound does not increase the contracting strength, or fully utilise fast twitch fibres. Therefore, long distance walking over flat terrain in a fit Greyhound, in fact, does little to tone up muscles or maintain strength. Contractile speed and power in fast twitch fibres is only maintained and conditioned by regular fast work and racing. However, Greyhounds do not need the high specificity of training often adopted by human athletes, or the over muscle development stimulated by uphill running, as the animal will become tired and sour, and too heavy and awkward for streamlined sprint racing.

EVALUATING MUSCLE FIBRES
Research over the past decade in Greyhounds and other animals, particularly racing horses, has shown that samples of muscle fibres, called biopsies, can be taken to determine the ratio of slow and fast twitch fibres. Greyhounds have a high proportion of fast twitch fibres in their muscle profile. However, for fast muscular activity towards the end of the race, the high performing Greyhounds are thought to have a greater number of fast twitch fibres, that utilise energy, without the need for oxygen, more efficiently. On a theoretical basis, using a muscle biopsy, it would be possible to predict the future racing ability of a Greyhound during training.

It was hoped from the original studies in racehorses, that the muscle fibre biopsies could be useful in predicting the potential performance and speed of a young foal. However, other studies have shown that there are many other factors that are involved in the speed of muscle contraction process. Unfortunately, predicting performance on muscle fibre types alone, is not regarded as being an accurate way of selecting an animal at an early age. Although muscle fibre biopsies in Greyhounds are technically possible, there has been little research work on racing Greyhounds.

CONDITIONING MUSCLES
Studies have shown that stepwise increase from walking to galloping exercise is desirable in early training to strengthen muscle fibres as well as allow the cardiovascular system to adapt to fast work. Experience has shown that a stepwise increase in speed and distance helps reduce the risk of muscle injuries, perhaps by increasing the amount of supporting tissue within each bundle of muscle. This conditioning period is useful to reduce the incidence of muscle tears and injury, once the Greyhound starts regular galloping. Certainly, Greyhounds that are not conditioned slowly, tend to have an increased incidence of muscle tears and muscle soreness once they start trialling and racing.

It is true of course that very fit Greyhounds, and particularly fast Greyhounds, generally have a reduced risk of muscle injuries when racing. These Greyhounds have the acceleration speed to get ahead of the field early in the race and are therefore less likely to be interfered with, particularly on the first corner on a typical circle track. Conditioning work also improves local circulation within the muscle, by increasing the number of blood vessels penetrating into the muscle to supply oxygen and nutrients to the individual muscle bundles and fibres. In the racing Greyhound, where most of the galloping is done without total reliance on oxygen to produce energy, the increase in the number of blood vessels feeding the muscle is not maximised to the extent that it would be in a slower endurance type animal. However, as compared with other breeds of dogs, Greyhounds have a much darker, more vascular muscle structure, to sustain speed and stamina during racing.

It has also been shown that the mechanical stress produced by training increases the strength of the junctions between ligaments or tendons and the bones. It is well known that cartilage and joints thicken in response to training. However, this is a slow process and must be conditioned over a period of time. Therefore, in early conditioning, it is important to give a Greyhound at least four to five weeks of walking and low trot type work on the lead, with short handslips over 100 metres from the third week, to strengthen the muscles, their attachment to bones, and the membranes around the muscles themselves. This will help to increase the amount of support tissue within the muscle, strengthen ligament and tendon attachment to the bone and muscle and ensure that the cartilage and joints are thick enough to withstand the wear and tear of high speed galloping.

Obviously, a diet must be provided that is adequate in protein to build muscle and blood, and various minerals and vitamins, particularly Vitamin A, Vitamin D, Vitamin E, calcium, magnesium, zinc and iron, are required to assist in strengthening the ligaments, bones, and muscles respectively, as well as to develop the blood. Vitamin E in particular is an important aid to muscle development and strength in racing Greyhounds.

THE HEART AND LUNGS

The Greyhound's cardiovascular system is particularly adapted to sustain speed and stamina. Studies have shown that racing Greyhounds have a greater left heart wall thickness than other breeds of dogs, and a greater magnitude and amplitude of the heart beat. This corresponds to the Greyhound's need to pump high volumes of blood to the working muscles during exercise. In fact, during exercise, up to eighty per cent of the blood is delivered to the working muscles, reducing the circulation within the bowels and kidneys to a maintenance flow. During exercise in other animals the kidney flow itself is cut to less than twenty per cent of its normal flow during rest. A well planned conditioning programme also helps to increase the efficiency of heart and lung function.

Studies in other performance animals have shown that training increases the number of blood vessels in the heart by up to forty per cent as compared with untrained animals. However, heart size becomes limiting for efficient action, and the per cent of fast twitch fibres and the muscle bulk or fibre number are more important. In untrained animals, a large proportion of lung tissue is actually closed off for breathing, and these deflated areas of lung are brought into service with increasing training and speed, increasing the expansion of the chest and depth of breathing.

The cardiac output in a racing Greyhound increases from about 200mls per kg per minute to over 1000mls per kg per minute when racing. This corresponds to about 30kg of blood pumped each minute, or roughly its own bodyweight. The excitement in the traps increases the heart rate and, at the moment of jumping, one study showed that the heart was delivering 1500mls blood per kg per minute just as the animal leaped at the lure. In fact, the racing Greyhound actually circulates its entire blood volume five times during the 30 second gallop.

The racing Greyhound is also unique in its rise in heart output during exercise. Whilst human runners can increase heart output by up to twenty per cent during sprint work, the cardiac output of a racing Greyhound commonly rises from about 2.2mls per kg at rest to about 2.9 during galloping, or a rise of up to thirty per cent in stroke volume. One of the main reasons for a Greyhound's high cardiac output is its high blood volume, in relation to other breeds of dogs. A fit racing Greyhound will have up to 11.4 per cent of its bodyweight as blood, compared with about 7.2 per cent for other breeds of dog.

The ability of the Greyhound to deliver high volumes of blood and circulate it during exercise is a combination of larger stroke volume and a higher heart rate. A peak heart rate of 300-320 beats per minute is common during a high speed gallop. Studies have shown that after a gallop, the heart rate does not return to normal for up to twenty minutes during the recovery phase. The heart rate in a sleeping Greyhound is by comparison 29-30 for a well-performed, fit animal, and possibly even higher for animals that are not good performers.

Heart size is about 4.5-11 grams per kg, or about 0.5 per cent of bodyweight, in most breeds of dogs. Greyhounds have a range from 0.9 to 1.73 per cent of bodyweight with an average of 1.2 per cent The Greyhound heart, despite its larger size and mass, is able to reach very high rates of beating during racing. The heart of an average human athlete is about the same size as a Greyhound heart, but a Greyhound's heart delivers blood at a much faster rate, and it beats at a much faster rate, than an athlete's heart in a comparable sprint race.

The racing Greyhound also has a much higher number of red blood cells and packed cell volume (PCV) than other breeds of dogs. Although, in a sleeping Greyhound studies have shown that the PCV can be as low as 42-44 per cent, once a Greyhound is walked or excited by the noise or site of a lure, the PCV rises to 60-63 per cent. In a fit Greyhound the average PCV would be at least 63-65 per cent. Although the reserve is not as large as the racing horse, extra red blood cells are stored in the spleen during rest, and are released in response to excitement and galloping.

Generally, winning Greyhounds have a much higher PCV average of 62-66 per cent than lesser performing Greyhounds. Although blood counts are not used in Greyhounds to the same extent that they are in assessing adaptation to training in race horses, it is most important that PCV and red cell counts are interpreted specifically for racing Greyhounds, and not compared with other breeds of dogs.

OXYGEN UPTAKE

The Greyhound has a superior oxygen transport system to most other athletes, delivering oxygen to working muscles at about twenty-five per cent higher rate than a human sprint athlete. This is largely due to the greater blood volume, the elevated heart rate, and the higher PCV in the Greyhound. In comparison to other breeds of dogs, the Greyhound has a larger blood volume, a higher PCV percentage, more fast twitch muscle fibres, an increased number of fibres, and a higher proportion of muscle to bodyweight, as compared to other tissue.

It is also considered that Greyhounds have a thinner skin, and a short hair coat, which decreases weight and enhances heat loss, with overall less wind resistance than most other breeds of dogs. Their muscle structure has less connective tissue and more muscle fibres than other dogs, and their gut volume when fit, is one of the lowest volumes of any racing animal. However, a large heart and a high blood count does not necessarily guarantee a top racing animal. Poor or weak conformation, and a lack of mental attitude, may be other limiting factors of ability to perform on the racetrack.

 Treadmill studies have shown that during galloping, a racing Greyhound takes in 4-6 litres/kg/minute, of air into its lungs or about 60-90 litres of air in a thirty second race. In the race, a Greyhound breathes from 2 1/2 to 3 breaths per second, synchronised to the stride action of the leading front leg. The major objective of any training programme should be to adapt and condition the Greyhound's system to improve its delivery of blood and oxygen to the working muscles, as well as improve the size and strength of the muscles to maintain stamina and speed during racing. However, high muscle bulk and water retention as promoted by anabolic steroids is not beneficial, due to increased overall bodyweight and loss of power to weight ratio.

DIGESTIVE PHYSIOLOGY

The digestive tract of the racing Greyhound is relatively short and adapted to a concentrated high energy, relatively low fibre diet. Authorities believe the racing Greyhound has adapted to physical proportions of larger heart and lung capacity, and high muscle ratio to bodyweight, and therefore has a lower gut volume and gut weight proportion to bodyweight than other breeds of dogs.

Although food can be retained in the stomach for up to eight to sixteen hours after eating, depending on the texture of the food, the fat content and the relative temperature of the food, it is the small intestine that plays the most significant role in digestion in the racing Greyhound. Bile from the gall bladder is released into the first part of the small intestine to emulsify fats to allow them to be attacked by digestive enzymes released in the pancreatic juice. This starts primary digestion of proteins, fats and starches into their various components. Alkaline pancreatic juice neutralises the stomach acidity, which enhances the enzymatic action on the food in the small intestine.

The majority of food materials are absorbed from the small intestine, primarily soluble sugars released from cereals and other starches following digestion by pancreatic enzymes. Protein from meats and dry foods is split by pancreatic enzymes into the constituent amino acids. These are then absorbed by the small bone, muscle and organ proteins.

Many minerals and vitamins, particularly calcium, are also absorbed from the small intestine during the digestive process. Therefore, by the time the food mass reaches the end of the small intestine, most of the useful nutrients have been removed, leaving only the residue of indigestible fibres from plant origin and some starches.

In the large bowel, the growth of fermentative and digestive bacteria promotes the breakdown of the remaining residues, and in normal healthy Greyhounds, the stool residue is low as compared with the total amount of food consumed. Most of the stool mass is made up of undigested fibre, bacteria and moisture from a well-balanced adequate diet. As most racing Greyhounds are younger animals compared with the rest of the canine population, with a relatively controlled diet and reasonable quality foods, the typical digestive upsets and common bowel diseases that occur in other breeds of dog due to aging or scavenging-type diets, do not occur in the racing Greyhound.

However, one of the most common causes of compromised digestion in racing Greyhounds is high levels of internal parasites – roundworms and tapeworms interfering with digestion. The sheer physical volumes of heavy worm burdens restrict intestinal flow and irritate the bowel, causing diarrhoea. Other types of digestive problems include food allergy, with red meat allergy reported in Greyhounds, but not as commonly as in other breeds of dogs. Intolerance to milk, particularly in adult dogs that have been weaned early in life, and have lost the lactate enzyme activity necessary for the digestion of milk sugar or lactose can also reduce digestive efficiency by increased transit time.

Other main causes of digestive upset are an imbalance of dry food to moist food, the use of highly contaminated foods such as salvaged meat from dead, dying, diseased or debilitated animals, and poor storage and unhygienic preparation methods, that increase counts of abnormal bacteria and the risk of diarrhoea. High fibre and carbohydrate diets also enlarge stool bulk and weight, due to increased water retention diverting water flow from the kidneys. This can lead to reduced urinary flow and build up of metabolic wastes in the blood, reducing vitality and health.

THE NERVOUS SYSTEM

Basic anatomy of the nervous system is similar to other breeds of dogs. However, many young Greyhounds have to learn an efficient galloping action, using their left hind leg as the driving leg next to the rail. The repetition of training with free galloping is important to coordinate the nervous and muscular system during the gallop. However, Greyhounds have adapted their senses of sight, scent and hearing by careful selection over hundreds of years. It is considered that racing Greyhounds gallop and hunt using a combination of sixty per cent sight, twenty per cent scent, and twenty per cent noise. Therefore, in the racing Greyhound running after a lure on the racetrack, sight and noise of the lure are the major stimuli to the Greyhound to gallop and chase the lure.

The level of intelligence of the racing Greyhound is also considered to be superior to many other breeds of dogs. While some authorities believe this is due to careful selection for alertness, good eyesight and hearing, recent tests in retired greyhounds have shown their quick adaptation to obedience training, and greyhounds are currently being trained as seeing eye dogs for the blind, and as drug sniffers for law enforcement. Although it is a common belief that greyhounds have a poorly developed sense of smell, observations have shown that Greyhounds have retained the keen sense of smell common to other breeds of hounds.

Chapter Three

FEEDING AND NUTRITION

An adequate and well-balanced diet is paramount for the health and development of the Greyhound. This starts from the time of conception, during its growth and rearing stage, when it is coursed or raced, for its well-being when used as a companion or show animal, and finally in retirement as a household pet. A well-planned feeding programme during the early developing stage in a young Greyhound improves the chances of a successful coursing or racing career. Although much of the science of feeding and the practical aspects of making up a diet have been researched or adapted from other breeds of dogs, the coursing and racing Greyhound has requirements more specific than many other breeds of working dogs.

Feeding the Greyhound as a performance animal is both an 'art' and a 'science'. The science of feeding matches and balances the dietary composition, intake and exercise, the nutritional value of feeds, and likely deficiencies and imbalances, to ensure that the Greyhound maintains its health and performance, usually within a set bodyweight range. The art of feeding is knowing an individual's likes and dislikes, feeding habits, how to select good-quality feeds and when to feed.

On retirement to a show or companion lifestyle, the Greyhound is prone to obesity if it is not regularly exercised. The diet must be carefully formulated and adjusted to maintain the animal in the desired proportions for the show ring, or as a companion or household pet during this time. Greyhounds generally are easy dogs to care for, consuming a wide variety of meat and other foods, with few likes or dislikes, as can occur in many other smaller breeds of dog. A good dietary programme must be complemented by adequate exercise and by health care such as regular worming, vaccination and teeth cleaning. However, the ration must be adapted to suit the individual Greyhound's appetite, comparative feed conversion, temperament, seasonal conditions, and the amount of daily exercise. Regular assessment and adjustment of the diet must be made to achieve the desired purpose as a racing, show, companion or working animal.

FEEDING THE GROWING GREYHOUND

GENERAL CONSIDERATIONS

Most Greyhound puppies are weaned at about five to six weeks of age depending on the number in the litter, and their general development. Introduction to good-quality puppy food from three weeks of age will help the young animal accept and adapt to the weaning diet with minimal setback. Once weaned, the nutritional management of growing Greyhound puppies must aim at providing the foundation for proper skeletal, muscle and body development necessary for a racing or coursing career.

It is absolutely essential that the weaner be fed an adequate and balanced diet to achieve an even

Once a Greyhound puppy is weaned it is essential to provide a diet aimed at developing sound skeletal, muscular, and body development.

growth rate, without excessive bodyweight or development at any stage. This must be complemented by daily access to an exercise area to encourage the development of a strong musculo-skeletal system. It is unwise to aim for maximum growth rates in a growing Greyhound puppy. Although providing feed on an ad lib or continuous basis to demand will ensure good growth and development, overfeeding and restriction of exercise can lead to skeletal abnormalities, the risk of breakdown and a shortened coursing, racing or show career.

Some bloodlines of Greyhounds tend to overdevelop as puppies and weaners even when the diet and exercise is within the normal standard. Therefore regular fortnightly appraisal of a young animal's growth rate and development is essential, to avoid setbacks or spurts in growth. As a general rule, the young Greyhound should be maintained in a fleshy condition, preferably with the outline of the wither and lower back spinal bones, the pin bones, and the last two or three ribs still visible, until about one year of age.

FEEDING MANAGEMENT

It is important to monitor the daily feed intake and adjust it as required to ensure that the young Greyhound grows at a steady rate. Most weaners are fed up to four times a day, depending upon the diet composition and facilities. Diets can be based on a good-quality dry food, containing 22-24 per cent protein, 10 per cent fat, 5 per cent fibre, and a range of vitamin and minerals including the correct calcium and phosphorus ratio for bone and muscle development.

Care must be taken to ensure that larger, more aggressive or greedy weaners are identified and monitored regularly to ensure that they do not put on excessive body weight or overdevelop. Overfeeding is a particular danger in pups that do not have adequate room to exercise, or have less than 30 minutes individual exercise per day. Greyhounds are best raised in a group rather than as individuals. This helps to develop the competitive sense, group interaction and confidence that is needed for a successful racing or coursing career. Many breeders select pups on aggression displayed when feeding and playing.

ENERGY: Energy provides the fuel for growth, development and exercise. Extra energy is needed for warmth in colder conditions and for panting during hot weather. Over-supply of energy in the ration, particularly when weaners are given ad lib access to dry food as a snack during the day, will often result in overweight and excessive development. Heavyweight pups are also often reluctant to exercise adequately, further increasing the risk of musculo-skeletal damage. However, if pups are allowed to exercise freely in a large rearing yard, then they may burn up energy that should be channelled to growth, and not grow in ideal proportions. In this case, exercise may need to be restricted to ensure a balance between an adequate growth rate and suitable body development. Although weaners can be reared in large groups up to six months of age, they should be segregated into smaller groups of three or four of the same sex from nine months of age.

PROTEIN: Protein provides the 'building blocks' in the form of amino acids for growth of the body, bone and muscle. A growing Greyhound should be provided with a 24-27 per cent protein diet, and where the meat content exceeds 50 per cent of the diet by weight, a dry food containing 22-24 per cent protein should be provided. If the amount of dry food exceeds 75 per cent of the diet, then its protein content should be increased to 24-27 per cent. Where a total dry food diet is fed then a 27 per cent protein dry food can be used as a basis for the diet.

MINERALS: In all other breeds of growing animals, the primary concern is an adequate intake and balance of calcium and phosphorus on meat-based diets. As meat, without bone, is very deficient in calcium, a supplement of calcium should be provided, along with trace minerals and Vitamin D, particularly where puppies are raised during the winter months or indoor kennels, to ensure the requirements of these important bone and muscle building nutrients are provided. Although there is no need to provide extra calcium during the growth phase of the young Greyhound over and above other breeds of dog, an adequate and balanced amount of calcium to phosphorus is absolutely essential. The ideal ratio for the diet is 1.3 calcium to 1.0 phosphorus. Although there are many proprietary supplements available on the market, on meat-based diets it

A meal of mutton ribs or soft brisket bone with dry food, twice weekly, helps develop the teeth and jaws and keeps the pups interested in their diet.

is preferable to supplement calcium and phosphorus in proportion to the amount of meat fed so as to achieve the optimum range.

A young growing puppy requires about 320mg of calcium per kg of bodyweight daily to meet its needs. Many dry foods contain a balanced amount of calcium to phosphorus, and if 75 per cent of the diet is provided by dry food, then only about 1g of elemental calcium need be provided as a supplement each day. However, where meat constitutes 50 per cent of the diet, then at least 2.5g of elemental calcium must be provided each day to balance up the meat portion of diet. Other minerals that are required for proper bone and body development, besides calcium and phosphorus, include magnesium, zinc, copper, manganese, iron, iodine and selenium. Most of these minerals would be provided in a dry food base in the diet, or by a proprietary general vitamin and mineral supplement formulated for growing puppies, preferably one dosed to balance the meat content of the ration.

It is essential that, once the young Greyhound is given regular exercise, or is introduced to light training from 12 months of age, it receives adequate levels of calcium and phosphorus in the diet to remodel toes, shins and limb bones in response to faster exercise. Where meat constitutes more that 50 per cent of the diet, it is recommended that a proprietary vitamin supplement, given at the general dose for growing puppies, be provided daily.

VITAMINS: As the growth and development of the Greyhound is the basis for ultimate performance as a coursing or racing animal, then supplements of Vitamins A, D and E in particular are considered by many breeders as being essential for optimum growth and development. A supplement of approximately 2iu of Vitamin E per kg of bodyweight over that which is contained in the feed itself, as well as a proprietary supplement containing Vitamins A, D and B-complex, is recommended to balance the diet.

Although many dry foods are fortified with vitamins and minerals to meet the needs of growing dogs, loss during storage and preparation may result in a less than optimum intake, so an additional supplement of vitamins formulated for Greyhounds is recommended. Because many natural foods such as yeast and wheatgerm provide B-complex and Vitamin E, small amounts (about 2 teaspoonfuls a day) may improve digestion and health. A scientifically formulated proprietary supplement may also be of benefit to ensure daily needs are satisfied.

It is important to ensure that amounts of all supplements, including calcium and vitamins, are increased as the young Greyhound develops, with adjustments at monthly intervals. When using supplements, be sure to feed only the recommended amounts. Avoid feeding excessive amounts of Vitamin A and D, in particular, as these can have detrimental effects on the animal's growth rate and its future health as a racing Greyhound.

EXERCISE
It is essential to provide all young growing Greyhounds with adequate facilities for regular daily exercise. Although long runs of up to 100 metres (110 yards) in length encourage young pups to gallop freely, generally a large, almost square, yard at least 50 metres in length and breadth will provide an adequate exercise area for up to six weaners. Some breeders raise pups from 6 months of age in long curved runs with a crescent shape to strengthen the skeleton by galloping around a curve.

A larger area will encourage them to play, gallop and turn sharply at speed to develop their whole musculo-skeletal system, particularly their toes, lower limbs and joints. If possible, access to a larger yard or a small field once or twice a week will encourage the young animals to gallop freely, turn, chase and learn group social behaviour. This is most important to their general

Greyhound puppies need regular free-running exercise.

development as strong athletic animals. The exercise yard must be provided with safe boundary fencing, adequate drainage and a grassed surface that is even and without holes, obstacles or other surface debris that could lead to injuries.

FEEDING METHODS

In most cases, it is best to provide individual bowls for the daily measured feeds. This will ensure that each animal can be assessed regularly, and the diet adjusted to its individual growth and development. Where large groups of Greyhounds are reared, they can be segregated and grouped according to size, aggressiveness at feeding and general development. However, where only one litter is being raised at a time, it is important that each animal be given a measured amount of feed to ensure a steady, uniform growth rate. Usually a dry food snack can be provided on an ad-lib basis, but if an individual puppy is eating excessive amounts, then consumption may need to be restricted.

Access to an adequate amount of cool, clean water is particularly important to young growing dogs on a diet high in dry food, or those that are exercising in hot weather. Greyhounds will generally drink more water when it is cool and clean, preferably located in a shady area within the yard or in the kennel. Normally it is best to dampen dry food with either a small amount of milk, if available, or water or even a meaty gravy, to ensure acceptance. The dry food alone will usually contain adequate electrolytes to meet needs for growth and light exercise. There is no need to add extra salt to the diet, even during hot weather, in growing Greyhounds. A regular worming and kennel hygiene programme is essential to complement a balanced and adequate ration.

FEEDING GREYHOUNDS DURING EDUCATION

Most Greyhounds are introduced to the lead, and schooled to coursing or lure racing, from about 12-15 months of age. It is most important that the diet is adequate in calcium and phosphorus to provide the foundation for the development of strong "shins" or metacarpal bones in the feet, in the Greyhound being educated to run on a circle track. In many cases, it is best to feed a smaller amount of a typical racing diet to a young Greyhound during its breaking-in period, as this will provide an adequate intake for development, including galloping and competitive training.

It is best not to school excessively overweight Greyhounds on a tight circle track as this increases the risk of them injuring themselves when allowed to gallop under competitive situations. It is best to feed the young Greyhound simply to maintain bodyweight during its four week education period, adjusting according to the amount of exercise. As the young Greyhound is subjected to physical and competitive stress for the first time, it is important that its appetite be monitored, and its intake adjusted, to ensure that it eats sufficient food to meet its exercise demands, and maintain its bodyweight during basic training procedures.

FEEDING RACING AND COURSING GREYHOUNDS

Just as an adequate and well-balanced diet is paramount for growth, the ration for the competitive Greyhound must meet its specific needs, maintain the animal at a relatively constant weight, and provide adequate nutrients, not only for performance, but to counteract the physical and mental stress of competitive racing, and provide nutrients for maintenance and repair of the musculo-skeletal and other body systems.

The diet must be economical, palatable, highly digestible with a low bulk to maintain minimal gut volume for competiveness, and health and vitality when racing on a repeated basis. It is essential to ensure optimum fluid balance under all weather conditions, particularly during warmer months when dehydration can adversely affect performance and recovery rate. The feeding programme may be modified to suit the kennelling or racing routine, or adapted to match the stage of training or an individual Greyhound's preferences.

Ideally, a racing Greyhound should be fed to maintain it in a slim condition, with "condition" lines from ribs to flank and the outline of the pin bones and last two ribs visible under the skin. Feeding the racing and coursing Greyhound is based on practical observation and scientific principles, but there is also a good deal of folklore associated with feeding. In all countries where Greyhounds are raced or coursed, diets were based traditionally on meat, with added dry food or cereal grain mashes to balance the ration. Other foods such as cooked vegetables, eggs, honey, cheese, liver, kidneys, heart and tripe are often used to provide variety, and also to formulate a well accepted, nutritious, and economical ration.

Although in recent years, there have been a number of significant advances in the scientific aspects of feeding for sprint performance, most diets still remain relatively simple. In most cases, trainers are reluctant to incorporate changes or substitute new feeds if Greyhounds are maintaining their bodyweight, vitality and performance.

ENERGY

In the adult racing Greyhound, energy is the most important constituent in the diet with the exception of water. Energy provides the fuel for muscles, nerves and metabolic function, and without adequate energy the Greyhound will not perform. If there is too much available energy, particularly in the form of carbohydrates, the Greyhound is more likely to put on weight, or cramp when trialled or competed. The energy supply and exercise level are interrelated, and can vary between individual Greyhounds, with the distance of racing or coursing and with the environmental conditions.

Changes in workloads and climatic conditions have the greatest influence on the amount of energy required on a daily basis to maintain a static racing weight and optimum performance. The

Ideal racing condition for a racing Greyhound. Note the lower rib and mid-rib lines that converge as a fold of skin in the flank, and the visible outline of the last two or three ribs; the pin bones behind the back are visible but covered with flesh.

racing Greyhound requires extra energy during cold weather to maintain its body temperature. In most cases the amount of energy is increased by boosting the amount of dry food, or adding extra fat to the diet. In hot weather, extra energy is required to fuel panting as a Greyhound expels heat during rest or following exercise. This is usually best provided by increasing the level of fat in the diet, without increasing the bulk of the ration consumed. Racing Greyhounds require up to twice the amount of energy in their ration during hot weather to fuel respiratory muscles for panting. Greyhounds in training are usually highly muscled with little reserves of their own body fat, so that extra fat is the simplest way of boosting the diet to meet shortfalls in the day to day energy needs without increasing the amount the animal has to consume.

Excitable, barking, 'hard walking', nervy and highly-strung Greyhounds that run or course their race before the start, often expend valuable energy reserves in the pre-race period due to this hyperactivity and anticipation. Many of these Greyhounds benefit from additional fat to boost the energy levels without making them too excitable. Extra fat in the diet, combined with supplementary electrolytes, also reduces the risk of dehydration in this type of Greyhound.

On traditional 70 per cent meat diets, about 50 per cent of the energy is provided by the meat part of the diet. Meat contains low levels of carbohydrates, with most of the energy being contributed by protein in the meat. The major portion of energy supplied by the cereal grain based dry foods is provided by 40-50 per cent of carbohydrates and an average 20 per cent protein content. Many dry foods also contain added fat, up to 10-12 per cent, to boost energy levels, which helps reduce the need for a large bulk of dry feed. It is always important to compare the various brands of dry food available for both energy and fat levels (as listed on the outside of the bag). The lower protein (12-17 per cent), lower fat (3-5 per cent) dry foods are suitable for mixing into a high meat-based diets. The higher protein (20-24 per cent), high fat (8-12 per cent) dry foods are formulated as a more complete food, on minimal meat or meat-free rations.

Traditionally, Greyhound diets contain up to 70 per cent meat, with 25 per cent dry food by weight. Although Greyhounds can utilise a wide variety of different types of meat, lean beef still constitutes the standard on which most diets are formulated. However, the fat content of any type of meat used should be at least 10-12 per cent to provide adequate energy, as well as enhance the digestibility of the meat contained in the diet.

Over recent years it has been popular to add a pre-race snack of carbohydrates or sugars as an energy boost prior to coursing or racing. As a rule, it is unwise to feed short-chain simple sugars (e.g. glucose, honey, etc.) as an energy boost within 4-6 hours of racing. As they are absorbed, blood sugar rises quickly, and in turn triggers secretion of insulin, which acts to limit the blood glucose level. This can make the Greyhound lethargic, and if raced within four hours it may lack performance. Longer chain, more complex carbohydrates such as rice, pasta, or even potato (100-150 grams) given about 6-8 hours before racing is considered more suitable as a form of extra energy in a pre-race period, particularly in nervy, highly strung Greyhounds that anticipate the thrill of coursing or racing.

PROTEIN

The Greyhound diet should contain about 30-35 per cent of high-quality protein, on a dry matter basis, or about 20 per cent overall in the combined meat and dry food mix as fed. Excessively high protein diets reduce energy which can be readily metabolised, as energy is lost in urine as urea. When meat or vegetable proteins are taken in with the feed, digestive action splits the food proteins into individual amino acids. These amino acids are then recombined in the Greyhounds liver to form the proteins that make up the tissues and cells in the animal's body.

Up to 85 per cent of the total protein requirement in the racing Greyhound is normally provided by the meat base in a high meat diet. Therefore, for most meat-based diets, a lower protein dry food is adequate to satisfy needs, without providing excessive protein levels. However, if very lean meat is used, the dry food must contain adequate fat (10-12 per cent), or additional fat should be added to boost the energy level, especially during particularly hot or cold weather. Without adequate fat content, digestive and metabolic action is not maximised.

Although excess protein in the diet can be used as an energy source, it is less efficient than sugars and fats. As Greyhounds become fit and ready to race, they actually use less protein as an energy source for muscles during exercise. However, adequate protein must be provided to maintain and repair body tissue following hard competitive exercise. When Greyhounds commence initial training, the muscles may need building up, whilst the body fat reserves need to be reduced. During this time, if a Greyhound needs to put on muscle mass, then it is a good idea to boost the protein level in the diet by feeding a higher protein dry food for the first four to six weeks of training. After this time a lower protein dry food (from 13-17 per cent protein) can be offered, where meat constitutes 70 per cent of the total diet by weight.

It has been found that some meat proteins are not as well digested as beef protein. For instance, studies have shown that horse meat proteins digested only 80-85 per cent as well beef proteins, and vegetable proteins in dry food are only 80-85 per cent on average digested as compared to meat protein. Generally, more protein is passed out in the stools of Greyhounds fed on high dry food diets because the proteins are digested less than those in a meat-based diet containing the same amount of protein.

Over recent years, it has become popular to add higher protein dry foods to the ration for the first two meals after a hard course or race. This is aimed at boosting the protein levels to help repair muscle and other tissue. It is best done by simply substituting a 24 per cent protein dry food for a normal 17-20 per cent dry food for two meals, or by providing two lightly poached eggs, or three tablespoons of chopped liver, to boost protein levels after racing. The digestibility of certain proteins, such as egg white and soybean proteins is improved by cooking, but proteins in meat sinews (tendons) and feathers are poorly digested, even when cooked.

Low protein diets in coursing and racing Greyhounds have been associated with reduced liver function, and the development of anaemia and poor blood counts. However, an excessively high protein diet, although not affecting health directly, is not only expensive to feed, but does not increase performance in competitive Greyhounds. Furthermore, the elimination of excess poor-quality protein particularly is an energy-consuming process. It results in increased urinary ammonia and other wastes, water loss and extra body heat production. Therefore there is no advantage in feeding high protein meals once a Greyhound is fit for coursing or racing, with perhaps the exception of increasing protein levels for two meals after each race to help maintain muscle tissue.

FAT

Although traditionally very lean meat or meat with fat trimmed off was fed to racing Greyhounds, it is now accepted that at least 10-12 per cent fat in the diet is important for efficient digestion and performance in Greyhounds. Fat has a very high energy value, being 2 1/4 times higher than carbohydrates or protein, on a weight for weight basis. This means that relatively small amounts of energy dense fat will boost the energy content of the diet dramatically without significantly increasing the volume of food the animal has to consume.

For example, each 12g (1 tablespoonful) of fat or oil added to the diet provides the same amount of energy as 30-40g of 20 per cent protein, 10 per cent fat, dry food. Although over past years the feeding of fatty meat has been blamed for building up bile, with 'biley throats' and symptoms described as 'fat inside' in racing and coursing Greyhounds, this is now considered not to be directly related to fat levels in the diet. However, there is a limit to the amount of fat that can be fed, as Greyhounds will put on weight if the diet has too much energy.

An overall fat level of 12-15 per cent is considered to be suitable for most Greyhounds. Lean meat contains about 10 per cent fat, and dry foods up to 12 per cent fat. Therefore in diets with only 3-8 per cent fat content, it is beneficial to add extra fat to the diet. Under hot climatic conditions, feeding extra fat to increase the energy density of the ration will help to reduce the risk of dehydration, aid recovery and maintain the Greyhound at a more uniform bodyweight. Fat is the cheapest form of energy available, and fat trimmed from meat, or suet or kidney fat, and polyunsaturated cooking oil can be used as sources of fat to boost energy. The fat must be fresh, because if it oxidises or turns rancid, it is not only less palatable, but vitamins such as Vitamin E can be destroyed in the ration.

It is unwise to add cooked fat, such as that contained in roasted or grilled meat, to Greyhound diets, as in the long term this may lead to fat accumulation in the liver because the liver cannot utilise fats damaged by high-temperature cooking. Fat from stews is relatively safe because boiling temperatures do not damage the fat. Racing and coursing Greyhounds that are in training and being exercised daily, can tolerate relatively high levels of fat without apparent ill effects, as compared with other less active breeds of dogs. However, to avoid digestive upsets, the fat levels should be increased in a step-wise manner over one or two weeks, and the bodyweight monitored regularly every three to four days during this time. This progressive addition will also enable the racing Greyhound to adjust its metabolism to utilise fat for energy.

Obviously, if too much fat is added to the diet, the Greyhound will put on weight, hampering its speed and competitive potential. As mentioned above, up to 15 per cent fat in the total diet is considered ideal for racing Greyhounds to provide energy for exercise and boost energy levels during hot weather. During metabolism the breakdown of fats for energy releases additional water within the body tissues which can help to counteract dehydration, particularly in nervous, hard walking Greyhounds. These animals often suffer from chronic dehydration, which often causes them to reduce their water intake.

It is also well known that fats and Vitamin E have an inter-relationship. Vitamin E prevents

COMMON FEED INGREDIENTS: Values per 100g as fed
MEAT
(Best fed raw, either coarsely minced or diced)

Type of Meat	Average Energy Kcal Metabolisable Energy	Average Protein %	Average Fat %	Approx Substitution rate to Lean Beef for Energy	Comments
Lean Beef	200	21	12.5	100g	May be too low in fat for energy during hot weather, add 5g fat/100g beef.
Medium Beef	260	18	20	80g	Suitable energy source during hot weather, or long distance coursing races.
Horse	150	18	7	130g	Low in fat, add 7g/100g horse meat. Some greyhounds develop diarrhoea if horse meat substituted totally for beef - introduce slowly or feed only 50:50 mixture.
Chicken	200	20	12	100g	Low in iron and copper - add these minerals in a supplement during long term chicken use.
Mutton	265	15.5	22	75g	Ideal energy source during hot weather, and animals with symptoms of red meat allergy.
Beef Kidney	88	18.2	1.6	Limit to 30% substitution	Often used in stews. Low in fat, add 15g fat per 100g kidney.
Beef Liver	157	20	8.6	Limit to 100g twice weekly	High in purine compounds - may affect performance
Beef Heart	100	18.2	3	Limit to 50% substitution	Low in fat - add additional fat 10g/100g heart
Meat trimming fat	800-900	-	-	Max 10% substitution for meat as an energy boost	High energy content - ideal during hot weather, or for dehydrated greyhounds.

COMMERCIAL DRY FOODS
Soak for 15 minutes to moisten before feeding. Ensure water is always available

Low Protein/ low fat	270	12	2	Formulated to mix with diets containing 70% meat. Provide about 200-250g daily.
Medium Protein/ Medium Fat	290	17	5	Formulated for 50-60% meat diets. Provide about 250-300g daily.
High Protein/ High Fat	330	20-24	10	Suitable for 20-30% meat diets, or higher amounts to replace meat. Provide about 350-700g daily depending on meat content.
Very High Protein/High Fat	400	30	15	Complete dry food diet. Refer to manufacturer's recommendations for feeding rate.

All substitutions should be observed by monitoring appetite, body weight and performance on a weekly basis uncontrolled oxidation of polyunsaturated fats to harmful compounds in the muscle cells. Therefore, for every tablespoon of fat added to the diet, an additional 25iu of Vitamin E should be supplemented in the daily ration, above the normal supplementary level of 50-100iu of Vitamin E per day. Where stamina and endurance is required, such as in coursing Greyhounds, additional fat added to the diet will ensure adequate energy reserves for long-duration coursing.

FIBRE

Greyhounds require about 5 per cent fibre in the diet for efficient digestion. Meat contains relatively low amounts of fibre and most Greyhounds obtain their major fibre source from dry foods or vegetables. Greyhounds cannot digest large amounts of fibre effectively, which reduces gut transit time, as well as increasing the overall bulk and water content of the stools. Excess fibre can bind water in the bowel, diverting it away from urinary excretion, increasing urine concentration and the risk of urinary tract problems.

   If the diet is excessively concentrated, without adequate fibre levels, many Greyhounds will suffer from low grade constipation, often straining to pass small concentrated motions. They may develop a craving to eat their own stools, or seek out grass to eat on a regular basis. Regular checking of the consistency of the stools and the ease with which a Greyhound empties out, is a practical way of assessing relative digestive function and the adequacy of fibre in the diet. Low-fibre diets resulting in small concentrated motions being passed can be made more suitable by adding extra dry food, a cup of cooked vegetables, or even 1-2 tablespoons of wheat bran. If, however, Greyhounds on a high dry food diet are emptying out a comparatively large volume of stools, then the bulk of the dry food can be reduced by adding extra fat to make up the energy shortfall.

WATER

Greyhounds must be provided with an adequate supply of clean fresh water at all times. Water must be available during hot weather, after racing and when electrolyte supplements are being added to the diet. The requirement for water depends on the amount supplied in the feed, the environmental temperature, the type of exercise and individual animals' electrolyte balance. The dry food should be soaked to a moist consistency preferably at least 15 minutes prior to actually being fed.

   On average a Greyhound will drink upwards of 1 1/2-2 cupfuls of water per day in cool weather. However, some Greyhounds are poor drinkers and often suffer from a dry coat and a chronic dried out or dehydrated state. Adding electrolyte replacers, or physiological salt mixes to the diet, will encourage extra water intake. However, when these are added to the diet it is important to provide clean, cool water at all times.

DIETARY CONSTITUENTS

MEAT

The main components of meat are protein, fat and water. Unfortunately, muscle meat has no bone, and is deficient in many important minerals and vitamins, particularly calcium, so it is not a complete food for coursing and racing Greyhounds. They also need organ meats such as liver and kidneys, bones, and vitamin and mineral supplements. As dogs in general digest animal protein more efficiently than vegetable sources, authorities consider that meat or meat byproducts must be included to ensure the most efficient absorption of food energy and protein in the competitive animal. Raw meat, minced to a coarse consistency, or even in small chunks, is better utilised than cooked or finely minced meat. Additional information on each individual type of meat, as well as the feeding amount and the relative benefit to racing diets, is summarised on Page 36.

DRY FOODS

Over recent years, dry foods have become more important as a major dietary constituent for Greyhounds. Traditionally, dry foods were added to a meat-based diet to make up the shortfall of energy and protein. They also provided additional fibre needed for the digestion, as well as some minerals and vitamins.

Generally, dry foods fall into two categories. Dry foods containing 12-17 per cent protein are formulated to supplement a meat-based diet, and usually have a fat content of just 4-6 per cent. Dry foods containing 20-24 per cent protein, with up to 10 per cent fat, are formulated as a more complete food. Many lower protein dry foods need the fat level boosted by an extra 1 1/2-2 tablespoons of fat to meet basic needs for panting. Dry foods contain a maximum of 15 per cent moisture, and they should be moistened to a mushy but not sloppy consistency up to fifteen minutes before feeding. This not only improves overall digestion of the dry food component, but also ensures that it does not have a dehydrating effect on the bowel mass once it is consumed.

In Greyhounds prone to dehydration, the feeding of moistened dry food with a maximum of 5-7 per cent fibre retains more moisture in the bowel due to its fibrous content and provides a reservoir for replacement fluid in the animal. When dry foods are mixed into a meat-based bulk mix, extra fluids such as milk or water should be added to the mix to prevent dehydration of the meat component, and provide adequate water to meet digestive needs.

Most commercial dry foods contain added vitamins and minerals, including calcium, as a complete feed for Greyhounds. However, because of the general structure of dry foods, and their fibrous content, it is possible that iron, calcium and magnesium, in particular, are not fully absorbed as they are bound up in the structure of the fibrous portion of the dry food. Therefore it is important not only to ensure that the dry food is moistened and softened prior to use so it opens up during digestion, but also to add 25 per cent of the recommended dose of calcium, as well as a general vitamin and mineral supplement, to the diet, even where a complete dry food constitutes a major proportion of the diet.

VEGETABLES

Although traditionally vegetables were a popular feed for Greyhounds, there is no real need to feed vegetables at all when good-quality dry foods are incorporated into the ration. In general, vegetables provide a source of fibre and moisture, and in some cases they contribute a limited amount of vitamins and minerals without providing much energy to the diet. However, high levels of carbohydrate-containing vegetables, such as potatoes, rice or pasta, can be used as an energy boost to the ration. It is unwise to cook vegetables by boiling for long periods as this destroys many of the vitamins, and releases soluble minerals and salts into the cooking water. This water can be added back to the diet to provide additional fluid to dampen and soften the dry food component.

Although vegetables are probably not a necessary additive, they do provide extra fibre and bulk to the diet and valuable fluid reserves. This is of particular benefit to a Greyhound that is prone to dehydration during hot weather due to excitement, or to fluid loss through panting under hot kennel or travelling conditions.

Where vegetables are not fed, wheatbran can be used to boost the fibre content of the diet to aid moisture retention in the bowel and help keep stools soft for ease of emptying. About 1-2 tablespoons of bran per day is recommended for high meat diets where minimal amounts of dry foods are fed, or vegetables are not included. If stools become too soft, reduce the amount of bran until they return to normal.

MILK

Depending on its availability, milk can be used as a source of fluid and a limited protein supplement for racing and coursing Greyhounds. However, in many areas, milk is not readily available, and therefore dry food should be dampened with either a meaty broth, lukewarm water, or vegetable cooking water. Milk is palatable to Greyhounds, and it is useful to add to a breakfast meal, if breakfast is provided, to help soften the dry food for puppies and younger racing Greyhounds.

However, it is most important to avoid sudden reintroduction of milk, or products containing milk powder, to older Greyhounds which have not been given milk for at least two to three months. Basically, Greyhounds do not need milk, but if available, it is a palatable and appetising fluid to moisten dry food with, particularly during the warmer weather when every chance should be taken to give Greyhounds extra fluids mixed into the food to reduce dehydration.

MINERALS

The major mineral requiring particular attention is calcium, together with the relative balance of calcium to phosphorus in the racing Greyhound's ration. Meat-based diets usually have a deficiency of calcium relative to phosphorus; and although balanced dry foods can counteract some of the calcium deficiency, it is necessary to add a supplementary source of calcium to most

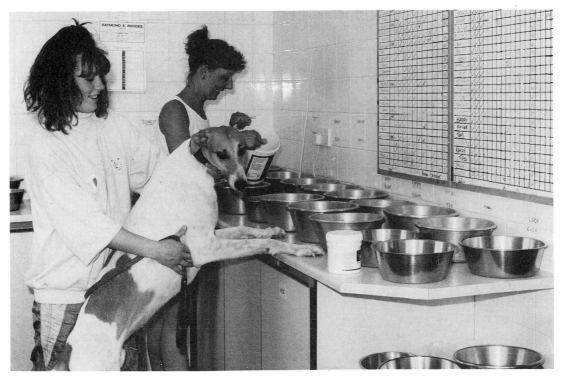

Mineral supplements may be added to the diet according to individual needs.

MAJOR MINERAL AND VITAMIN REQUIREMENTS

Nutrient	Recommended Daily Intake		Deficiency (D)/ Excess (E) Signs	Likely dietary Imbalances	Therapeutic Uses
	Resting	Racing			
Calcium	3,570mg (0.6% dry diet)	6000-8000mg (1.0-1.2%) dry diet	(D)Lameness, stiffness, bone growth problems, bone weakness. (E)Slow growth, decreases copper, zinc, iron uptake.	High meat or cereal based diets. High fat decreases blood levels.	Counteract high fat diets. Bone strength for young greyhounds in training.
Phosphorus	2,670mg (0.5% dry diet)	5000-6000mg (0.8-1.0% diet)	(D)Reduced appetite, lameness. (E)Causes relative calcium deficiency, kidney damage.	Meat diets relatively deficient, or excess calcium supplementation	Balance Calcium: phosphorus ratio to 1.35-2.0:1.0 in meat diets.
Sodium	330mg sodium (Requirement relatively low as greyhounds do not sweat)	Maximum 5000mg salt daily (0.8% of diet)	(D)Weight loss, fatigue slow growth, reduced milk in brood bitches. (E)Excess thirst, lack of appetite, heart and kidney damage. Death.	Dry foods contain 1-1.3% salt. Bore water. Excess causes urine loss of water and potassium.	Do not add additional salt if more than 300g dry food daily. Do not use salt mixes formulated for sweating horses.
Potassium	2670mg	4500mg slow release coated supplements recommended	(D)Develops due to diarrhoea, kidney tonics. Causes weakness, poor performance, dehydration. (E)Lack of adequate water - heart damage.	High salt content, excess bicarbonate in diet. Extra loss in excitable, hard walking greyhounds. Meat based diets marginally low.	600-1200mg as a supplement daily to prevent dehydration and cramping in nervy animals.
Magnesium	246mg	800-900mg	(D)Retarded growth, poor performance, weak toes, hocks and wrists. (E)Diarrhoea and urine crystals.	High fat and calcium levels in diet reduce uptake.	Add half RDI in hot weather, nervy or cramping animals.
Iron	20mg	60mg maximum	(D)Anaemia and lack of stamina (E)Loss of appetite, weight loss.	Low in white meat (chicken and fish) diets. High milk diets.	Supplement white meat diets, or during recovery from anaemia.
Copper	1.8mg	5.0mg	(D)Slow bone growth, anaemia, joint weakness. (E)Not reported.	High calcium, excess zinc in diet. Low in chicken meat diets.	Supplement chicken diets with half RDI and all young growing greyhounds.
Zinc	21.6mg	65mg	(D)Slow growth, poor appetite hair loss, skin scurf. (E)Results in signs of calcium deficiency.	Reduced uptake in cereal dry food diets or high calcium diets.	Add half RDI for optimum skin condition and bone growth.
Iodine	0.36mg	1mg	(D)Poor growth, lack of performance, hair loss. (E)Similar to deficiency.	Low in cereal based diets.	Add half RDI on cereal dry food based diets.

Recommended Daily Allowance (RDI) Adult 30kg (66lb) racing Greyhound

Vitamin A (Retinol)	2,250iu (0.675 mg)	3375iu (1.0mg)	(D)Reduced fertility, poor skin, weak tendons, poor eye sight. (E)Loss of appetite, bone weakness.	Lean meat based diets.	Supplement routinely on meat diets. May assist disease resistance, tendon healing.
Vitamin D (Cholecalciferol)	240iu	360iu	(D)Bone growth problems (rickets), poor teeth. (E)Debility, diarrhoea, vomiting.	Kennelled greyhounds, winter months, lean meat based diets.	Add RDI to lean meat based diets, or kennelled greyhounds.
Vitamin E (Tocopherol)	15iu	30-100iu	(D)Reduced fertility, birth of dead pups. Muscle weakness, poor stamina. (E)Poor appetite.	Freezing meat destroys Vitamin E. Often combined with selenium 0.1mg daily for muscle strength.	Add to high fat and meat based diets. May help reduce cramping and enhance stamina in deficient animals.
Vitamin K	No known requirement. Synthesised by bacteria in large bowel		(D)Risk of haemorrhage. (E)High intake likely to be dangerous.	Excess Vitamin A in diet. High temp cooked foods. High dose sulpha drug therapy.	Certain drugs and antibiotics can reduce natural bowel synthesis.
Vitamin B1 (Thiamine)	600ug	1.8mg	(D)Poor appetite, weight loss, muscle weakness. (E)Not toxic.	Raw fish (carp). Cooked foods for long periods.	High doses may assist in settling nervous behaviour.
Vitamin B2 (Riboflavin)	1.5mg	4.5mg	(D)Dry skin, muscle weakness, reduced fertility. (E)Not toxic	Cooked foods, excess bicarbonate salt in diet	High fat diets, or during cold weather.
Vitamin B3 (Nicotinamide)	6.75mg	20mg	(D)Black tongue, ulcers in mouth, anaemia, poor performance. (E)Skin vessel dilation.	Long term sulpha drug therapy.	Add half RDI for race performance.
Vitamin B5 (Pantothenic Acid)	6.0mg	18mg	(D)Poor appetite, gut disorders, liver damage. (E)Not observed.	Cooked feeds.	Supplement racing diets.
Vitamin B6 (Pyridoxine)	0.6mg	2mg	(D)Anaemia (E)Not observed.	High protein diet increases requirement.	Add half RDI to high meat diets.
Vitamin B12 (Cobalamin)	15ug	45ug	(D)Anaemia (E) Not observed.	Combined vitamin B6 deficiency, high chicken diets.	Supplement RDI on high chicken diets.
Folic acid (Folacin)	120ug	360ug	(D)Anaemia (E)Not observed.	High hookworm burdens. Cooked foods long term sulpha drug therapy.	Add half RDI in heavy training on low meat diets.
Vitamin C	Natural liver synthesis 1200mg daily	250-300mg supplement	(D)Poor skin healing. (E)Poor repeat performance observed.	Contact with iron and copper supplements destroys Vitamin C.	Supplement 250-1000mg daily for 1-2 days before racing.

Greyhound rations to meet requirements. There are many forms of commercial or proprietary calcium supplements available, but in general a calcium supplement containing both calcium and phosphorus, with vitamins A and D, which is formulated for Greyhounds and fed in direct proportion to the amount of meat in the diet, is the best one to balance the calcium need in the racing Greyhound. Greyhounds require additional calcium over and above other breeds of dogs because they need to maintain a strong bone structure during long-term training and competitive coursing and racing. As a guide, a Greyhound on a meat-based diet should be provided with an additional 2-3 grams of supplementary calcium per day to balance the diet and meet basic calcium requirements during training. Where milk is used as a constituent to moisten dry food in the amounts offered to racing Greyhounds, milk provides relatively small amounts of calcium. One cupful of milk contains 300mg of calcium. The amount of milk is often limited by its cost, the risk of lactose overload and subsequent loosening of the bowels in an adult Greyhound.

Bones can provide an additional source of calcium, but these are not usually fed to racing Greyhounds on a regular basis. For instance 200-300g of good-quality brisket bone, with a fat covering, provides a source of calcium, as well as fat, when given once or twice weekly to a coursing or racing Greyhound in training. The abrasive action of gnawing bone also helps to clean the teeth and provide relief from boredom in Greyhounds confined to kennels. Large beef bones to gnaw once a fortnight or so can also be provided to relieve boredom in racing kennels. However, it is unwise to cook any form of bone added to Greyhound diets as this only increases the risk of splintering and possible injury to the gut system during digestion. This applies particularly to rib bones, often fed to Greyhounds during training.

Other minerals that are important in the diet are magnesium, zinc and iron, as constituents of blood and body fluids. Generally, a commercial vitamin and mineral supplement formulated to meet the needs of racing Greyhounds is recommended to provide a source of these important minerals to meet requirements in the diet. A supplement containing iron and copper is particularly important on white meat diets, such as chicken or fish, which contain only about one quarter of the levels of these blood-building minerals found in red meats such as beef, horse or sheep.

VITAMINS
Meat-based diets are generally deficient in a wide variety of vitamins, notably Vitamins A, D and E, particularly where lean meat is used as a base. Although many dried food formulations contain a vitamin package formulated to meet the requirements of non-sporting or sedentary dogs, the racing Greyhound requires additional levels of Vitamins A, D and E, including a wide range of B-Complex vitamins, to maintain a strong musculo-skeletal system, muscle stamina, appetite and digestive function.

Generally, a commercial vitamin and mineral supplement, containing a wide variety of vitamins, is adequate for the majority of racing and coursing Greyhounds. However, additional Vitamin E supplements (up to 50-100iu daily added to the feed), may be beneficial to improve endurance and stamina in Greyhounds racing and coursing over longer distances. Guidelines for minerals and vitamins are included on pages 40 and 41 with appropriate comments on the dose rate, and benefits of supplementation.

ELECTROLYTES
Although Greyhounds sweat little compared to horses and human athletes, an adequate supply of electrolytes is required to meet the daily requirements particularly in Greyhounds prone to stress, nervousness and pre-race anticipation. As a non-sweating animal, a Greyhound does not require high amounts of sodium salt added to the diet on a regular basis, and sufficient amounts usually

are provided by the dry food component in the diet. However, Greyhounds that are excitable, or easily stressed by race day and coursing procedures, are often unable to conserve potassium, and benefit from physiological electrolyte mixtures containing high levels of potassium over and above that required by non-sporting dogs. In nervous, hard walking Greyhounds an additional supplement of slow- release potassium, usually provided as a coated tablet, is often recommended during periods of high stress, during hot weather or when an animal is dehydrated due to repeated racing and travelling. It is essential that an adequate supply of cool fresh water be provided at all times, and dry food be dampened prior to feeding, when electrolytes or body salts are added to the diet.

FEEDING SHOW GREYHOUNDS

The racing Greyhound is a highly intelligent, lovable and gentle dog that is becoming increasingly popular as a show animal in sporting and hound classes in many countries. As a dog specifically bred and maintained for competitive exhibition, the racing Greyhound should be well developed, strongly structured, without blemish or obvious injury related to poor conformation.

The animal should exhibit vitality and good behaviour, complemented by a well groomed haircoat and a fleshy, but not obese condition. There are a number of dietary alternatives that can be used for show Greyhounds, ranging from the traditional fresh meat and dry food dietary blend commonly provided for racing Greyhounds, to complete dry food, or canned, semi-moist commercial pet foods used for other show dogs. If meat is used as a base, it should contain 10-12 per cent fat for energy and to ensure efficient digestion.

Consideration must be given to providing a balanced diet, together with access to large bones at least weekly, or brisket bones twice weekly, to keep the gums and teeth healthy and free of the tartar build-up common on soft food diets. Descaling of teeth may also be necessary to avoid gum disease and premature loss of teeth as an animal ages.

The amount of feed is generally only 10 per cent less in weight than that offered to a racing Greyhound in training, with adjustment in energy content to match the amount of exercise and weather conditions in order to maintain optimum show body condition. Twice weekly supplements of 100 grams of fresh liver or kidney often help maintain the appetite.

One of the major requirements for a show animal is a fine, glossy haircoat which can be achieved by regular grooming and the provision of polyunsaturated fatty acids, such as contained in one teaspoonful of blended vegetable oil per 10kg bodyweight, added to the daily ration. A supplement of vitamins and minerals containing Vitamin A (2500iu), Vitamin D, as well as zinc, copper and iron, in particular may be beneficial in promoting a deep coloured, smooth glossy coat. Regular worming and flea control is mandatory to achieve the vitality and haircoat condition required in the show ring. When show Greyhounds are travelling and being exhibited on a regular or repeated basis, it is essential to provide electrolyte or body salt replacers in the food, and clean, cool water to drink during travelling and prior to ring work and exhibition to avoid dehydration. The use of specialised rehydration drinks is recommended in nervy or highly excitable animals to replenish fluids quickly after travelling or between show ring workouts. Show Greyhounds should be given regular daily exercise on the lead, and because some standards require a trim bodyline with prominent muscle development, short straight-line handslips over 200-300 metres up a slight grassy rise will assist in promoting a strong, fit, race-ready appearance.

FEEDING RETIRED GREYHOUNDS

Once their show or racing careers have ended, Greyhounds are often adopted out as household pets or as companions for senior citizens. Retired Greyhounds, by way of their placid nature, easily-maintained, low-shed short haircoats, and house-trained habits of kennel life, make adorable family pets. They make faithful companions for young and old. Once taught that jumping up is taboo, and that cats and other dogs can be affectionate companions, ex-racers make considerate and easily cared for pets. Greyhounds of both sexes are generally safe with children, postmen and visitors.

In fact, Greyhounds tend to be very playful and quickly learn their names, to be obedient and exhibit watch dog behaviour, and to enjoy ball chasing and other canine pastimes. Diets commonly fed to other pet dogs to maintain them in a slightly fleshy condition can be given in proportion to bodyweight, combined with adequate exercise. However, Greyhounds can become obese once retired to a sedentary lifestyle if they are not exercised daily by walking on the lead, or in a large house yard. In common with other dogs, regular worming and teeth care is essential for health and well-being.

As Greyhounds age, muscle and joint injuries sustained during their racing career can cause arthritic pain and discomfort. Eye cataracts are also relatively common in the aged Greyhound, with partial blindness often developing by 8-10 years of age. An elevated bed above concrete or stone flooring is helpful in slowing the onset of old age symptoms, and anti-inflammatory medication, as prescribed by a veterinary surgeon will enable the aged animal to lead a comfortable lifestyle as a pet and companion.

Chapter Four

GENETIC PRINCIPLES

CHROMOSOMES AND GENES

All mammals are made up of millions of tiny cells in the centre of which is a nucleus, examination of which, with a high-powered microscope, would reveal thread-like structures within. These structures are known as chromosomes. Closer examination would show that each cell had the same number of chromosomes and that in a dog this number would be 78. This is not peculiar to a single breed but is seen in every breed of dog from a Chihuahua to a St Bernard and is also seen in the wolf, from which the dog, regardless of breed, is almost certainly descended. The coyote and the golden jackal also have 78 chromosomes.

The 78 chromosomes come in distinct shapes and sizes but they are actually classifiable into similarly shaped pairs to the extent that it is more accurate to speak of 39 pairs of chromosomes than of 78 individual ones. Chromosomes of a pair are termed homologous chromosomes, and one member of each such pair has come from the sire of the animal being studied, while the other stems from the dam.

Chromosomes are composed of various products, one of which is DNA (dioxyribonucleic acid) which is the substance of which genes are made. A gene is the unit of inheritance and specific genes are always found on particular chromosomes and at a specific location or locus (plural: loci) on that chromosome. Thus a gene may be found at an extreme end of chromosome pair number 14. Because the animal has two chromosome 14s, it must have two of this specific gene.

ALLELES

A specific gene will always be involved in the control of a particular feature, though some genes may influence more than one trait. It may be a gene which has a massive effect (e.g. a gene causing dwarfism) or it may be a gene with a very tiny effect (such as adding a fraction of a cm to wither height). Not only do specific genes have an influence on a particular feature, but genes can come in more than one version. Different versions of a gene are termed alleles, and although these alleles will always affect the same feature in the dog, they may affect it in different ways.

This can be illustrated by the gene S which brings about solid coat colour. This gene has several alternatives or alleles, one of which is termed s^p or piebald spotting. Thus S and s^p are two of the alleles at the S locus (others being s^i and s^w). Because a dog has two of each chromosome, it must carry two versions of the S gene, one having come from the dam and the other from the sire.

If a dog carries SS or $s^p s^p$, then it is said to be homozygous (the same) in that it carries a specific gene in duplicate. If, on the other hand, it carries Ss^p then it is said to be heterozygous (different) for this gene. What a dog cannot have is three versions of a gene because it only has two chromosomes on which this gene is found.

DOMINANTS AND RECESSIVES

In the S series we have used upper and lower-case letters and there is scientific precedent for this. An allele which only needs to be present in a single dose for it to work is said to be dominant. An allele that must be present in duplicate to work is termed recessive. Generally, it is conventional to use upper-case letters for dominants and lower-case letters for recessives.

A dog carrying SS would be solid-coloured and essentially free of white markings. Similarly, an Ss^P dog would be self-coloured because the S allele masks (is dominant to) the s^P allele. In contrast, the $s^P s^P$ animal would be principally white in coat colour, albeit with darker patches in certain locations. Dominant alleles are easy to deal with, since, if the allele is present, it will be exhibited in some attribute. In contrast, recessive alleles are only identifiable when present in duplicate, or, in other words, if two apparently 'normal' animals give rise to an individual exhibiting some recessive trait. We would then know that *both* parents carried this recessive. Recessive traits can lie dormant in a population for generations and can 'skip' generations. Many anomalies in the dog are recessively inherited.

GENOTYPE AND PHENOTYPE

The phenotype of a Greyhound is what we can see or measure, whereas its genotype is the underlying genetic make-up. The SS and Ss^P dogs would have identical phenotypes (i.e. self-coloured) but quite different genotypes. Our objective as Greyhound breeders is to try to assess the genotype of the dog so as to allow us to predict possible results from using specific dogs. We cannot always do this, but we are attempting always to assess genotype from the basis of phenotype. This applies whether we are measuring relatively simple traits like coat colour or important attributes like racing ability or coursing prowess.

The speed with which a dog runs is a measure of its phenotype for racing. It is not necessarily a good guide to its genotype, but from the phenotypic racing performance we are hoping to assess the dog's genetic merit for racing. The same is true of other behavioural traits.

SEX INHERITANCE

Although it was said that there are 39 pairs of chromosomes with each member of a pair resembling its partner, there is a slight exception to this rule. In females there is a fairly large pair, whereas in males only one such large chromosome is seen and its partner is a small chromosome. These are termed the sex chromosomes and conventionally the female (large) one is termed X and the male (small) one Y. Thus all females are XX and males are XY.

When germ cells (sperm and ova) are formed it would clearly be illogical for them to have 78 chromosomes, because on uniting sperm and ovum, there would be 156 chromosomes. Accordingly, when sperm cells and ova are being formed there is a reduction division whereby only one member of each chromosome pair goes into each sperm/ovum, thus giving germ cells only 39 chromosomes, but with each pair being represented once. Thus when sperm and ovum unite at conception, we are back to 78 chromosomes, again in 39 pairs.

It should be obvious that at this point a great deal of chance is involved. Every sperm has one of the 39 chromosomes, but it is pure chance which these are. One sperm can have chromosome 14 that came from the dog's sire, another could have the one that came from the dog's dam. In addition to this chance element of which chromosomes go to which sperm (or ovum), there is the issue of the sex chromosomes. All ova carry an X because the female only has two Xs. In contrast, sperm can be either X- or Y-bearing. If the Y sperm gets to the ovum first, a male is conceived. If the X sperm is first there, a female is conceived. Thus the male determines the sex of its offspring.

There is some evidence that Y-bearing sperm either move faster, or the ovum has a predeliction for such sperm. At all events, more males are conceived. Though more male embryos may die, at birth there are about 106 males for every 100 females, which is termed the sex ratio, and this value is common to most breeds. Normal growth differs from the formation of sex cells in that normal growth consists of cells duplicating themselves, so that each contains the same number of identical chromosomes. In other words, no reduction division occurs.

It must be obvious that if sex cells are produced with a random half of the chromosomes (the only proviso being that one member of each pair is present), and then there is randomness in terms of which sperm meets which ovum, the element of chance in dog breeding is enormous. Aside from identical twins (extremely rare in dogs) no dog is going to be like any other, particularly as we may be dealing with many thousands of genes.

SEX-LINKED TRAITS
Any gene carried on either of the sex chromosomes will be transmitted to specific sexes. Thus, anything carried on a Y can only pass to a sire's son, while anything on an X can only pass to his daughter. Fortunately, few important genes are carried on the sex chromosomes. An exception is haemophilia A, which is carried on the X chromosome. Thus haemophilia A (probably existing in every breed) is 'carried' by females and expressed in males. A haemophiliac male (if he survives) will have a defective X chromosome, in that it carries the haemophilia gene. He will pass this to all his daughters, who will *all* be 'carriers', but his sons will be quite safe. In contrast, his daughters – regardless of who they mate – will, on average, give rise to fifty per cent haemophiliac males.

SEX-LIMITED TRAITS
Sex-limited traits are those expressed only in one sex. Examples would be milk production (seen only in bitches) and cryptorchidism (failure of testicles to descend – seen only in males). Although expressed only in one sex, these characters are caused by genes carried by both sexes. A bitch carrying high numbers of cryptorchid genes may produce defective sons, but she herself will show no symptoms or indications of the problem.

SEX-CONTROLLED TRAITS
Sex-controlled traits are seen in both sexes, but more frequently in one. In man, spina bifida and hip dysplasia are features of females more than of males and, in the dog, hip dysplasia tends to be more severe in the female than the male.

VARIABLE EXPRESSIVITY
Specific traits can express themselves differently in different animals. Two dogs could inherit the same genetic defect by carrying the gene in duplicate, and one dog may show an extreme form while the other shows a less extreme form. A type of dwarfism seen in the Alaskan Malamutes and Collie Eye Anomaly found in several Collie breeds are both examples where different degrees of severity are seen, but in both cases the condition is a simple recessive.

Using an affected dog that seems only slightly affected is just as dangerous as using a dog with the extreme form, since both are genetically alike. The least affected one could produce a severe case and vice versa.

EPISTASIS
Sometimes, genes at one locus interfere with or affect the expression of genes at another locus. This is best explained with coat colour. A Greyhound with the gene combination AA can form

black pigment. If it also carries B, either in duplicate or in single dose, then it will have black coat colour. However, for that black coat colour to express itself, it is essential that the gene D is present. If, instead of D, the dog carries dd, then this will prevent black pigment being formed, and instead of a black coat the dog will be blue.

Thus A-B-D- or A-B-Dd will be black, but A-B-dd will be blue. In this example, the dash indicates that the second gene at the A or B locus is unimportant. Thus, an AABBDD animal will be just as black as an AABBDd animal, but all combinations of AB with dd will be blue. This is an example of epistasis. It is, of course, important to realise that the AABBDD dog will only ever produce black offspring. In contrast, the AABBDd dog could give rise to blacks and blues, depending upon what mates are used. Thus their identical phenotypes hide different genotypes.

POLYGENIC TRAITS
Although, thus far, we have been looking at simple traits caused by single genes, most of the really important features which affect the dog (of any breed) are not inherited in this simple fashion. Traits such as wither height, litter-size, body-weight, physical construction and behaviour are all characters controlled by many genes. The individual genes will act as dominants, recessives, epistatic genes and the like, but each gene will tend to have a tiny individual effect, whereas the sum of the genes may have a large cumulative effect.

Characters which are influenced by many genes are termed polygenic, and such characters exhibit a format which follows a curved pattern termed a normal curve. There will be few animals at the extremes – most around the centre or mean area. Thus, if we were examining wither height, we would see very few tiny animals and very few giants, but most would be around the mean height for the breed, with numbers declining as you moved away from that centre. The same would apply to a feature such as racing performance in the Greyhound, with the complication that there would be differences in type of racing (sprinters versus long distance racers), and the features sought in a coursing dog might be slightly different from those desired in a track racer.

Suppose, for the sake of argument, sprinting ability was controlled by three gene pairs with alternatives being + or O at each pair, and with + indicating an increase in performance. Thus you could have dogs which ranged from 000000 through to ++++++. The numbers in each category would depend upon what breeding programme would apply, but if you mated a six + animal to a six O animal, the progeny would all be +0+0+0 in genetic make-up. If two of these were then mated together, all possible combinations from six O through to six + would exist. In a large number of such mating you would end up with the proportions shown in In the following table. It can be seen that the distribution follows the typical normal pattern, with few at the extremes and most around the centre.

Distributions of genes with three gene pairs.

Number of + alleles	Number of dogs	Percentage of population
0	1	1.56
1	6	9.38
2	25	23.43
3	20	32.25
4	15	23.43
5	6	9.38
6	1	1.56
Total	64	100.00

Of course, this is very much an over-simplification. Sprinting performance is unlikely to be controlled by as few as three gene pairs and, moreover, it is not controlled solely by genes. The ability of a Greyhound to run will depend upon genetic make-up coupled with a series of environmental influences, which will comprise (among other things) nutrition, exercise and training, as well as the dog's mental approach to the job, itself a trait partially under genetic control.

Some dogs, quite capable of running quickly, may have no interest in so doing within the constraints of a track and with other dogs racing alongside, yet that same dog in a field might express its potential. Greyhound trainers need a dog with the ability to run *and* the willingness to do so.

The colour of a dog's coat will be exclusively an inherited feature, and a relatively simple one at that, but his ability to run will depend upon many genes inherited in different ways, each with a relatively small influence, but with a large influence collectively. It will also be influenced to varying degrees by the environmental conditions imposed upon that dog. In contrast, coat colour will be unaffected by the way the dog is fed, managed, or trained.

These provisos apply to many of the important features listed above. The eventual height, weight, physical construction, litter-size and racing potential of a dog will depend upon the interaction between its genetic make-up and the environmental influences to which it has been exposed.

A breeder of Greyhounds is seeking to assess the potential of his dogs, identifying the best and breeding from these. The extent to which he will succeed will depend upon many things, including knowledge of the breed, understanding of pedigrees, and a great deal of luck. It will also depend upon the extent to which high performance is inherited. Only with inherited traits can superiority of the parents be transmitted to the next generation.

Of course, Greyhounds are kept for different purposes. As sight hounds they were used initially as hunters of game, which today corresponds to coursing. The racing track represents a modification of that hunting instinct by making the dog chase a moving object around a track for varying distances. In contrast, breeding Greyhounds for the show ring is an illustration of a dog being retained solely as an object of beauty.

Regardless of which of these three objectives exists, the chart on page 48 shows what a breeder is trying to do. The upper curve shows the parental population assessed for a particular feature e.g. wither height or racing speed over 400 yards. The breeder has selected as parents those in the hatched area and the lower curve shows the result. The pattern of the population is unchanged but the mean has moved along in an upward direction. However, the superiority of the parents has not been transmitted in its entirety because it was not 100 per cent inherited.

The extent to which selection will succeed will depend essentially upon two things:

1. The superiority over the population of the parents selected.
2. The extent to which the character is inherited.

Item 2 is termed the heritability of the character. If a character had a heritability of 40 per cent then 40 per cent of parental superiority would be transmitted to the offspring. Unfortunately, in dogs, estimates of the heritability of traits are not readily available in the way that they are with cattle, pigs and sheep and are increasingly becoming in the horse. However, it is likely that reproductive traits such as litter-size will have a low heritability value (around 10 per cent), while wither-height will be in excess of 50 per cent and body-weight about 40 per cent.

Racing performance has hardly been studied, but Timeform ratings in thoroughbred horses are

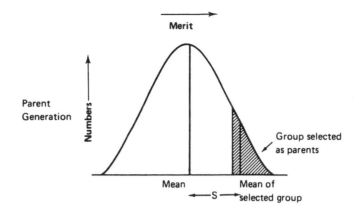

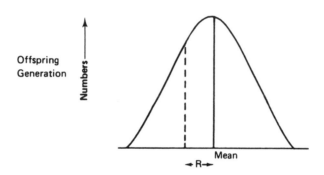

known to be about 40 per cent heritable, and it may be that racing performance in sight hounds is of a similar order. Heritabilities differ from breed to breed and from population to population within any breed, but traits that are less than 20 per cent heritable do not respond well to direct selection. In contrast, traits that are moderately heritable (25-50 per cent) or highly heritable (over 50 per cent) will respond well to selection.

FEATURES OF SPECIFIC INTEREST TO THE BREED

FITNESS TRAITS

Despite the name, fitness traits do not refer to athletic features but rather to traits concerned with 'fitness' of the species. Thus fertility, embryonic mortality, litter-size and viability of pups are all fitness traits. These tend to be of low heritability (under 15 per cent), but they are still traits with a large genetic influence. Unfortunately, they are controlled by combinations of genes and are thus difficult to select for.

QUALITATIVE TRAITS

These are traits concerned with coat-type or colour and tend to be simple in their mode of inheritance, essentially involving one or two genes operating in simple Mendelian ways. They are of less importance to the dog in functional terms but can be important in the show ring.

Greyhounds are not selected for any specific colour, and so breeders do not have to restrict themselves to certain colours but can concentrate on more useful attributes.

QUANTITATIVE TRAITS

These are features of great importance concerned with structure and conformation, as well as physical attributes. Most tend to be polygenic in origin and to be influenced by both genes and environment. Heritabilities vary but can be quite high for some features. These are the really important factors affecting the conformation and functioning of the dog.

BEHAVIOURAL TRAITS

These concern not only character (shy, aggressive, dominant, submissive, etc.), but also functional traits such as racing performance. Most of these features are only now being studied and many are complex in mode of inheritance, but usually polygenic. Fear, for example, is a highly inherited trait, with a value around 50-60 per cent.

ANOMALIES

Anomalies are not wanted but can be important. Most are simple Mendelian traits, usually inherited recessively, but some features are sex-linked (e.g. haemophilia A and B) and others polygenic (e.g. hip dysplasia and OCD). Breeders do not want these traits but have to take account of them in breeding programmes so as to reduce their incidence or avoid their occurrence. Greyhounds are virtually free of hip dysplasia, but from time to time other defects may crop up. It is, therefore, sound policy to discard from a breeding programme those dogs that are affected by any defect of genetic or presumed genetic origin.

Chapter Five

BREEDING GREYHOUNDS

THE GREYHOUND'S ROLE

Greyhounds are bred for three main purposes: to course, to race on the track, and to compete in the show ring. Historically, the Greyhound was bred to hunt by sight, and coursing is merely a refinement of this in-bred instinct. Sportsmen have channelled the Greyhound's natural desire to chase so that two dogs are pitted against each other – in pursuit of a hare – in a display of speed, endurance and courage. It can therefore be argued that coursing Greyhounds are the most typical examples of the Greyhound as it was meant to be. Track racing is a further refinement of the hunting instinct, with the chasing instinct aroused by a mechanical lure. Greyhounds run at top speeds for short bursts, competing against five or more dogs, and negotiating bends in the track.

Theoretically the racing Greyhound and the coursing Greyhound should be virtually interchangeable – both are bred to hunt at speed. In the early days of track racing, coursing Greyhounds adapted to the new sport with great success. However, the two disciplines diverged as it became apparent that a different type of Greyhound was needed in the highly competitive world of track racing. Increasingly, Greyhounds were bred specifically for the track, and as Greyhounds were also bred specifically for coursing, two distinct types emerged.

Greyhounds bred for show must conform as closely as possible to the Breed Standard (the written blueprint for the breed) in terms of general appearance and character. Although the stated aim of the Standard is that the breed should be able to carry out the function it was originally bred for, there is no test to see whether a Greyhound has the instinct to chase or has the speed to hunt successfully. The show Greyhound is therefore judged by its looks alone, with the breeder attempting to produce the structure and conformation of a dog that is capable of running at speed.

Today, there are enthusiasts for all three types of Greyhound – and breeders work with great skill to develop lines that will be successful for their particular discipline. In order to understand the differing requirements of these breeders, three major lines have been highlighted. Diana Ellis has founded a coursing dynasty, culminating in Evening Mail, winner of the 1992 Waterloo Cup. Nick and Natalie Savva are leading breeders of racing Greyhounds with countless major competition winners carrying their Westmead prefix. Barbara Wilton-Clark established her show kennel of Shalfleet Greyhounds in the 1960s, and her dogs have had a profound influence on bloodlines all over the world.

COURSING BLOODLINES

Evening Mail, winner of the 1991 Waterloo Cup, was a remarkable Greyhound. In a way he was something of a dinosaur as he was the first one hundred per cent English traditionally-bred coursing dog to win the classic since 1983, and he was the first puppy with his kind of breeding to

Evening Mail:
Winner of the
1991 Waterloo
Cup.

triumph since Linden Eland in 1972. People had become used to only Irish-bred coursing dogs winning the Waterloo Cup when Evening Mail emerged from a different time-warp and proved them wrong.

Before the 1970s when the Waterloo Cup became swamped with Irish dogs and Irish winners, English purpose-bred dogs won the Waterloo Cup almost as a matter of course. Coursing breeders produced a stream of puppies from traditional lines, usually reared on hill walks in Cumberland and the Borders, which filled the vast produce stakes of the time at Altcar, Druids Lodge, and Postland. In the 1970s, however, the big kennels of the landed gentry were seen no more and, with the added threat of imminent abolition of coursing by a succession of hostile Labour governments, coursing breeding was a shadow of its former self, allowing Irish imports to take over.

Diana Ellis, however, continued to breed from traditional lines, although she was not above using a smart track sprinter to inject early pace into her stock when she thought necessary. Her success at Altcar was phenomenal, breeding the winner of the Waterloo Cup in 1975 with Hardly Ever, in 1981 with Timworth Edward, and in 1992 with Evening Mail. She also bred two runners-up, as well as Southland Melody, one of the best Greyhounds fated never to triumph at Altcar.

Even so, no-one except Mrs Ellis could have expected her mating of Coley with Excuse Me to produce a classic winner. Coley never ran as a puppy, and he did little to excite attention in his second season until he went to the 1987 Waterloo Cup. Starting at 50-1 he reached the semi-finals,

Evening Mail in action.

just getting caught in his last course by the eventual winner Mouse Tail. He ran with some distinction in his third season, running up under handicap for the Altcar 1000 and for the Waterloo Plate to the very fast Irish bitch, React Molly. Coley had been beaten in the Waterloo Cup proper by the eventual runner-up, Crafty Roll On, in a poor little course which allowed neither Greyhound to show their true worth. He came out again in his fourth season, but the old spark was gone and he suffered three ignominious defeats before he retired.

Coley hardly seemed the stuff of which great stud dogs are made, but Mrs Ellis sent her bitch Excuse Me to him. Coley was by her 1981 winner Timworth Edward from a very solid English bitch line. Excuse Me was the only bitch that he covered, as soon afterwards he died from a tumour. Excuse Me's record was not very distinguished, she lost almost as many courses as she won. But this mating proved the Eldorado that all bloodstock breeders search for – the mating of two parents which produces stock superior to themselves.

This can only be done with faultless lines which have been bred from patiently for generation after generation. Both Coley and Excuse Me came from lines which were rooted in traditional English coursing, and which could be traced back for year after year through some of the best-known names in the sport. All Mrs Ellis's Greyhounds sprang from her two original brood bitches, Treble Stitch and Dendera Lena. The blood which flowed through their veins came from the days when English open coursing was considered the only legitimate Greyhound sport, when Irish 'park' coursing was thought of as a quaint joke, and track racing was regarded as a commercial confidence trick.

Evening Mail was a very good Greyhound. He had sufficient pace to lead the Irish runners, he had a good mouth, and he could run on gamely. He was a dog which would have been at home at Altcar a hundred years before in the palmy days of the sport. He was at his peak when he won the Waterloo Cup as a 22-month-old puppy and, despite a niggling shoulder injury, he reached the semi-finals again in his second season. There he was led two lengths by the eventual winner, Johns Mascot.

The final test for Evening Mail will be whether he can pass on his traditional virtues to his stock. He may well be the last of his kind.

RACING BLOODLINES

Nick and Natalie Savva have consistently bred top-class Greyhounds for the track for over twenty-five years, and their Westmead prefix is universally respected in sporting circles. The Savvas have been single-minded in pursuing a breeding programme geared to produce fast, sound, consistent Greyhounds that could compete with the highest company. They have valued their Greyhounds who have triumphed on the track, but they have also nurtured their brood bitches and stud dogs with the aim of improving and developing the Westmead line.

"I started in the beginning with a bitch called Pink Hannah, who cost just £30 back in 1968," said Nick. "She was no world-beater on the track, but I used Maryville Hi on her and it turned out to be a good litter. Westmead Villa was the star of the litter. She won some forty races and equalled the record at West Ham for 700 yards before she was two years old. That litter was bred purely out of enthusiasm, as an experiment.

"I then bought Cricket Dance from Phil Rees, and I bought Hacksaw from Patsy Brown. Cricket Dance was bought for racing, but she got injured. Hacksaw was also bought for racing, but she had problems with her wrist and did not stand up to it. So I eventually decided to breed from both of these bitches.

"To be honest, I did not know much at the time, although I followed the open racing scene and was aware of who were the best dogs around. I also knew how these dogs were bred, but I did not have the knowledge that I have acquired after years of studying pedigrees. I asked Patsy Brown which dog I should use on Cricket Dance, as I could not decide between Clonalvy Pride or his son, Yanka Boy. Patsy's advice was to use Clonalvy Pride, as at this stage the dog was twelve years old and therefore he was unlikely to be around for much longer. We could always use Yanka Boy later on.

"That was the beginning of our success story. The litter produced Westmead County, W. Lane, W. Pride and W. Silver. Then I mixed Cricket Dance's progeny with Hacksaw, which also worked very well. In fact, the Westmead line was founded on these two bitches and has continued ever since. The first Greyhounds I stood at stud commercially were litter brothers Westmead County and Westmead Lane, and they were very successful. I have had Glenroe Hiker and Fionntra Frolic who were both popular as stud dogs, but I would say that Flashy Sir has certainly been my most successful stud dog.

Nick and Natalie Savva with representatives of the Westmead kennel.

*Westmead Move
in her racing
days.*

*Westmead Move
has now become
highly successful
as a brood bitch.*

"The stud business in England is at a low ebb at the moment, and it is significant that the two stud dogs who I think have the most potential have left this country. Right Move is standing at stud in Ireland, and Balligari was sold to stand at stud in Australia. These dogs would not have got the same opportunities in England as they will in their new homes.

"It is more difficult to assess the strength of the male line of your breeding programme compared with the dam line, as you always use a lot more bitches. Westmead County was an outstanding sire of all classes of dogs – middle distance, stayers, and marathon runners. He used to throw very good dogs to moderate bitches. His brother, Westmead Lane, was also a very good sire. At the moment I am using one of his daughters, Westmead Satin, for breeding.

"What I am aiming to produce is a Greyhound that has the speed and the ability, and also the trackcraft to compete successfully at the highest level. A Greyhound must be keen – the chasing instinct must be one hundred per cent. I also like good travellers and good kennellers, and I look for these attributes in both the males and the females that I select for breeding.

"Size is not important. Cricket Dance was only 55lbs, and she had no problems with whelping. Bitches are generally bigger now, and I would generally like a brood bitch to be around 60lbs. As long as a bitch is in good condition, I am not too worried about age. When Westmead Seal was nine years old she whelped two litters which included Westmead Lodge, Phantom Flash and Westmead Chloe, who all became stars on the track.

"I would not breed from a bitch if she was hopelessly slow on the track. However, if she was of average ability and her litter sister was classy, then perhaps she would become a brood bitch. The expense of keeping a brood bitch means that you do not want to take too many chances, and you either want to see proven ability on the track, or you would look at a previous litter in the paddocks and see if they were showing potential.

"We have been fortunate in having few problems with the Westmead line, physically or temperamentally. The temperament of our dogs has been impeccable, with only the odd one proving difficult. They have all been very easy to school and very easy to handle. The only variance in them has been their speed.

"A lot more of my bitches than my dogs have come closer to the ideal. It is hard to put into words, but having dealt with their mothers, grandmothers, and great-grandmothers there is something that I can sense in a litter. When I bred the litter which included Westmead Move and Westmead Call, some Swedish buyers had pick of the litter. There were three bitches, and they left me with Westmead Call and Westmead Move. The pups were only four or five months old at the time, and I had no idea how good Westmead Move would become."

Move was to make up into one of the best stayers in training in Britain and in 1986 she landed the big race double of the Castford Gold Collar and the Walthamstow Grand Prix – a feat which earned her the title of Best British Bred Greyhound of the Year. Incidentally, the following year the award when to her litter brother, Oliver's Wish.

"Westmead Move has certainly been my most successful brood bitch of recent years. Everybody expects stayers from her litters, as the dominance of the dam line is so strong. But I have tried to instil early speed into her offspring. It is only recently we have been able to get the likes of Balligari and Right Move – two dogs with good early pace. By going to Daleys Gold with Westmead Move it did give me the early pace that I desired. For her next litter, I will probably go to a son of Daleys Gold or a son of I'm Slippy. She has now had seven litters for me, and she is nine years old. At our kennels we have a schooling track, which is 400 yards in circumference. We started off with grass, but after a few Greyhounds were injured, we changed the bends to sand. I have an outside hare which resembles the McGee system. I also have a sand straight of around 250 yards which runs parallel to the back straight of the schooling track. There are seven paddocks that can be used for pups, and I can keep up to twenty pups at a time. This averages to between two and three litters which can be bred per year.

"The pups are never shut in. As soon as they can walk they follow their mother out to a decent sized paddock. When they are old enough they have access to a field which is two or three acres in size, and they also have access to the middle of the schooling track every day for about an hour. When they are saplings they are galloped every day. They go around the track on their own and around the fields.

"I used to start my schooling quite early because I was impatient, but having injured a pup at eleven months old, I have changed my ways. I don't start formal schooling until the dogs are thirteen or fourteen months old. However, I have a small circuit with a whirlygig system, and I find this invaluable. I have a single trap, and the dogs get used to the box and going round bends. You can encourage a pup to chase a skin on a line from as early as three months of age, and you can try him with the whirlygig at five to six months. I would give a pup three or four tries with the whirlygig, and once he has chased, I stop work until he is thirteen months old.

"We feed our puppies a variety of milk, cereals, bread, stale cakes, eggs, and a dried biscuit called Febo. The puppies get as much as they want to eat and drink in the morning. As soon as the pups get off their beds in the morning, they follow their mother and they will eat from her bowl, which introduces them to different types of meat. Their main meal will consist of Febo, and I mix bread with it, and then a choice of chicken, beef, horse or tripe. I give them a variety as I find that the puppies eat better if they are given a change of diet.

"If the puppies are getting on well together and not fighting, I leave them in the paddock until they are twelve months old. If youngsters becoming too aggressive, I bring them in at nine months. At this stage the puppies get experience of being handled and the routine of kennel life. I kennel my Greyhounds in twos, and we work out according to individual temperament whether to kennel a dog and a bitch together, or two Greyhounds of the same sex. We are then ready to start schooling, and getting the puppies prepared for the race track."

SHOW BLOODLINES

In 1960 a very young Barbara Osborne (now Wilton-Clark, and in-between-times Odell) made up her first Greyhound Champion, the beautifully elegant bitch Treetops Ringdove, who was sired by the Crufts Best in Show winner Ch. Treetops Golden Falcon out of Ch. Treetops Liberty Light. Golden Falcon was, of course, a son of that fabulous stud dog, Ch. Treetops Hawk. Ringdove was to become the foundation bitch upon which generations of Shalfleet Champions would be based, through a very carefully considered close line-breeding programme back to Hawk.

Mated to Shalfleet Wicked William, a Hawk son, Ringdove produced the bitch, Shalfleet Enchantment, who became a most important brood bitch. Enchantment was mated to Ch. Shaunvalley Mudlark (who had lines back to Hawk on his sire Riverbank Playboy's side) to

Ch. Shalfleet Sir Lancelot: An important sire for the Shalfleet kennel.

Diane Pearce.

Shalfleet Silver Moon: One of the most prolific producers of Champion offspring the breed has ever known.

produce Frank Brown's dominant stud dog of the 1970s, Ch. Shaunvalley Cavalier. Mated to Ch. Seagift Sheriff (who again had two lines back to Hawk on his dam's side of the pedigree), Enchantment produced Ch. Shalfleet Swing High and Val Webb's Ch. Padneyhill Shalfleet Spring Greeting. Swing High was mated twice to Ch. Shalfleet Sir Lancelot (again strongly line-bred to Hawk) to produce, amongst many other winners, the Champions Shalfleet Spanish Town (owned by Rita Bartlett) and Shalfleet Sophisticate of Courthill (owned by Roger Stock). Spring Greeting, mated by Val Webb to June Minns' Cavalier son, Ch. Shaunvalley Bombardier, produced June's Ch. Padneyhill Prince Charming, the dominant sire of the late 1970s and early 1980s. When Prince Charming was mated to Gaysyde Nimbus (a Sophisticate daughter by Ch. Starbolt Cetus), he produced the leading stud dog of the 1980s and l990s, Ch. Gaysyde White Christmas.

Another Enchantment daughter by Mudlark was the beautiful parti-coloured Shalfleet Spanish Moon who, before going to California to become the foundation of Claire Kelly's Clairidge kennels, produced a litter by Ch. Seagift Sheriff which included the blue-and-white bitch Shalfleet Silver Moon. This bitch later became one of the most prolific producers of Champion offspring the breed has ever seen. She was an incredible bitch who was little shown, but she was worth her weight in gold as a brood, having the ability to produce quality offspring when line-bred not only back to Hawk, but also when mated to dogs of different breeding, thus allowing any out-crossing which Barbara may have considered necessary.

Mated twice to Hortondale Treetops Mighty Grand (an unshown double grandson of Hawk), she produced in the first litter Ch. Shalfleet Silver Fortune, who later went to the Sundridge kennel in America. From the repeat mating came the Chs. Shalfleet Sir Lancelot and Spode, thought by many to be the best Shalfleets ever. Lancelot was a strong, beautifully balanced, brindle dog, very reminiscent of his famous ancestor Hawk. Spode was the most exquisite blue bitch, absolutely teeming with quality. Lancelot went on to become the breed record holder with a total of nineteen CCs, this at a time when only eight to ten sets of CCs were on offer each year – a truly remarkable achievement. A mating of Lancelot and Spode produced the Chs. Shalfleet Stop That Tiger and Shirley Ann, who were so similar in type to their parents. In another litter by Cetus, Spode produced the outstanding bitch Ch. Shalfleet Sarah Fraser, who so sadly died without producing the puppies which Barbara had so looked forward to. Silver Moon was then mated to Ch. Cormoran Qattara Beau Brummel and produced the black dog Ch. Shalfleet Sporting Knight and other CC winners. She was then mated three times to Ch. Starbolt Cetus (Starbolt Argo – Starbolt Qattara Black Pearl), a combination which produced several Champions including Shadow Light, Spotlight, Sandpiper and Snow Bunting, as well as other CC winners.

The list of English and overseas Champions and CC winners bred in the Shalfleet kennels over the period from around 1960 to the time when Barbara gave up the dogs in the mid-1980s is much too long to be detailed here, but special mention must be made of one or two others. It is said by some that the best Shalfleet ever (indeed, I have read the best Greyhound ever, in some people's opinion) was the blue brindle bitch, Ch. Shalfleet Starlight (Ch. Shalfleet Scandal – Ch. Charm of Chellheath), who won seven CCs each with BOB, and was Best in Show at Windsor before leaving for the Foxden kennels, owned by the Farrells, in America.

Around 1980, Barbara surprised the Greyhound world by importing Am. Ch. Aroi Sea Hawk of Shalfleet, a white-and-blue brindle parti-colour, bred by Georgianna Mueller in California. Although he was little shown in England, he was used at stud to great effect. The first of his Champion offspring were Shalfleet Stormlight and Socialite (out of Ch. Spotlight), who eventually went to America and gained their titles there, as well as becoming important breeding stock. Other Champions by Sea Hawk were Shalfleet Sea Devil, Windspiel Northern Style (top brood bitch all breeds in the UK, 1993), Ballalyn's Hurricane Higgins and High Cloudsbay, Hubbestad Famous

Grouse, and Hubbestad Silver Dollar. Shalfleet Sea Dancer (Sea Hawk – Ch. Shalfleet Shirley Ann) was the last of the Shalfleet Champions in England and was owned by Gerd and Geir Flyckt Pedersen, who have since returned to their native Sweden with their dogs.

Sadly for the breed in the UK, Barbara gave up first the Greyhounds and then her other breeds and left the UK to go and live in Tenerife in the Canary Islands. It was a big enough blow to lose the expertise of such a fine breeder, but added to this, most of the dogs went abroad as well, either to America or Europe, leaving a gap in the breeding of Greyhounds in the UK which it may take generations to retrieve. When a kennel has been so dominant for so long in a country – and when that country has strict quarantine laws making the importation of new (or old) blood extremely expensive – the effects on the quality of the breed may only be measured in the very long term.

Chapter Six

MATING, WHELPING AND REARING

Greyhounds present few problems when it comes to mating and whelping, and provided breeders use stock that is fit and healthy, and the mating is timed correctly, most Greyhound bitches will prove to be admirable mothers. However, breeding dogs should never be undertaken lightly. It is an expensive, time-consuming hobby, and unless you have ambitions of founding your own kennel, it is wiser to leave it to the experts.

BREEDING PROGRAMMES
Regardless of whether you are breeding Greyhounds for the show ring, for the track, or for coursing, there are basically three programmes to follow when establishing a line.

IN-BREEDING: This is the mating of very close relatives – mother to son, father to daughter, brother to sister, etc. This type of breeding has the advantage of fixing certain qualities, but it is equally likely to cement faults into a line. If you are doubling up on pedigrees to this extent, any fault – no matter how small – can become a major problem. For this reason, in-breeding should only be used by experts who are fully conversant with the pedigrees they are using. Even then, it should not be used too often as it will weaken a line.

OUT-CROSSING: This is the complete opposite to in-breeding and involves mating two dogs who have no relations in common – at least for the first four generations. This method of breeding is used when fresh blood is needed to invigorate a line. The difficulties arise as the breeder cannot predict with any accuracy what the resulting offspring will be like. With luck, a good specimen may be produced, but there is no guarantee that this individual will breed true to type.

LINE BREEDING: This is the programme consistently used by most breeders. It involves mating dogs that are related, such as grandfather to to grand-daughter, uncle to niece, etc. This has the advantage of fixing family traits, but it does not involve the risks of in-breeding. Most breeders found their kennel on one or possibly two brood bitches, and all their stock will relate back to these early Greyhounds.

THE IN-SEASON BITCH
Before deciding to breed from a bitch, you must ensure she is in good health, fully mature, and of sound temperament. Obviously, the qualities that you are hoping to produce in the offspring will depend on your discipline – show, track or field – but these essentials remain constant. The bitch should be wormed before mating, she should be up-to-date with her inoculations, and she should

be the correct weight for her size. Most Greyhound bitches come into season every nine months, although some will cycle every six months. When you are planning a mating, it is helpful if you have kept a record of your bitch's seasonal cycle, and then you will have a better chance of ear-marking the correct date for mating. A season generally lasts for twenty-one days, and this should be counted from the first day she shows colour – a blood-stained discharge. You can usually tell when a bitch is coming into season, as she will pay more attention to her rear-end, her vulva will become swollen, and she may squat to urinate more frequently. It may be helpful to bed your bitch on a piece of white sheeting so that you will be able to detect the first signs of the discharge.

Most bitches are ready for mating between day twelve and day fourteen, although this can vary enormously. Bitches in some family lines may ovulate earlier or later, and only experience will teach you what is the right time to mate your bitch. The vet can take a vaginal swab from the bitch and from this he can work out the optimum time for mating. This test also has the advantage of showing up if the bitch has any infection which could hinder conception or could harm the stud dog. If this is detected early enough, a course of antibiotics can solve the problem in time for a successful mating. When the bitch is ready for mating, the discharge will change to a straw-colour, and the vulva will be swollen. A good test is to stroke the bitch's rear end. If she twitches her tail to one side, she is indicating that she is receptive and ready to be mated.

THE MATING

You will have chosen a suitable stud dog depending on your discipline and the breeding programme you have adopted. Again, it is essential that the dog is fit and healthy and of sound temperament. It is always advisable to select a stud dog that excels in an area where your bitch is lacking. Never double up on faults. It is customary for the bitch to visit the stud dog for the mating, and in most cases the stud dog owner will supervise proceedings. You may be required to help by holding the bitch steady. All dogs are individuals and all matings are slightly different. However, the most usual course of events is to introduce the dog and bitch, and allow them to play a little together. The stud dog will quickly make it clear whether he considers the bitch is ready for mating. A maiden bitch (one who has not been mated) may resent the stud dog's attentions to begin with, and some stud dog owners prefer the bitch to be muzzled.

When the bitch settles down she will stand and allow the stud dog to mount her. As the dog's penis penetrates the vagina his thrusting becomes more forceful. He will then settle, and may turn so he is standing rear-end to rear-end with the bitch. The ejaculation of the male occurs in three parts. The first fluid passed is semen and any other residue in the penis; this lasts for the first couple of seconds. The sperm is passed within one or two minutes of penetration, and the third part is the seminal fluid which follows as a drip feed during the tie period, helping the sperm on their way. A tie is always preferable in a mating, but a slip mating can be successful as long as the male organ is held inside the bitch for a few minutes.

The tie can last for a few minutes or for much longer. However, the average duration is twenty to thirty minutes, and the dog and bitch must be held steady during this period. The tie is caused by the swollen gland, the bulbus glandis, at the base of the penis, which is held by the muscles of the bitch's vagina. The pair cannot part until the swelling has reduced in size. After the mating, the bitch should not be allowed to urinate for half an hour or so.

PREGNANCY

When you return home after your bitch has been mated, life should continue as before. There is no need to change your bitch's diet or exercise routine until you know she is in whelp. For the first four weeks there will be little change in your bitch to tell whether she is pregnant or not. Some

A Greyhound bitch, seven weeks into her pregnancy.

bitches go off their food and appear slightly off-colour about three weeks after mating, and then quickly resume their normal appetite; others will show a slight change in behaviour, becoming more loving and affectionate. However, the first sign is when the nipples become a brighter pink in colour, and by five weeks you may be able to detect a slight bulge just behind the ribcage. An ultrasound scan will confirm pregnancy, and can also give a fairly accurate indication of the number of whelps being carried. From five weeks onwards the pregnant bitch should have a slight increase in her rations, making sure she is fed high-quality food. It is important not to over-feed, as an obese bitch can have problems when it comes to whelping. From six weeks it will be obvious that your bitch is in whelp, and from this time onwards it is advisable to divide her food into two meals a day, rather than one large meal. Regular exercise will help to keep her fit, but make sure the exercise is not too strenuous. Some bitches become more sedate as their pregnancy advances, taking good care of themselves. Others seem quite heedless of their condition, and will gallop round a paddock, playing with other dogs, if given the chance.

The average pregnancy last for nine weeks – sixty-three days – although a couple of days either side of this is not unusual. In the last week before the puppies are due, you should get your bitch used to her whelping quarters. Whether you choose to whelp your bitch in the house or in a kennel, you must make sure the area is warm (70-75 degrees Fahrenheit), and is draught-free. Most breeders use a specially constructed whelping box, and this must be large enough for your bitch to lie fully stretched out along one side, with ample space for the puppies to move away from the bitch, if desired. A 'pig-rail' should be fitted to the back and sides of the whelping box. This is a safeguard against puppies being crushed by their mother in the first days after whelping.

A week before the puppies are due you should make your final preparations for whelping. You will need:

A large supply of newspaper (to change the bedding during whelping).

Old towels (for drying the newborn puppies).

A container of antiseptic and a pair of blunt-ended scissors (for cutting the umbilical cords, if necessary).

Lengths of thread (for tying the cords).

Lubricating jelly (in case you need to help with a delivery).

A cardboard box box with bedding (this can be used for existing puppies while the bitch is delivering a pup).

A lidded bucket (for discarded placentas).

Waste disposal sacks (to dispose of soiled newspapers etc.).

A pair of scales (if you wish to wish to weight the puppies at birth).

A notebook and pen (to write down the time of arrival of each puppy, the time between contractions, and the weight of the puppies).

THE WHELPING

When whelping is imminent the bitch will become increasingly restless. She will probably pay a lot of attention to her rear end, she may start panting heavily, and she will start scrabbling at her bedding – nesting before the puppies are born. Some bitches will refuse food, and this gives a fair indication that whelping is drawing close, although others will be quite happy to eat a hearty meal as they go into labour. A drop in temperature is a certain sign that whelping is imminent, and as labour commences the temperature will have dropped to 99-98 degrees Fahrenheit from the usual temperature of 101.5 degrees.

If this is the first litter you have bred, it is advisable to recruit a more experienced breeder to be with you during the whelping. Most bitches will cope perfectly well, only needing reassurance and encouragement, but if problems arise you will be in need of expert advice. It is wise to inform your vet when your bitch goes into labour, and then he can be on stand-by in case he is needed.

The contractions during the early stage of labour serve to dilate the cervix, and the puppies cannot be born until the cervix is fully dilated. The length of time this takes varies, but if your bitch is straining for more than two hours and is failing to produce a puppy, you should consult your vet. The water bag, which looks like a black balloon at the vulva, heralds the birth of the first puppy. The bag may appear and then retract until the contractions are forceful enough to expel it. The first puppy will appear shortly afterwards, although the first-born may take slightly longer to arrive than subsequent whelps.

Puppies may be delivered head-first or hindlegs first. The hindlegs presentation does not constitute a breech birth – this is when the rump is presented first with the hindlegs tucked up along the stomach. The easiest delivery is head-first, as the body follows out very swiftly as soon as the head emerges. The hindlegs presentation requires slightly stronger contractions from the bitch in order to expel the head. If you have a breech presentation, you may need to help with the delivery. This is when the help of an experienced breeder is invaluable. In order to help your bitch, you must scrub your hands and fingernails, and then apply a small amount of lubricating jelly just inside the vagina, trying not to get any on the portion of the puppy that has emerged. Then, using a piece of towelling, grip the puppy firmly but gently, and as the bitch strains, a simultaneous rotation and downward pull should pull the puppy free.

EARLY DAYS

ABOVE: Fullerton with his mother, Bit of Fashion. Fullerton divided the Waterloo Cup in 1889 as a puppy, and then won it outright in three successive years. Bit of Fashion divided the Waterloo Cup in 1885.

BELOW: The Greyhound became highly-prized in the mid-19th century when coursing reached new heights of popularity. The Ashdown meeting was always particularly well attended.

P.J. Gates Photography.

THE VERSATILE GREYHOUND

ABOVE: Success on the track demands speed, stamina, and the mental attitude of a highly competitive athlete.

BELOW: On the coursing field, the Greyhound fulfils the function it was originally bred for.

FACING PAGE: In modern times the Greyhound – the sporting dog par excellence – is highly prized on the race track and on the coursing field, and also finds favour in the show ring and as a companion dog.

RIGHT: Ch. Hewly Hispanic II: A big winner in the American show ring.

BELOW: The Greyhound, with its gentle nature, makes an ideal family dog.

FACING PAGE TOP: Greyhounds waiting in the slips, wearing the traditional coursing collars.

BOTTOM: Fearless Mustang, trained by Geoff De Mulder, at full stretch.

GREYHOUND COLOURS

Greyhounds can be any colour, and although all colours are permitted in the show ring, many of the top show winners are predominantly white.

ABOVE: Two blue-coloured litter brothers.

FACING PAGE – TOP RIGHT: The distinctive markings of a brindle Greyhound.

TOP LEFT: The black Greyhound may be all black or may also have white markings.

BOTTOM: Ch. Ransley Fortune Seeker, bred by Rita Bartlett, winner of nineteen CCs.

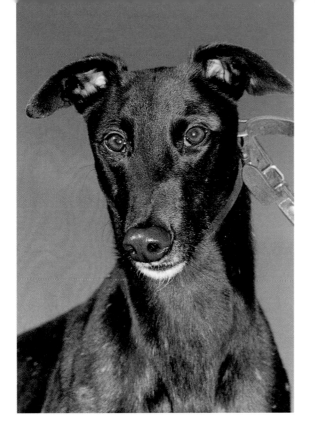

The fawn colour can range from a pale cream to a rich red-fawn.

Most bitches will cope with their newly-born puppies, licking them to remove the birth-sac, and severing the umbilical cord. However, a maiden bitch may be confused by what is happening, and she may require some help. If the bitch displays little interest in her new-born puppy, you will need to free it from the birth-sac, making sure its nose and mouth are clear of the membrane. The puppy should then be rubbed dry with a towel to stimulate breathing. By this time, your bitch will probably be responding more positively, and after she has licked it, you can put in on to a nipple and, hopefully, it will begin to suckle.

A bitch will instinctively eat the placentas, which are highly nutritious. However, it is preferable if she does not eat more than one or two, as they will make her motions very loose. The bitch will normally sever the umbilical cord with her side teeth, but if she is reluctant to do this or if she is being a bit clumsy, you will need to do this for her. This should be done by tying the cord with a length of thread, and cutting with your blunt-ended scissors about two inches from the puppy's abdomen. Before you cut, massage the blood that is visible in the cord towards the puppy.

The interval of time between births varies; sometimes two or three pups are born close together, and then the bitch rests before starting up again. You can take this opportunity to get rid of the soiled newspapers, and replace them with clean bedding. You can also offer your bitch a drink of warm milk with honey or glucose, to help her keep up her strength.

If, at any time, your bitch is straining for some time and appears to be suffering discomfort, call your vet. It could be that a puppy has become stuck and the bitch may require a caesarian section. The other whelping problem to be on the look-out for is uterine inertia. This is when the contractions are not strong enough to bring about a normal birth, and it can occur at any stage during the whelping. Again, a caesarian will probably be needed.

POST-WHELPING
When your bitch has finished whelping, take her outside for a few minutes to relieve herself. She may be reluctant to leave her new family, and you will probably have to put her on a lead. While you are outside, get someone to change the bedding, so the bitch will be able to settle down comfortably on her return. Make sure the puppies are warm, and check that they are all suckling, and then you can go off for a well-deserved rest! It is a good idea to ask the vet to call in after the birth to check the bitch and the puppies. He may give the bitch an injection to ensure that she has expelled all the afterbirths. A contented litter will be very quiet in the first few days after whelping. The mother will provide for all their needs, feeding them and cleaning them. At this stage, your job is to supply good-quality meals for the bitch, and to make sure she has plenty of fluids available which will help her milk supply. For the first couple of meals after whelping, feed your bitch a light diet, such as white meat and boiled rice, so as not to put too much strain on her digestion.

THE FIRST WEEKS
In their first week of life, puppies will sleep ninety per cent of the time. Occasionally a puppy will stray too far from the dam, and you will need to help it back to her side. Some breeders like to weigh their puppies at birth and then at regular intervals thereafter in order to ensure there is an even weight gain throughout the litter. However, you will soon see if any of the puppies are failing to thrive, and if this occurs you may need to supplement with bottle-feeding. There are many good products of milk powder on the market to choose from, and it is surprising how quickly a puppy will learn to feed from a bottle. One of your regular tasks from the first week onwards is to trim the puppies' nails. They can be very sharp, and if they scratch the dam while they are suckling she will end up with a very sore tummy. Make sure you only cut the tips of the nails. If you cut into the quick, it will be very painful for the puppy and will bleed profusely. The puppies' eyes will

The newborn Greyhound puppy bears little resemblance to the adult.

open from the seventh day onwards. To begin with, they can only distinguish light from dark, and it is important to avoid bright lights during this sensitive stage. Depending on when the eyes first open, vision will become more distinct from the tenth to the fifteenth day. The ears open from about the fourteenth day, and the hearing is acute by five weeks. The puppies will be able to stand upright by three weeks of age, and they will be walking and running by four weeks. At this stage they will discover each other, and start playing together. This is the start of the most fascinating time of all, as you watch the puppies emerging as individual personalities.

POTENTIAL PROBLEMS
ECLAMPSIA
This condition affects nursing mothers, and is also known as milk fever. The bitch becomes increasingly restless; she will lose coordination and will eventually collapse. It is essential to seek veterinary assistance immediately or the bitch will die. The condition is caused by lack of calcium, and the bitch will swiftly recover if she is given a large injection of calcium and glucose. The nursing bitch is most at risk when her milk production is at its highest – usually when the puppies are two to three weeks old. It may also occur if a bitch is feeding a large and demanding litter. The condition is unlikely to recur if the bitch is given a calcium supplement in her rations. However, it is unwise to over-supplement with calcium during pregnancy, as it is thought that this can actually increase the likelihood of a bitch experiencing eclampsia.

MASTITIS
This is an inflammation of one or more of the mammary glands of a nursing mother. The glands become very hard and hot, and are painful to the bitch when touched. The milk in the glands will

LEFT: Most Greyhound bitches make good mothers and enjoy caring for their puppies.

BELOW: Once weaning is under way, the puppies will become increasingly independent.

be discoloured or even blood-stained, and the puppies will avoid suckling from the affected glands. The bitch may also show signs of fever. Application of warm towels and expressing the milk at regular intervals may bring some relief, but antibiotic treatment is usually required.

METRITIS
This is a bacterial infection which can occur in the uterus after whelping. It can result from a difficult whelping, retained placentas or other foetal membranes, or unhygienic conditions. The signs are a putrid or blood-stained discharge from the vulva coupled with fever. Antibiotic treatment will be required.

WEANING
Depending on the size of the litter and your bitch's milk supply, this is usually started when the

*Play is an
important part
of development.*

puppies are about three weeks. Most breeders begin by giving each puppy a morsel of finely-ground, top-quality beef. Offer this to each puppy individually, giving the puppy time to lick the meat and to get used to having solid food in its mouth. In no time the puppies will learn the smell of food, and will be only too happy to co-operate. Do not offer too much food to begin with, or you will upset the puppies' digestion.

A week after introducing solids, you can graduate to giving about one ounce of meat three times a day, with the puppies feeding from the dam in-between times. You can build this up, introducing a couple of milky cereal feeds. Learning to lap is a messy business, and the best plan is to separate the bitch from her litter when they are feeding, and then bring her back to clean the puppies. If you have a reluctant feeder, you should offer food to that puppy away from the rest of the litter to ensure it is getting enough food. However, most breeders find that communal feeding stimulates the puppies' competitive instinct, and most will thrive in these conditions.

Remember that when you start weaning, the mother will stop cleaning up after her puppies, and you must take on the task of keeping the bedding area and the play area clean at all times.

WORMING

All puppies carry a roundworm burden, even though you will have wormed your bitch before mating. It is important to start a worming programme when the puppies are two weeks old, and to repeat the dosage according to the instructions. It is a good idea to ask your vet to recommend a treatment.

INOCULATIONS

All puppies need to be vaccinated against the major infectious canine diseases which include distemper, parvovirus, hepatitis and leptospirosis. Vaccination programmes vary from region to region, but most puppies are vaccinated at around twelve weeks, and again at fourteen weeks. Ask your vet for advice.

SELLING YOUR PUPPIES

Your responsibilities do not end when you sell your puppies – you should be on hand to offer advice if needed, and to take the puppies back if problems arise. For this reason, do not sell your puppies to the first buyers that come along. Make sure prospective purchasers understand the responsibilities of owning a dog, and do not agree to a sale unless you are confident that the dog will be well provided for throughout its life.

Chapter Seven

GREYHOUND RACING

BRITAIN AND IRELAND

THE BIRTH OF GREYHOUND RACING

The concept of Greyhound racing was born out of the desire to offer a humane alternative to the highly popular sport of coursing. It was in Hendon in 1876 that six Greyhounds were first sent after a mechanically propelled lure. However, with the track being straight and with few people being interested in the humane aspect, the idea failed to take off. But the seeds were sown and some forty-five years later in 1921 Owen Patrick Smith opened the first Greyhound track, circular in shape, in Tulsa, Oklahoma. Coursing was illegal in many states in the United States, and this new sport proved to be an immediate success. Within six years Smith was the owner of twenty-five tracks and the proud father of a sport which was to touch the lives of millions worldwide.

Smith died in 1927, but lived long enough to hear that his invention had reached Britain. It was on July 24th 1926 that Mistley (Jack In Office – Duck) became the first official winner of a Greyhound race in England at Belle Vue, Manchester. The concept of Greyhounds racing around a track proved to be much more interesting than simply up a straight field. This, combined with evening meetings and the small investment involved in ownership, meant that racing soon became a firm favourite with the working man. Within six months crowds of 17,000 were packing the terraces at Belle Vue and tracks were springing up all over Britain. By the time of the sport's first anniversary there was a track in Liverpool and four in London – White City, Harringay, Wembley and Wimbledon. Celtic Park in Belfast preceded Dublin's Shelbourne Park by a month, and when Harold Park opened in Australia a fortnight later, it was clear that Greyhound racing was here to stay.

THE FIRST SUPERSTAR

It was by good fortune that the sport's first superstar was arguably its finest ever. In 1929 Mick The Miller was bought from Ireland for 88 guineas. Such an enormous sum ensured that Mick The Miller became a household name literally overnight with the coverage of his sale hitting that evening's papers. His debut in the 1929 Greyhound Derby – the sport's premier event – fuelled the fire when he set a new national record of 29.82 for 500 yards. Mick went on to win the Derby and hit the headlines again when sold for 2,000 guineas. He held the public's imagination for another two years, winning the Derby for a second time in 1930 and losing a re-run final in 1931.

MIXED FORTUNES

For the next twenty years, Greyhound racing was as familiar and accessible as soccer or horse racing, with crowds in excess of 80,000 turning up at White City to witness the Derby final. Why the sport's popularity declined in the sixties has never been fully documented, although many will argue that the legalisation of betting shops at the same time was more than just a coincidence. In the seventies and early eighties many tracks were forced to close, with none more lamented than White City – the sport's flagship – in 1984.

The arrival of superstars Scurlogue Champ and Ballyregan Bob, backed by an economic mini-boom in the country as a whole, provided Greyhound racing with a shot in the arm in the mid-eighties, and the long decline in attendancies was, temporarily, reversed. But as Britain stumbled into recession so the old problems of falling crowds returned, and the sport entered the nineties with the spectre of track closures looming once more amid growing fears that it was only a matter of time before off-course betting shops were allowed to open in the evenings.

In 1993 those fears were realised, but the result was not the devastation that many promoters had predicted. For many years Greyhound racing had been demanding a levy from off-course bookmakers similar to that awarded to horse racing. But despite a series of strong campaigns at Parliamentary level, the Government refused to help. However, once it had paved a way for the betting industry to keep its doors open in direct competition to the tracks themselves, the Government became more sympathetic to the needs of the Greyhound racing industry and urged bookmakers to assist the sport by way of a voluntary 1/4 per cent levy on off course bets. While many small bookmakers have ignored the call, the major companies have played ball, deducting the levy from punters' returns and handing it over to the newly-formed British Greyhound Racing Fund, headed by Lord Kimball. A potential pot of around £3 million ($4.5m) a year has softened the blow of increased competition from betting shops. Integrity services, prize money, track improvements and retired Greyhound welfare schemes have been among the main benefactors, but in theory any track or individual with a proposal for the benefit of the sport can apply for a grant from the Fund.

In May 1994 Greyhound racing enjoyed another boost with the announcement that Government Sunday trading laws were to be revised, allowing Greyhound racing, and betting, to take place on Sundays for the first time. If, as many believe, the lifting of restrictions on track-to-track totalisator betting follows, allowing the creation of huge Jackpot pools designed to attract new customers, the sport can face the future with more optimism than for many years.

THE RULING BODY

In the early years of Greyhound racing, following in horse racing's footsteps, cons and coups were immediately put into practice in a bid to make quick money out of the new sporting epidemic. It soon became apparent that, like horse racing, Greyhound racing needed its own regulatory body, and so the National Greyhound Racing Club (NGRC) was founded on January 1st, 1928. The basic objective of the NGRC is to police Greyhound racing and to ensure that the written rules are adhered to. When rules are broken, the NGRC has the power to fine the offending person, and can in more serious cases ban the offender from attending a track for the rest of their lives.

A steward is appointed at every NGRC venue to witness that all pre-race procedures are correct and that facilities are up to standard. The steward is also responsible for visiting the kennels of each track's appointed trainers, who must have a licence to train issued by the NGRC. Regular meetings are held at the NGRC's London headquarters under the Chairmanship of the Chief Steward. These meetings are, in effect, Greyhound racing's trials. Witnesses will be called and evidence heard concerning certain cases of misconduct by trainers, and sentences are passed or cases dismissed.

Today most tracks insist that Greyhounds must provide a sample of urine before racing, which is subsequently tested for performance-enhancing properties. This has increased the workload of the NGRC manyfold, but it maintains Greyhound racing's image. The most common cause for a stewards' inquiry is that of time-finding, i.e. where a Greyhound has improved in time between two races or trials. Improvement of over half a second would usually arouse suspicion, and if the dog was heavily gambled on, the stewards would feel they had a strong case. Other common causes for stewards' inquiries are a Greyhound running well below his ability, and the dog's sample showing positive for prohibited substances.

NGRC TRACKS

The tracks licensed by the NGRC fall into two categories: fully licensed tracks and permit tracks. Trainers licensed by the NGRC fall into three categories: professional, owner-trainers and permit trainers. Fully licensed tracks, which are in the majority, have around ten professional contract trainers each, and they supply the dogs for racing at every meeting. These trainers must have kennels that meet up to stringent NGRC rules and regulations. Permit tracks can have any number of permit trainers, who are allowed to train up to four dogs which must be in their ownership. Owner-trainers must have at least a 50 per cent share in the dogs they train, and are then eligible to race at fully licensed tracks. In May 1994 there were 36 NGRC tracks in Britain.

INDEPENDENT TRACKS

There are a further 52 tracks which operate independently of the NGRC. Generally these venues are much more of a low-budget operation, although venues such as Bolton and Kinsley offer better facilities than the poorer of their NGRC rivals. Independent tracks cater for the person who wishes to train their own dog without having to apply for a licence and its subsequent red-tape. Because identity cards are not used at Independent tracks, and there is a lack of security, no one involved in NGRC racing may race a dog at an Independent track. Most Independent tracks charge an entry fee for runners and this is then distributed as prize money between the first and second dog.

THE BORD NA gCON

In Ireland, racing at the Republic's eighteen venues was governed by the Irish Coursing Club until the 1950s when Bord Na gCon was founded by the Government. Bord Na gCon (Board of Greyhounds) is a semi-state body operating out of Limerick. Its purpose is exactly the same as the NGRC, although, in practice, its rules are less stringent.

Only a small percentage of trainers are licensed, namely those who train for others, and rules for time finding are virtually non-existent. Instead it is left to the track manager's discretion to report a suspicious run. This rule is harder to enforce in Ireland, as any dog is allowed to race at any track and can therefore find time (or lose it) through lack of familiarity with the venue. Limited drug testing was brought into Ireland in 1992. A travelling squad from Bord Na gCon tests all big race finalists and holds the trump card of maybe turning up when least expected at any ordinary meeting.

THE RACING FORMAT

The transition from new-born pup to racing Greyhound takes roughly fifteen months. After being earmarked – an identifying tatoo inside the ear – at three months of age, the puppy is then reared and schooled until it is old enough to race on an official track. Before its debut a Greyhound must complete three satisfactory trials within certain time limits laid down by the track management. When the racing manager is happy that the pup is running genuinely and consistently, he will allow it to compete in graded races. The concept of a graded race is to bring together a field of similarly gifted Greyhounds in order to provide a tight and exciting finish. When a Greyhound improves it is promoted to a higher grade, with the best rating over the standard distance being referred to at most tracks as A1. Prize money for graded races ranges widely around the country. Top class winners in London can earn £150 ($225), while at some provincial tracks the prize is less than £50. Even at the leading tracks, graded prize money is substantially lower than in the United States and Australia.

Due to the various circumferences of the tracks in Britain, many racing distances are used. The shortest is the sprint at Mildenhall, which covers 220m, and the longest is Romford's 1100m maxi-marathon trip. Hurdle races offer a popular variation for spectators, and Greyhounds have their own Grand National held at Hall Green, Birmingham. The fences were once made of solid wooden bricks, but today flexible brushes are used, which, if hit, simply collapse.

Handicap racing is also increasing in popularity. This system involves giving a low-grade dog a head start against better rivals. All six traps will be arranged according to each dog's ability and this provides many exciting close finishes. Hurdle and handicap races are also held over various distances, but for the purist, the standard trip of four bends (450-500m) is the only real test of a Greyhound.

THE TOP RACES

Greyhound racing is held all year round and trainers familiarise themselves with the annual calendar of events in order to give their dogs the best chance of winning the most lucrative competitions. When a dog is able to rise above the top grade at a track he is regarded as 'open class', meaning he is of the ability to take on all-comers. Open races consist of the very best Greyhounds. The Greyhound Derby, now held over 480m at Wimbledon in June, is the top accolade any Greyhound can win. Unlike other major races, where the participants are selected on merit from those entries that wish to take part, any Greyhound can run in the Derby provided the owner will pay the entrance fee. Entries are drawn into groups of six who will then race against each other, with the first three home progressing into the next round. This pattern is followed until just six Greyhounds are left. and the final is run for a first prize of £50,000 ($75,000). The Irish Greyhound Derby, held at Shelbourne Park in September, also offers a £50,000 prize.

Elsewhere other major races over the standard trip offer prizes of up to £20,000. The maximum for top staying events and sprint races is £10,000.

THE BREEDING INDUSTRY

Breeders in Britain and Ireland registered 5,008 litters in the latest volumes of their respective Stud Books. The lion's share of 4,128 was recorded in the Irish tome, which covered the period January to December 1992, while the British book, reporting the twelve months from June to May 1993, weighed in with 880. Individual registrations amounted to 23,297 in Ireland and 6,984 in Britain.

The busiest stud dogs, each with around 160 litters registered in the two books, were Greenpark Fox (Citizen Supreme – Stern Satoo) and I'm Slippy (Laurdella Fun – Glenroe Bess). I'm Slippy died on New Year's Day 1993, a few months short of his twelfth birthday. Satharn Beo (Wise Band – Linda's Zest) was responsible for some 120 litters, and in fourth place was Murlens Slippy (I'm Slippy – Murlen's Chill) with almost 100 litters. Another twenty sires were credited with more than fifty litters.

The only track sires' standings published are those relating to NGRC open races. I'm Slippy headed the list in 1993, when his stock won nearly 400 events, confirming his initial championship, gained the previous year. The Laurels hero, Slipaway Jaydee was his most notable

Greyhound racing in Britain is set for a new lease of life following legislation making betting on Sundays legal.

winner. Runner-up for the second consecutive year was the former champion, Whisper Wishes, whose offspring notched up over 200 open wins. The son of Sand Man also finished second in the brood bitch sires' table, which was led yet again by Linda's Champion (Monalee Champion – Merry Linda).

Whisper Wishes' daughters have made a cracking start to 1994, producing the winners of 28 NGRC opens during January. This score places the 1984 Derby victor ahead of Linda's Champion and Moral Support, who are tied on 22, and suggests he could clinch this title in 1994.

AMERICA

"Heeeeeeeeeeeeeere comes Wooooooooooooodeeeeeeee," track announcer Randy Birch screams into the microphone at the start of the 100,000 dollar Sprint Stake at The Woodlands in Kansas City, Kansas "Here we go for the big one!"

Ten-thousand eyes turn to the starting-box as eight pure-bred Greyhounds charge out of the box in hot pursuit of the mechanical lure.

"It's number 6 out early, EJ's Douglas. The Douglas dog has never lost, 6, 3, 8 on the turn," Birch calls the race.

The 32 stilt-like legs send sand flying everywhere as the Greyhounds round the first turn.

"Out in front it's the Douglas dog followed by By Tar. Running third the number 8, Ready To Narrate, ready to put his name in the record book."

The two speediest Greyhounds, EJ's Douglas and By Tar take a big lead charging down the track at speeds up to 45 mph, while the rest drop back to avoid jams and bumps, intent on staging late rallies.

"We're ready for the final turn, oh man, it's a 2-dog race."

Fans tightly clench pari-mutuel tickets which totalled over $150,000 for this one race alone.

"The Douglas dog is two lengths ahead of number 3, By Tar. As we go into the final turn By Tar takes the lead. By Tar knocks the tar out of them again."

So went one of the United States' top sprint stakes as R.G. Beckner's By Tar won his second major race and a $50,000 cheque. Previously, By Tar raced to victory in the World Classic at Hollywood in Miami, Florida, winning another $70,000. In the USA, Greyhound racing is big business. From the fans at the track to the breeders on the farm, the one-time sport of racing has turned into America's sixth largest spectator sport. Its annual attendance is higher than that of the National Basketball Association.

EARLY HISTORY

The origin of the sport can be found on the dirt farms of the midwest. Millions of pesky jackrabbits were eating farmers out of house and home back in the mid-1800s. It did not take settlers long to import four-legged pest control from Ireland and England, and thus the Greyhound became a common sight on farms in Kansas, Missouri, Oklahoma and Texas. America's competitive spirit led to the discovery that Greyhounds were also a great source of sport and entertainment. One of the first national Greyhound meets, covered at the time in the nationally known magazine *Harper's Weekly*, was held in Kansas in 1886.

The sport of Greyhound racing took a revolutionary turn in 1921 when O.P. Smith perfected a mechanical lure in Emeryville, California. Smith's new invention did not take root in the West but became successful the following year in Tulsa. Six years later Greyhounds were racing in Florida, Montana and Oregon. Fuelled by the ability of the Greyhound to run without jockeys and at night under the lights, the sport grew and grew.

THE MODERN SCENE

Today, nowhere is Greyhound racing more popular than in the United States. In 1992, attendance at Greyhound tracks reached almost 3.5 million. The 57 race tracks in the nation ran 16,827 performances and the fans wagered 3,471 billion dollars. A typical race track held eight cards a week, with 14 races per card. The biggest Greyhound track in America, Gulf Greyhound Park near Houston, Texas, averaged 5,000 fans and a pari-mutuel handle of $500,000 for each of its 467 performances.   Of course, not all Greyhound tracks are as lucrative as Gulf Greyhound Park. Kennel owners at an average track earned between 3,000 and 7,000 dollars per week in purse money, while at some of the smaller tracks 2,000 dollars was an excellent week. Phoenix Greyhound Park, a typical track in Arizona, averaged 221,955 dollars handle for the track's 402 performances.

THE RACING FORMAT

All but two of the race tracks in the US are quarter-mile ovals. Most of the races are held over the 5/16-mile (1,650 feet), with the next most popular distance the 3/8-mile (1,980) course. Some fans like to see the puppies run the longer 7/16-mile course (2,310 feet), and occasionally the sprint race will be held on the 3/16 course (990 feet).

The US boasts world records at three of the above distances. Earth Call, owned by Tom and William Denton, covered the 5/16-mile in 29.59 seconds. At Hollywood in Florida, P's Rambling, owned by James Paul, raced around the 3/8 oval in 36.43 seconds. And, again at Hollywood, Runaround Sue, owned by Leonard Wood, covered the longer 7/16-mile course in an incredible 42.57 seconds.

Most of the fifty-seven race tracks run eight-dog races. The Greyhounds are placed in grades— usually grades M, J, C, B, A – depending on their ability. As the pup wins, it moves up in grade. As the dog runs out of the money three times, it drops in grade. The track racing secretary draws the races under the watchful eye of the state judge and kennel representative. Post positions are based on a draw, called the shake. These days computers shake the post positions.

Most American tracks run eight-dog races.

Most of the race tracks have a kennel compound which houses the 1,000 or so Greyhounds it takes to operate a race track. Two hours prior to the races, the Greyhounds are brought to the paddock area of the facility to be weighed. If a Greyhound's weight varies more than 1 1/2 pounds above or below the established weight of the Greyhound at weigh-in time, the racing judge scratches the dog. This is to insure the Greyhound is in top shape to race. The Greyhounds are also examined by a paddock judge prior to racing, and drug testing is performed after each race.

All of the tracks in the US operate under a closed kennel system. Each track has a list of 16 to 20 kennels which are allowed to race there. Greyhound owners then lease their Greyhounds to the kennel operators at the track. Traditionally, the kennel owner receives 65 per cent of the Greyhound's earnings, giving 35 per cent to the owners. Stake races are split 50-50.

TRACK FACILITIES

Just about every race track has a climate-controlled club house for full service dining, serving everything from sandwiches to prime rib. The prime rib at St. Petersburg's Derby Lane is world-famous and takes a mighty healthy appetite to devour. The average track can seat up to 1,000 in the club house. Most seat over 6,000 with a track capacity of 10,000 or more. Gulf Greyhound Park, billed as the largest track in this country, can seat 8,400 and has a capacity of 16,000.

Some of the race tracks have adopted names for the artificial lures which are shaped as either a rabbit or a bone. At The Woodlands the lure is named Woody. At the Wichita, Kansas track the lure is Ozie in honour of the Wizard of Oz. At Lincoln, Rhode Island, fans hear the track announce proclaim, "Here comes Rhodey." At Dairyland in Kenosha, Wisconsin the lure is called Barney, and at Waterloo, Iowa the lure is called Napoleon.

WAGERS

A variety of wagers can be placed by the fans. All tracks offer the traditional win, place, show, quiniela and trifecta wagering. Many tracks have experimented with exotic wagers – superfectas

Greyhound racing is big business in the USA – fans wager over three billion dollars a year.

The Greyhound Review.

(picking the top four places), pick six (winners of six straight races), twin trifecta and quiniela double (select quinielas for two consecutive races). A few years back, two race tracks even went so far as to experiment with a pick nine wager that guaranteed a one million dollar pay-off to anyone hitting the bet. To win the wager, called The Big One, fans had to pick the fourth place finisher in eight straight races. Needless to say, no one ever hit the 1 million dollar pay-off.

All of the money wagered at US tracks goes through the totalisator and bookmaking is not allowed. A per cent of the total tote, or handle, is then divided among the state government, Greyhound purses, and the track. The average purse at US tracks is 4 per cent of the handle. Gulf Greyhound Park's 5 per cent purse is the highest, while a couple of tracks in Alabama pay the low 2.7 per cent.

PRIZE MONEY
The Greyhounds are paid depending on the grade and finish. A Grade A victory will return between 100 and 2,000 dollars depending on the race track. Stake races sweeten a pup's earning potential. The added money can mean big bucks for the winners. Ben G Speedboat, for example, pocketed 125,000 dollars for 30.21 seconds of work in 1986, winning the Greyhound Race of Champions at Seabrook, New Hampshire. That is the most money won in a single race. The past three years the GROC has paid 100,000 dollars to the winner. The 1991 winner, Mo Kick, has career earnings of over 290,000 dollars, and as of October 1993 he was still racing. It is expected that Mo Kick will overtake Homspun Rowdy's 297,000 dollars in career earnings before retirement.

THE TOP RACES
As mentioned, the top paying and top stake in the United States is the Greyhound Race of Champions. Sponsored by the American Greyhound Track Operators Association, it is a rare occasion that this stake does not attract the top Greyhounds in the country. The Greyhound Race of Champions has been held since 1982, and all but three of the dozen Race of Champions have been over the 3/8-mile course. While it pays the most money, and attracts the most Greyhounds, seldom have winners gone on to greater things.

None of the GROC winners have made the Greyhound Hall of Fame, for example. And none of the winners are in the Top Ten sire or brood standings. However, with Mo Kick still running, it is too early to say he will not break this trend. The 1985 runner-up, Dutch Bahama, went on to become a number one sire and was inducted into the Hall of Fame.

Other top distance stakes are the 170,000 dollar Wonderland Derby held at Wonderland near Boston, Massachusetts, and the 150,000 dollar Sunflower Stake at The Woodlands in Kansas City. Though the purse money is not as high, the 60,000 dollar American Derby held at Lincoln, Rhode Island, the 75,000 dollar International Classic held at Flagler in Miami, Florida, and the 45,000 dollar Hollywoodian held at Hollywood near the Miami, Florida area, are all major open distance stake races.

The Wonderland Derby started in 1935 and it has been won by a number of Hall of Famers. Never Roll won the stake in 1942. On The Line was victorious in 1952, and K's Flak was in the winner's circle in 1979. The American Derby dates back to 1945. Real Huntsman won the race two consecutive years in 1950 and 1951. Downing won the race in 1977, and Dutch Bahama won back-to-back Derbys in 1984 and 1985. The International Classic dates back to 1961. Miss Whirl won this stake twice. The Hollywoodian started in 1971. Unruly earned a spot in the Hall of Fame with back-to-back victories in this stake in 1981 and 1982.

The Woodlands has only been open since 1990, but the Sunflower has quickly established itself as a top distance stake attracting stellar fields. The top sprint stakes include the $125,000 Hollywood World Classic, $160,000 Grady Memorial Sprint at Wonderland, $125,000 Irish-American Classic at Biscayne in Miami, $125,000 Florida/World Classic at Biscayne, $100,000 Winter Sprint at The Woodlands, and the $100,000 Great Kansas Shootout at Wichita, Kansas.

The Irish-American Classic started in 1970. The stake matches the best American Greyhounds with Ireland's best. The Irish racers must be close descendants of Irish Greyhounds. Downing won the event in 1977 and K's Flak followed two years later. It was also one of Dutch Bahama's greatest moments in 1984. The Florida-World, started in 1983, matches the top Florida-bred Greyhounds with those of the rest of the country or the world, as the stake name implies. It should be noted that the Biscayne course is 165 feet longer than a typical 5/16 track, making it a demanding course for sprinters.

The World Classic at Hollywood, started in 1975, is also a prestigious sprint stake. Downing won the race in 1977. Wonderland's Grady started in 1978 and the two sprint stakes in Kansas have only been held for the past four years. Derby Lane in St. Petersburg, Florida also holds two very prestigious stake events, the $100,000 Distance Classic and the $100,000 Sprint Classic. These stakes, however, are not open stake events but rather closed to just those Greyhounds on the St. Pete roster.

Onie Jones, a Hall of Famer, won the Distance Classic in 1974. Keefer, who may some day be enshrined, won back-to-back Distance Classics in 1986 and 1987.

AMERICAN BREEDING

Americans breed close to 8,000 litters of Greyhounds per year. Over 38,000 race Greyhounds are individually registered with the National Greyhound Association each year. It is obvious, then, that the breeding farm is also big business. Greyhound owners claim it costs some $2,500 to train a pup to track age.

A good stud dog can be bred over eighty times a year. In 1992 HB's Commander was bred 147 times. However, only nine Greyhounds were bred over eighty times that year. The vast majority were bred between two and ten times a year.

Stud fees range from $2,000 (for Dutch Bahama) to $200. The average stud fee is $500. Over 2,000 sires recorded at least one breeding in 1992. Of those, only 520 are advertised at public stud in *The Greyhound Review*, the official magazine of the National Greyhound Association. Obviously, there is a relationship between the number of breedings, thus number of pups, and position on the sire standings. The top sire in the country for 1992, Dutch Bahama, produced 99 litters in 1991, producing 519 pups.

In the early 1980s, Downing (Big Whizzer – Hookers Flower) dominated the top of the sire standings. Downing, a product of Australia's Tell You Why through Big Whizzer's sire, Westy Whizzer, was the top sire in 1983, 1984 and 1985. Unruly (Kelly Jones – Skillful) took over the top spot in 1986 and stayed number one in 1987 and 1988. Unruly is also from Tell You Why through Kelly Jones' sire, Hoefer. Kelly Jones' dam, Elsie Jones, is by Ireland's Julius Caesar.

This Tell You Why – Julius Caesar cross with American dams Nettler and Hurry Bones is one of the top-producing lines in the US through brothers Onie Jones (sire of Corbin, K's Flak and Placid Ace), Kelly Jones (sire of Unruly, Dark Rumor and PK's Jet), and Demon Jones (sire of Journalist Jicha and Mac Leroy). In 1987 this pedigree dominated the sire standings as Unruly finished on top, followed by Placid Ace and K's Flak. That year Black Aztec, an Australian import, finished fourth in the standings for the third straight year.

Since 1989 two Greyhounds have been battling for the top spot. Dutch Bahama (Hairless Joe – Dutch Debit) became the number one sire in 1989. The following year My Unicorn (Rocky T –

Flying Slipper) took over the top spot in the standings. In 1991 My Unicorn was back at number one, just one win ahead of Dutch Bahama. Dutch Bahama regained the title in 1992. Sire standings in the US are based on top grade wins by offspring racing at the top twenty tracks.

The Greyhound Review compiles a table of dam standings based on wins by their progeny for all distances at Bicayne, Cloverleaf, Dairyland, Flagler, Gulf Greyhound, Hollywood, Jackonsville, Kansas City, Lincoln, Mile High, Mulnomah, Orange Park, Palm Beach, Raynham-Taunton, Southland, St Johns, St Petersburg, Tampa, Victoryland and Wonderland. In 1993 top place went to Wild Dunes C (K's Flak – Ciara) with a tally of sixty-seven top grade wins by her progeny. Runner-up was Nice Gal (Kunte Kinte – Fargo Lil) with her offspring notching up sixty-three top grade wins.

My Unicorn is a fourth generation descendant of Tell You Why. His dam, Flying Energy, is by two Irish imports, Shining Glory and Stoneview Beauty. Dutch Bahama is a third generation son of Tell You Why, while Australian imports Rocker Mac and Sky Jet appear in the fourth generation on his dam's side. Needless to say the American-Australian-Irish mix has worked well in the US. A perfect example is the Friend Westy – Miss Gorgeous line (Miss Gorgeous is also by Tell You Why). Sons Highway Robber, Rooster Cogburn and Prairie Dog have been outstanding sires in this country, while Sand Man travelled to Ireland to make his mark.

Artificial insemination is common in the US. More recently the National Greyhound Association has approved frozen insemination where the semen is collected and frozen for transportation. The semen is then thawed and inseminated into the female. The AI program has been hampered with low percentages, but recently insemination techniques have improved conception percentages. In 1992, Richard Conole imported frozen semen from Australia and successfully produced litters in the US. These were the first intercontinental matings.

THE FUTURE

While Greyhound racing in the US flourished during the 1980s, the sport fluttered in the 1990s. Like any sport, Greyhound racing has shown its vulnerability to competition. The growing popularity of casino wagering on river boats and Indian-run facilities has hurt attendance and handle. Five of the smaller Greyhound tracks closed their doors in the 1990s and predictions are that more will follow.

AUSTRALIA

It seems Australians were destined to be hooked on Greyhound racing even before the birth of the island nations, so it is little wonder the country is now engrossed in the sport. So much so that, for a country with 17 million people (about the size of London), there are more than one hundred Greyhound tracks, many thousands of registered owners and trainers, and a seemingly endless supply of canine athletes.

Australia was certainly born into Greyhound racing. When English explorer Captain James Cook discovered the nation in 1770, on board was botanist Joseph Banks. Among Bank's prized possessions on the ship, *The Endeavour*, were two Greyhounds. They stepped ashore and 'coursed' local game, minutes after Cook, Banks, and the landing party claimed Australia for Mother England. If only Banks could see Greyhound racing now! It has developed into a multi-million dollar business, proudly acclaimed by the Aussies to be among the best in the world. Those who have seen racing in all parts of the world are adamant Australia has the best dogs and the best racing.

While thoroughbreds might be the passion of the rich and famous, Greyhound racing is the sport of the family in Australia. Dad, Mum and the kids often go Greyhound racing with their pride and joy, in search of riches – up to A$300,000 (£135,000 or US$ 200,000) for the highest stakes earner this country has seen.

GREYHOUND RACING HISTORY

Cook, Banks and *The Endeavour* were behind the Greyhound's first steps on to Australian soil, but it was not until the 1880s that Greyhound racing was established. Because Australia was once a colony of England, most of the formation was along English lines, and Greyhound racing was no different.

At that time, coursing was the sport of the gentry in England, and many of the rich and titled had a team of coursing Greyhounds. This pattern repeated itself in Australia. Coursing flourished in the colony, especially around the states of New South Wales, Victoria and South Australia. It was much later that Greyhound racing spread to Queensland, Western Australia, Tasmania and finally the Northern Territory. Samuel Bladin was a household name in coursing circles in the late 1800s, winning a number of runnings of the Waterloo Cup, the Oaks, and the Derby, plus other feature events in Victoria with his all-conquering team. Bladin even took Australian-bred dogs back to England to contest the Waterloo Cup with satisfaction.

Australian fight promoter Jack Munro saw O.P. Smith's mechanical lure invention at the Chicago World Fair. He liked what he saw and tried to introduce it to Australia, but without success. It was left to Frederick Swindell to pick up the pieces from Munro a few years later. In the 1930s that mechanical lure racing was introduced. The first meeting was held at Epping Racetrack in Sydney, site of the now famous Harold Park harness horse track. Racetracks prior to this had been on a straight course, the dogs chasing a 'lure' of men on horseback at the side of the track chasing a hare up the centre.

Bicycle lures were also used. Today's training lures of a bicycle wheel, geared to drag a plastic bag at the end of a long cord, were utilised. It was commonplace for Epping Racetrack to attract average attendances of 12,000 to Greyhound racing in the 1930s. The record crowd at this time was 27,000. Bellamand (The Turf – King's Battery) won the first mechanical lure race held in Australia.

Horse racing officials lobbied hard against Greyhound racing soon after, and state governments were often swayed to cause the new sport much strife. However, by the 1940s and 1950s Greyhound racing was hitting back hard, and tracks sprang up throughout the country. Night racing was firmly established by the 1960s, and Greyhound racing took its place as the ideal alternative to horse racing.

THE RACING SCENE TODAY

More than one hundred Greyhound tracks cater for the many thousands of dogs registered in this country. Each state's capital city has its own top-class facilities for Greyhound racing. Brisbane in the state of Queensland races at Albion Park, a facility it shares with the state's major harness racing venue, racing twice weekly (Monday and Thursday nights). Sydney in New South Wales races twice a week (Saturday and Monday nights) at Wentworth Park, probably the premier track in the country. Melbourne in Victoria has two individual tracks, Sandown Park and Olympic Park, the former racing on Thursday nights, the latter on Monday nights. In Adelaide, the capital of South Australia, Angle Park races on Monday and Thursday nights. In Perth, in Western Australia, Cannington races on Saturday nights. Tasmania caters for major Greyhound race meetings at Launceston on Monday nights and Hobart on Thursday nights. All these tracks race on a sand-based surface. The city tracks have the highest prize money of all, racing generally from A$500 ((£225) in Melbourne to the winner of each low graded race, to A$2,500 at Wentworth Park for a low grade race at Sydney's premier track. Because of the high stakes, the best dogs race on the city tracks, generally after contesting a number of races on provincial tracks throughout their own state. Provincial racing caters for the majority of dogs, the best Free For Allers (top grade) at provincial tracks being well up to city standard and generally swapping between city and provincial racing.

The top-class dogs generally race only on the city tracks, where prize money can range for them from an average of A$1,500 to the winner of a normal graded event up to A$100,000 to the winner for the Golden Easter Egg run at Easter at Wentworth Park. However, provincial racing is strong in many centres where Greyhound racing clubs can offer prize money of A$10,000 to A$20,000 for major events. Facilities at the major city tracks are first-class. Dining is lavish at most of these centres, and the tracks' average attendances are between 1,000 and 5,000, with crowds bigger at nights when big races like the National Derby, Golden Easter Egg, or Melbourne or Australian Cups are run. Provincial tracks cannot boast the same facilities. However, there is a trend today to centralisation, and it is hoped in the future that some of these provincial tracks may close, leading to an increase in city racing. Some of the provincial tracks, like Parklands on the Gold Coast in Queensland, would be equal to any in the world.

Tracks are all shapes and sizes in Australia. Distances range from 300m sprints to 1000m marathons. Average distances are 520m and 720m on the city tracks, with the provincials' average ranging from 450m to 650m. Grading is generally different between provincial and city tracks. Surfaces are sand on the city tracks and on the majority of Victorian, South Australia and Western Australia tracks, but grass on most tracks in New South Wales and Queensland, although the latter state has seen a number of tracks switch to sand recently.

THE RACING FORMAT

Greyhound racing in Australia is unique, a sort of Free For All. There are no track-based trainers, only individuals who nominate their dogs for specific race meetings. There are major professional trainers, like Tony Zammit, John Reimer, Pauline Freund, Mike O'Byrne in Queensland, Alan Pringle, Paul Wheeler, Jim Coleman, Ken Howe, Ron Gill in New South Wales, Graham Bate, Joe Hili in Victoria and Doug Payne in South Australia.

These trainers have upwards of thirty dogs in training – and most have fifty or more dogs at any one time. They have lavish training complexes, huge kennel blocks, large galloping paddocks, long straight tracks, and a number of staff to help them. They achieve great success – but as we all know, they put in long hours to do so. There is also the average 'Aussie', who trains from one to sometimes three and four Greyhounds at his home. The competitive nature of the industry in Australia has forced this hobby trainer to be of the highest professionalism. Veterinary surgeons are held in high regard and conduct thriving business within the Greyhound industry in Australia. Trialling, training facilities etc. are first-class, due to the fact that Australians would refuse to race on inferior tracks.

BETTING

Greyhound racing is like every other racing industry, challenging for the gambling dollar – and a tough challenge it has to be. In Australia all off-course betting is run by the individual State Governments through the Totalisator Administration Board (TAB). Racing on track is a mixture of bookmakers and on-course tote, which is generally combined with the TAB holds. It makes for mammoth pools, and Australians are eager punters.

Most tracks have several bookmakers, but there is a trend in Australia for this traditional form of gambling medium to lose its popularity. Bookmakers are struggling to make a living on most provincial tracks, and the going is tough at the city tracks. Numbers dwindle every year. The economics of bookmaking in Australia make the industry hard going.

THE GLAMOUR RACES

Every state in Australia boasts classic races, big prize money and feature races which see the best dogs from throughout the country compete in search of riches. NSW is probably the leader, where the National Coursing Association and the Greyhound Breeders Owners and Trainers Association battle for supremacy. The NCA and the GBOTA often try to outdo each for prize money – and it is the owner who benefits.

In NSW, such feature races as the Association Cup (720m), the National Derby and Futurity (520m), the Golden Easter Egg (520m) which is worth 100,000 dollars to the winner, the Wentworth Park Gold Cup (720m), Peter Mosman Memorial (520m), Winter Stake (520m), Sydney Cup (720m), Vic Peters Memorial (520m), Summer Cup (720m) and the NSW St Leger (520m) all boast high stakes.

In the same state, provincial races like the Dapto Supercoat Petcare Classic (508m), which also boasts A$100,000 to the winner, and the Tweed Heads Galaxy (420m), Richmond Derby and Oaks (530m) are all glamour events, providing riches and fame and glory for their winners.

Queensland runs the Derby and Futurity (520m) at Albion Park, as well as the Gold Cup (710m) and the Coca-Cola Cup and Christmas Stocking (520m) – the latter three being worth A$45,000 to the winner. Provincial tracks like Lawnton and Ipswich run races worth A$35,000 down to feature events, which are restricted events open to dogs sold at an auction held every year, or pups entered at birth.

Victoria hosts such races as the Melbourne Cup (511m) and Australian Cup (511m), as well as such classics as the Maturity Silver Chief and Laurels (for bitches) over 511m. Provincial racing in this state is strong, with many country townships being able to run A$20,000 to the winner feature events. In South Australia, races like the Adelaide Cup at Angle Park carry A$50,000 to the winner. There are more than 200 races every year that would be deemed a feature race in Australia, although prize money for all of them varies.

SUPERSTARS

Australians believe they have the best Greyhounds in the world. They boast Chief Havoc in the US Hall of Fame, but believe such greats as Zoom Top, her sire Black Top, the legendary sire Temlee, his grandson Brother Fox, and in more recent times Highly Blessed and Sandi's McMum are as worthy of matching any dogs from anywhere in the world. Australians are quick to point out Tell You Why revolutionised Greyhound racing in the US when he went to stud there.

Zoom Top (Black Top – Busy Beaver) started 136 times in the late 1960s for 68 wins, 25 seconds, and 14 thirds, and the then record stakes earnings of A$59,000. She raced on 27 different tracks and won on all but one of them. Zoom Top captured the imagination of a Greyhound racing hungry public when she broke 16 track records over distances from 500 yards to 870 yards. Zoom Top is legendary in Australian Greyhound racing. The mighty Chief Havoc raced in the 1940s but has been immortalised with staggering performances. He trialled between races at Harold Park over 870 yards and broke a number of Australian records during the trial.

In recent years the mighty Temlee (Tivoli Chief – Temora Lee) was a Champion sprinter in Victoria, but established a siring dynasty the like of which has never been seen in this country. He, too, is Hall of Fame stuff. At one time Temlee had thirty-six sons standing commercially at stud in Australia. His grandson Brother Fox (Little Blade–Pitstock Park) is just as well remembered for his scintillating racetrack performance, breaking two world records for 500 yards and then becoming Champion sire. He, just like Temlee, had up to 30 sons at stud in Australia at any one time. Highly Blessed (Chariot Supreme – I'm Blessed) cut a swathe through Australia's glamour races in 1991 like no other Greyhound has done, winning the Melbourne Cup, the Coca-Cola Cup, the Adelaide Cup, and the Golden Easter Egg to become Australia's highest stakes earner. Only a few months had gone by before Jessica Casey (Amerigo Man – Osti's Shadow) took over that crown with victories in such races as the Golden Easter Egg, National Sprint Championship, Ladies Bracelet, Penrith Oaks and Penrith Cup, and was Greyhound of the Year.

Sandi's Mo Mum (Red Swinger – Sandilock) had held the record before Highly Blessed when she twice won the National Sprint Championship and won the Laurels at Sandown, the Adelaide Cup, and a host of other feature events. To twice win the National Sprint Championship is a staggering feat in Australian Greyhound racing. The mighty Worth Doing (Brother Fox – Versatile Miss) had to be seen to be believed, giving away big starts to his opposition in classic races and winning easily in recordbreaking time. He won the National Derby, Richmond Derby and the Young Star Classic.

Greats like Winifred Bale, National Lass, both twice winners of the NSW Greyhound of the Year, and the latter a Champion brood bitch, Bay Road Queen, Tegimi, Promises Free who won 19 of her 21 starts and five classics, Tangaloa who won the Melbourne and Australian Cups and became a Champion sire, and Blacktop, almost unbeatable as a sprinter in the early 1960s and a Champion sire, all go to make up the greats of Australian Greyhound racing

BREEDING

Like any other country, Australians are fiercely proud of their Greyhound stock. Champion sires of today are Amerigo Man, Chariot Supreme (a son of the hugely influential Irish import, Waverly Supreme), Worth Doing, Brother Fox (even though in the twilight of his days), and Tangaloa, whose son Pretty Short has established a dynasty of his own, most of them descendants of Temlee.

Damlines are many and varied. The great dams include National Lass, Osti Lee, who founded her own dynasty which accounts for such greats as Jessica Casey, Zulu Moss, and her litter sister, Riviera Moss, who are in the pedigrees of many of today's Champions, and the Dark Debutante line which boasts present-day stars like Golden Currency – all go to making Australian Greyhounds the fleet-footed animals they are.

Imports like Waverly Supreme have had a great bearing on Australian pedigrees, most particularly as brood bitch sires. There has been a recent influx of imported blood – such is the domination of Temlee – in a bid to introduce outcrosses to Temlee's male line.

THE FUTURE

Greyhound racing Australia-wide is running into problems. Rising costs are a problem everywhere in the world and just as much so in Australia. However, TAB distribution, where the state government-run betting medium returns a percentage to race clubs for use in prize money, is always available to help. Provincial clubs find it difficult to survive. The city tracks have only recently reduced prize money levels, although owners and trainers really have little to complain about when compared to other countries. The industry is fairly stable, and is run by Control Boards – state government elected bodies which run the industry in their respective states.

NEW ZEALAND
STRUCTURE

The New Zealand Greyhound Racing Association is in its eighty-fifth year of existence. It is made up of fifteen affiliated clubs, with the Association office situated in Auckland city. The

Association Board of Directors consists of a president, vice-president, immediate past-president, and six regional members. Each member is elected by the affiliated clubs for a two-year term, without restriction on the number of terms a member can act as a director. The Board meets approximately six times a year.

The Association conducts an annual meeting at which clubs are represented by a delegate and an observer. Constitutional rules and racing rules can be altered at annual conference by way of remit and voted upon. The Board can alter racing rules only at executive meetings. The Association is attended by the chief executive officer and an office manager. There are part-time stipendiary stewards who officiate at TAB totalisator race meetings, and honorary stewards who assist in the marking and earbranding of Greyhounds.

A representative of the Association serves on the New Zealand Racing Industry Board and the Totalisator Agency Board. Both positions are on appointment by the Minister of Racing, on the nomination of Greyhound clubs and/or Board, and they serve for two-year terms with the right of re-appointment. The Association is an affiliated member of the Australia New Zealand Greyhound Association, which has its office in Melbourne, Australia. This body acts as the Greyhound registration authority for the Association and is keeper of the Australasian Stud Book.

The Association acts on matters pertaining to the industry on behalf of its affiliated clubs. Such issues involve race licences and funding for major capital developments on tracks through the New Zealand Racing Industry Board's account. The Association is a non-profit organisation and operates through registration and licencing fees and club levies based on turnovers.

RACE LICENCES
The Association conducts over 120 TAB totalisator race meetings per season. The totalisator clubs are: Auckland, Walkato, Walrarapa, Manawatu, Wellington, Christchurch, Otago, and Southland. The non-totalisator clubs are: Tokoroa, Walkite (Rotorua), Gisborne, Taranaki, Wanganul, Ashburton, and Timaru.

The development of the code can be seen from the gain of TAB totalisator licences from 33 in 1987 to 84 in 1992, and currently over 120. The purpose of the non-totalisator clubs is to provide sweepstake racing for lower graded Greyhounds and trialling purposes. The totalisator clubs also conduct non-totalisator meetings. There are approximately 250 non-totalisator race meetings in a racing season, and these are held mainly on Saturdays or Sundays. Such meetings are conducted on the same lines as totalisator meetings, except no betting is permitted and stake monies are only based on sweepstake (portion of nomination fees).

Totalisator race meetings are conducted on a mid-week afternoon and are run for stake monies of no less than NZ$900 (£350) for lower graded Greyhounds and NZ$1,000 dollars for higher graded Greyhounds. A sum of NZ$750 is provided for each stake by way of a subsidy from the NZ Racing Industry Board. In addition, there are thirty-eight special subsidised races, providing for increased stakes of NZ$12,000 (Group One), NZ$7,000 (Group Two) and NZ$5,000 (Group Three). The stakes are subsidised fifty per cent by the NZRIB.

Ten races are programmed, and fields of eight runners are drawn with two reserves provided. The first on-course betting meeting on Greyhounds took place in 1975 and progressed to off-course (full TAB) betting in 1978.

THE RACING ENVIRONMENT
All but one of the Greyhound tracks in New Zealand are grass. The exception is a sand track (Forbury Park) in Otago. The Auckland Greyhound track at Manukau Stadium is the only purpose-built stadium for Greyhound racing. Distances vary from track to track, but they range from 290m

Our Hosanna: New Zealand's Greyhound of the Year 1993, pictured with top trainer Ray Adcock.

to the ultimate 805m. There are three distances: sprint (up to 400m), middle distance (400m to 600m), and distance races (over 600m). Some clubs conduct hurdle racing.

There are five grades from class 0 (non-winners) to class 5 and restricted age races. At totalisator races it is usual to run only class 2 to class 5. Class 0 and class 1 are usually run at sweepstake meetings. Greyhounds are graded on the winning of a totalisator race (or class 0 and class 1 at sweepstake meetings). The grade a Greyhound attains at any one track also applies to all other tracks. Combined grade races are run when nominations for any one grade are short. Hurdle and distance races have only two grades (class 1 and class 2). Failure by a Greyhound to win stake money (1st, 2nd, 3rd) in four consecutive starts at a totalisator race meeting allows the Greyhound to drop to a lower grade.

All clubs advertise their race meeting programmes through the *NZ Greyhound* – a monthly newspaper published in-house. The Association is committed to an industry drug-detection programme, and, on average, urine samples are taken from six Greyhounds at each totalisator race meeting.

TURNOVERS

Turnovers vary greatly depending on the day a meeting is held, with Thursdays being the most successful day. In a season when the Association conducts TAB totalisator racing on 102 occasions, a turnover of NZ$50million will be netted. The clubs exist on commissions from on-course turnovers (approx 10 per cent), and they share in the TAB profit (approx 3 per cent of their off-course turnover). In the last season the Greyhound industry received NZ$1million in the TAB payout from its profit.The wagering of TAB races does not differ from the sister codes, and it benefits from some exposure on the TAB television racing channel through live coverage (seven meetings this current season) and reviews. Television coverage of races in New Zealand is unique in that the TAB owns and operates its own racing channel (Action TV), thereby completely eliminating the spending of racing industry money on outside television commercial interests.

GREAT GREYHOUNDS

The current stake money allows Greyhounds to surpass NZ$100,000 in stake money should the opportunity present itself. The greatest stake winning Greyhound to race in New Zealand is Misty Anna, who won over NZ$115,000 during her career. Misty Anna was raced by an elderly couple, John and May Wilson of Mosgiel, near Dunedin, and she was widely travelled by her owners. There are about four other Greyhounds to have surpassed the NZ$50,000 stake money barrier.

RACES

The country's richest series is the NZ Championship conducted by the Christchurch GRC. It carries a stake of NZ$17,500 made up through Group One subsidy and sponsorship. Effern Foods sponsor the Pedigree Pal Meaty-Bites Classic, run throughout the country, with a final conducted by the Auckland GRC for a stake of NZ$15,000.

Other Group races of significance are the NZ Breeders Stakes, the NZ Derby, the Auckland and Wellington Cups, the NZ St Leger, and the NZ Sires Produce Stakes, all of which carry minimum stake money of NZ$ß12,000. There are only about 1,100 registered racing Greyhounds in New Zealand.

Chapter Eight

INTERNATIONAL BLOODLINES

THE BREED SPREADS

It is no coincidence that, outside the British Isles, the Greyhound has flourished chiefly in the USA, Australia and New Zealand – countries which received a high proportion of settlers from Britain and Ireland. Taking along their Greyhounds for assistance in their struggle for survival, these pioneers in due time translated their native affection for sport with hare and hound into organised coursing meetings in their adopted countries. The American Field Cup (later renamed National Waterloo Cup) was inaugurated in 1886, while in 1884 the London-published *Coursing Calendar* carried, for the first time, an account of the Victorian Waterloo Cup, established in 1873 and staged at Diggers' Rest, about twenty miles from Melbourne.

"Waterloo Cups are now quite the fashion in the Australian colonies," ran the report, "for this year New South Wales emulated Victoria, followed by South Australia, whilst New Zealand has had its blue riband of the leash for four years."

Reflecting the progress of the Greyhound from the old world to the new, this article charts three dynasties which influenced breeding on an international scale. The traffic in Greyhounds was initially almost entirely one way, although in 1878 the English-bred Registrar General returned from Australia to contest the Waterloo Cup, in which he suffered a comprehensive first round defeat.

Then, in 1882, a bitch from New Zealand, named Arama, made an impact on British breeding when throwing Britain Still (by Misterton), winner in 1884 of the 128-runner Gosforth Gold Cup. A very fast 'park' dog, Britain Still was the maternal grandsire of Fiery Furnace (1895-1906), Champion stud dog and male line ancestor of Mutton Cutlet, Sand Man, Monalee Champion and Newdown Heather, to name but four.

MUTTON CUTLET

Probably the most influential and successful stud dog of all time, Mutton Cutlet (Jamie – Miss Cinderella) was bred in England in April 1921 by Col. R. McCalmont. Three times an unsuccessful Waterloo Cup candidate, the 70lb brindle was bought by Irish Coursing Club secretary T.A. Morris at the termination of his career, taking up his new duties in Clonmel, Co. Tipperary, in 1925 – at ten guineas, a fee equalled in Ireland only by Jedderfield's, and exceeded solely by the twelve guineas asked for Three Speed's services.

Three Speed and Jedderfield were then the Republic's leading sires of winners, so Morris must have been extremely confident of his new acquisition's chances, confidence which was not misplaced. Mutton Cutlet's astonishing success was undoubtedly assisted by the almost simultaneous advent of track racing, at which his offspring proved particularly adept, and by the fact that Morris limited him – initially, at least – to approved bitches. A first-rate judge of a Greyhound, Morris carefully scrutinised the breeding, conformation and form of would-be mates, and did not allow him to cover any which failed his rigorous vetting.

The wisdom of this policy was evident at Clonmel in 1928, when the Derby final was contested by two pups from his first full crop, Keen Girlie and Porthos, victory going to the former. He struck again in 1929 with Debonairly, an August whelp, and in 1933 Floating Cutlet gave him a third success in the Classic. In all, thirteen winners or dividers of the coursing Derby came from Mutton Cutlet's male line, the last being Rahard Rebel in 1952.

His offspring similarly scored three times in the Clonmel Oaks, Keel Rose having landed the inaugural running in 1930 from Friend's Gift, another of his daughters, and in fact three of that year's four semi-finalists were by Mutton Cutlet. Monalogue registered a second victory for him in 1932, which was followed by Cutlet's Turn's win a year later. A unique double was accomplished by Monalogue when she added the 1933 Irish track Derby to her coursing Oaks triumph. She was Mutton Cutlet's only winner of the event, but progeny of his sons were successful in 1934 (Frisco Hobo), 1935 (Roving Yank), 1938 (Abbeylara) and 1939 (Marching Through Georgia).

Fourteen years elapsed before his male line produced its next Irish Derby hero, in the shape of Spanish Battleship, triple victor of 1953, 1954 and 1955, after which Colonel Perry's score in 1958 rang the curtain down so far as Mutton Cutlet's home-grown dynasty was concerned. In England, as in Ireland, just one Derby fell to Mutton Cutlet's offspring, the year in question being 1933, when Future Cutlet and Beef Cutlet scored a one-two for the king of stud dogs. Davesland, the 1934 winner, was by Mutton Cutlet's son, Kick Him Down, and in 1946 the honours were secured by Monday's News, by the Scurry Gold Cup winner Orluck's Best, who was by Mutton Cutlet's son Orluck. The English Oaks was won by two Mutton Cutlet bitches: Faithful Kitty (1930) and Queen of the Suir, dual heroine of the 1932 and 1933 renewals, along with the Irish equivalent in the former year. Beef Cutlet compensated for his narrow defeat in the White City showpiece with victories in the Laurels, Welsh Derby and Blackpool Hunt Cup. He then proved a powerful force at stud, siring the 1938 Gold Collar winner Junior Classic, his litter-brother Juvenile Classic, who won the 1938 and 1940 Junior Nationals, and their older brother, Jesmond Cutlet, Cesarewitch/Scottish Derby hero of 1937. In the long term, however, it was Larry of Waterhall, a litter-brother of Junior and Juvenile Classic, who was to safeguard the future of the line by establishing in the USA a branch which produced Sand Man.

UPSIDEDOWN

Well before the arrival of Larry of Waterfall, however, Mutton Cutlet's progeny had already made their mark on the American track and field scene, foremost among them being a March 1933 whelp named Upsidedown. In his native Ireland, this 80lb brindle qualified for Clonmel at Crohane and Killenaule, but went out of the Derby in the second round. Exported shortly afterwards to the USA, he won the National Waterloo Cup of that year (1934) before embarking upon a highly successful stud career. Brave Comrade (1939 National Waterloo Cup) and Good Sally (1940 National Derby) were prominent among his coursing winners, while on the track headlines were made in 1936 by Eddy Lee (Sapling Stakes), Wealthy Flirt (Futurity Stakes), First Son (Butte Inaugural) and Grey Tick (Wonderland Inaugural). Rather interestingly, the dam of Good Sally was Porte Special, an Irish-bred daughter of Mutton Cutlet, to whom the Derby heroine was thus closely inbred 2 x 2.

LARRY OF WATERHALL

Larry of Waterhall, bred by Miss P. Merrett in Llandaff, Cardiff, was a January 1936 whelp, from a repeat mating between Beef Cutlet and Lady Eleanor, whose sire Macoma was a brother to Mick the Miller. He was then transferred in 1940 to the ownership of Mrs T. Holmes, of Kent, Ohio, and took up covering duties at a time when American breeders had a wide choice of Mutton Cutlet line stud dogs. Upsidedown and over twenty of his sons were available, along with a dozen or so other sons and grandsons of the great sire.

Gun, Cameron and Harmony Red soon put Larry of Waterhall on the map, but as sires they were chiefly noted for the excellence of their daughters. However, the continuation of the male line was assured when Mixed Harmony was whelped in a September 1944 litter which Larry of Waterhall sired out of Thrilling Sport (Rural Rube – Sweet Harmony).

Thrilling Sport's pedigree epitomised the cream of American breeding, Rural Rube (My Laddie – Lady Gangdrew) being the most famous Greyhound ever bred in the USA. To digress for a moment, his sire, My Laddie, was by Traffic Officer, a son of the imported British-bred stud dog, Meadows, an April 1920 whelp by Husky Whisper II – Epergne. Meadows contested a number of stakes without ever gaining outright victory, his only success being the division of an 'eight' at Sydmonton, Berkshire, in November 1922. A measure of the esteem in which he was held can be gathered from the fact that when his owner sent him to a sale at the Barbican in April 1924, he made just four guineas, and was sent out to his new proprietor in Texas. Belying his lowly sale price, Meadows was within a year the sire of Traffic Officer, a track and field Champion, following up with the consecutive National Derby winners Peggy's Career (1929) and Sydney (1930).

Reverting to Thrilling Sport, her dam, Sweet Harmony (a daughter of Upsidedown), proved herself a top performer under both codes, landing the Palm Beach Inaugural on the track and running up for the 1937 National Waterloo Cup. Sweet Harmony's sister, Flashy Harmony, was the dam of Hall of Famer Flashy Sir. Mixed Harmony raced until the age of five, winning the 1948 Rainham Derby and scoring over distances from 550 to 770 yards. He left the track in a blaze of glory after running third in the 1949 Tijuana Derby in Mexico. However, greater fame was in store for him at stud, as he led the winning sires' lists in 1954 and 1955.

Through Ample Time, Johnny Leonard and Great Valor, Mixed Harmony established three powerful sire lines, and it was the first-named whose branch was to produce the modern king of stud dogs, Sand Man. A December 1951 whelp, Ample Time won 58 of his 148 races, including the Flagler Inaugural, the mid-season Biscayne Derby and two Flagler Derbys. Noted for both early pace and stamina, the 67lb brindle was effective from 550 to 660 yards and broke several track records during a career in which he amassed more than 30,000 dollars in prize-money. At stud, he sired his greatest son, Venerated, in 1961, but earlier, in 1955, had sired Ample Tip in a successful litter out of Your Telling Me, whose female line traced back to an imported British-bred bitch named Chocolate Candy (late Dee Maid), a 1925 whelp by Mah-a-Buacaill out of Dinara. Dinara's third dam, Forest Fairy, was the fifth dam of Mutton Cutlet.

Ample Tip scored his greatest hit as a stud dog when siring a March 1960 litter out of Win Dixie (Sunchek – Roseberry), whose dam line emanated from the imported British-bred bitch Ryston (Harbuckle – Binomial). Ryston was also the female line ancestress of the aforementioned Johnny Leonard and Great Valor. The litter contained two Champions, My Friend Lou and Sought After, who both rattled up identical race win tallies of 67. My Friend Lou was also honoured by selection in 1963 for the All-American team, and listed the Rocky Mountain Puppy Stake, Cloverleaf Inaugural and Mile High Timberline among his victories, along with a track record at the Mile High venue.

A mating between My Friend Lou and Westy Blubber (New World – Kinto Nebo) yielded in 1969 the red-brindled dog Friend Westy, unlucky when beaten in the 1971 Raynham Derby. Kinto

Nebo (by Johnny Leonard), bought cheaply for 250 dollars, ranks as one of America's greatest brood bitches, each of her seven litters having contained Grade A runners.

Friend Westy's stud career was founded upon two superb litters he sired out of Miss Gorgeous (Tell You Why – Miss Dilly Mar), who was recently elected to the Hall of Fame. Winner of 13 consecutive races and 34 in all, Miss Gorgeous threw three All-Americans among her produce: Highway Robber, Miss Friend and Rooster Cogburn. The first two named came from her initial litter by Friend Westy, whelped in August 1973, which included Sand Man. The repeat mating resulted in a November 1974 lot, among which were Rooster Cogburn and Gambling Fever.

SAND MAN

Sand Man, a Grade A performer, was sent to stand in Ireland by the expatriate Fr. Daniel Greene, a native of Doon, Co. Limerick. The phenomenal success he enjoyed in the Meelick, Co. Laois kennel of John Fitzpatrick rivalled the brilliant career of his male line ancestor Mutton Cutlet half a century earlier. At the time of Sand Man's arrival, Mutton Cutlet's domestic male line was extinct, and Irish breeding was in sore need of an outcross, a situation which the American dog fully exploited for a period of ten years until his death in 1988.

Just as Mutton Cutlet had brought off the English/Irish Derby double in 1933 with Future Cutlet and Monalogue, so Sand Man accomplished it in 1984 with Whisper Wishes and Dipmac. Ten other Classic victories in England included those gained by Sandy Sally (Oaks), Easy And Slow (St Leger) and Flashy Sir (Laurels). In Ireland, the Oaks fell to Strange Legend, the National Produce Stakes to Game Ball, and the Grand National to Sand Blinder. Three sons of Sand Man have sired Irish Derby winners: Overdraught Pet (Rathgallen Tady), Game Ball (Make History) and Manorville Sand (Manorville Magic); a grandson, Ardfert Sean, is responsible for Ardfert Mick. Gambling Fever followed Sand Man to Ireland and did well, but fell a long way short of his brother's achievements, as indeed have the numerous other American and Australian stud dogs introduced since then.

CAPRI

When, in 1882, Mr W. Cooper, of Sydney, imported Capri from England, he laid the foundation of a sire line which was to produce Champions in Australia, America, Britain and Ireland. Described as a 'great, raking dog', the 1880 son of Canute – Little Star shared a long division of the Kempton Park Derby and won a round of the Berkeley Derby before being acquired by Cooper for £50 and a contingency regarding a share of stake money won, upon which the NCC subsequently gave a ruling (Stud Book, Vol. 2 p. xii). Within a few months of his arrival in Australia, Capri won the 1882 Victorian Waterloo Cup, defeating another English import, Maid of Oborne, in the final of the 64-runner event.

He made a considerable impact at stud, establishing his male line through Heyfield – Young Heyfield – Senator to Comedy King (1908), top stud dog of his day in Australia and sire of Waterloo Cup winners King Comedy (New South Wales) and Brown Hawk (Victoria). It was, however, Comedy King's son Playful King who carried the inheritance on, via Agricola – Wharminda – Pharminda to Silver Chief, a first-class performer on track and field, and winner of the 96-dog Victoria Waterloo Cup in 1939.

Silver Chief sired Trion, whose son Chief Havoc broke or equalled 19 track records after being sold as a puppy for eight guineas. An equally brilliant chapter was then written at stud, where Chief Havoc reigned supreme in Australia and extended his writ to the USA in the shape of a son, Rocker Mac, who led the sires' table there from 1959 to 1965 – an unparalleled record. Rocket Fire, another of Chief Havoc's sons exported to America, fathered Rocket Ship, who was taken by

Pat Dalton to Ireland, there to sire the speedy Bright Lad in 1967.

A brace of Waterloo Cup heroes – Minnesota Miller and Minnesota Yank – gave Bright Lad considerable kudos as a dual-purpose sire, but tracking was primarily the game of his offspring. From Liberty Lad, Bright Lad's main outlet, the line spread out among Debbycot Lad, Echo Spark, Special Merchant and Citizen Supreme. Echo Spark's branch depends for continuation almost entirely upon his English Derby winner Signal Spark, whereas Citizen Supreme has a much stronger hand in Greenpark Fox (sire of the Irish Derby victor Manx Treasure) and Brownies Outlook.

MICAWBER

The Micawber sire line, for long one of the most dominant in Australia, has been transplanted successfully in the USA and Ireland, largely through the export to the United States of Tell You Why, the male line ancestor of such stars as Dutch Bahama, the top American stud dog, and Sail On II, who did well in Eire. The line was founded in Australia by The Dickens, a May 1914 son of Crombie – Cuckoo. Under his original name of Crafty Roger, The Dickens divided the Home Bred Produce Stakes at Sussex County Club in December 1915, and was sold at the Barbican a week later for 71 guineas.

From The Dickens, the line was passed on via Micawber – Andrew Micawber – Charlie Micawber – My Chriss Micawber – Alwin Chris – Menang to Tumble Bug, a January 1945 whelp possessed of tremendous pace. Tumble Bug's dam, Proposed, relied heavily in her pedigree upon close in-breeding to Cinbon (by the imported English dog, Cinder) and Lass O' Gowrie (by Andrew Micawber). Proposed's paternal granddam (Big Idea) and maternal grandsire (Dan's Gift) were sister and brother, by Cinbon – Lass O' Gowrie. Winner of 18 of his 27 races, Tumble Bug was reckoned to be the fastest Greyhound ever to have run in Tasmania, and he was no less impressive on the mainland when scoring at Sandown Park, Melbourne. Quickly establishing himself as one of Australia's best sires, he left behind a son named Rocket Jet when snapped up for export to America, where he sired Saddler and numerous excellent bitches.

He was by no means the first of the 'Micawber' line to make good in America. Twenty years before his arrival, Just Andrew (Andrew Micawber – Fanny) had been imported by wrestling champion John Pesek on the strength of his outstanding coursing performances in Australia. The hound proved equally effective on the track in the United States, prior to making his name at stud there when getting a September 1931 litter out of the imported Mutton Cutlet bitch, Mustard Roll, which included Lucky Roll, Ben Andrews, Perfect Roll and Just Roll.

Hall of Fame Lucky Roll won 60 races and was sire of Never Roll, who notched four world record times at Wonderland in September 1942. Never Roll sired Lucky Pilot (61 wins), Real Huntsman (won 27 consecutive races) and Lucky Sir, the Progenitor of Hall of Fame entrant Flashy Sir. Rocket Jet (Tumble Bug – Marnaleen) flourished at stud in Australia after the departure of his sire, getting winners of most major events, among them the Melbourne Cup victors of 1956 (Rocketeer), 1958 (Marine Jet) and 1959 (Capital King).

Another of Rocket Jet's sons, Tell You Why, won the Harold Park Classic and Bi-Annual Classic before being sent to America, where he topped the winning stud dogs' lists in 1967 and 1968. He sired Hoefer, Westy Whizzer, Trap Rock and a bitch named Miss Gorgeous, dam of Sand Man. Hoefer's son Kelly Jones got the champion American sire Unruly, while Westy Whizzer was responsible for Big Whizzer, the sire of Sail On II and Downing. The latter's son, For Real, produced Leaders Best, now prominent at stud in Ireland. Trap Rock is the sire of Hairless Joe, whose son, Dutch Bahama, is America's leading stud dog.

Chapter Nine

TRAINING RACING GREYHOUNDS

From the very early days when Greyhound racing was first developing as a sport, it soon became apparent that trainers conversant in the new discipline would be needed to provide Greyhounds for the track. Big money was at stake with wagers laid on the results of races, so it was essential to have handlers of integrity who could consistently produce top-quality Greyhounds. Over the years there have been many notable trainers who have graced the sport, displaying tremendous skill and dedication, and it is these individuals – as well as the Greyhounds – that have made the sport great.

All trainers have their own way of running a kennel, schooling a Greyhound, and preparing a top racer for a major competition. Sometimes the differences are due to circumstances, such as the way the sport is run in a particular country, but it also comes down to the way individual trainers interpret the needs of their dogs, along with the ability to get the best from their charges.

Linda Mullins – Champion Trainer of the Year, 1992 – has a consistent record of training top open-class dogs.

Britain, Ireland, the USA and Australia are universally acknowledged as the leading countries for Greyhound racing, and so top trainers have been interviewed, answering a series of questions on their methods of training racing Greyhounds. In Britain, Linda Mullins and Geoff de Mulder reveal their training methods; Michael O'Sullivan represents Ireland, Herb 'Dutch' Koerner and Ron Beckner give the American slant, and Paul Wheeler talks about training in Australia.

LINDA MULLINS
Following the sudden death of leading Greyhound trainer Pat Mullins in 1981, his wife, Linda, bravely decided to take out a trainer's licence herself, as well as bringing up her four young sons: John, David, Kelly and Ricky. She had been involved with Greyhound racing from an early age, working for her sister, Jeanne Chapelle, who was one of the pioneers of British Greyhound breeding and a successful open race trainer.

Linda then worked for the legendary trainer Leslie Reynolds, who guided a record five Greyhounds to Derby wins.

When working with her husband, Pat, the Mullins' name was associated with top open racers, and Lacca Champion was responsible for their finest moment when winning the 1978 Greyhound Derby. Linda has always maintained that Lacca Champion's success was down to Pat, and one of her ambitions is to win the great race herself. Her first classic victory came in the shape of Amenhotep, who won the Laurels in 1984. Of course, many more open race stars have passed through her hands, and she has proved herself second to none in training hurdlers, with Gizmo Pasha winning the Grand National in 1990. Linda was Champion trainer in 1992 – a remarkable achievement for someone who is committed to providing graded runners at Walthamstow three times a week. The following year, she notched up an amazing 207 winners on the open race circuit.

GEOFF DE MULDER

De Mulder was destined to be one of the best Greyhound trainers of his profession. His grandfather, Prosper de Mulder, was a leading racehorse trainer, his father, Joe, was an extremely successful owner of Greyhounds, and his mother, Beatrice, at one time had the highest number of greyhounds registered with the NGRC.

Geoffrey de Mulder took out his trainer's licence in 1959, and has won most of the prizes on offer in the sport. He has reached the Greyhound Derby final an amazing fourteen times, and has won the sport's premier race twice, with Jimsun and Sarah's Bunny. His Redlum kennel is an academy for canine stars, but also the staff who have worked under the maestro have gone on to greater heights. A perfect example is Tony Meek, who has now won the Greyhound Derby in his own right.

Geoff de Mulder, pictured with Fearless Mustang, is one of Britain's most successful trainers, with two Greyhound Derbys to his credit.

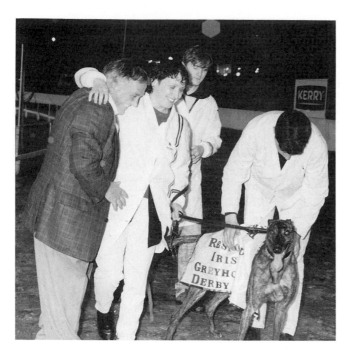

Michael O'Sullivan and his daughter, Marie, celebrating after Manx Treasure's victory in the 1992 Irish Derby.

Red Mills Photography.

MICHAEL O'SULLIVAN

O'Sullivan has sent out a stream of top-class winners from his County Tipperary kennels, but undoubtedly the high point of his career was when Manx Treasure won the 1992 Irish Derby. The dog suffered injury and in lesser hands might never have won a race at all, let alone scale the heights he did. Other dogs to have benefitted from O'Sullivan's compassionate but professional approach include: Aglish Aeroplane, McCalmont Cup winner; Coolamber Forest, Edinburgh Cup winner; Boher Ash, Paddy Whiskey stake winner; and the legendary Greenpark Fox. Add to these the numerous dogs bearing the Manx prefix, including St Leger winner Manx Marajax, and O'Sullivan's prowess becomes apparent.

DUTCH KOERNER

Koerner runs a successful Greyhound farm and kennel operation. Koerner raised and raced Dutch Bahama to a pair of American Derby victories at Lincoln Greyhound Park, Lincoln, Rhode Island, and a first-place finish in the Irish-American Classic at Biscayne Greyhound Track in Miami, Florida. Dutch Bahama was twice named to the All-America Team, he was the winner of the Flashy Sir Award and was inducted into the Greyhound Hall of Fame. Dutch Bahama has since become the number one sire in America. Koerner serves as a member of the National Greyhound Board of Directors and was recently elected to his fourth term as president.

Herb 'Dutch' Koerner

Ron and Dorothy Beckner accept the trophy for By Tar's victory in the Hollywood Distance Classic.

Sherry Seymour, Hollywood Greyhound Track.

RON BECKNER

Beckner has been raising and racing Greyhounds all his life. His grandfather, O.B. Beckner, raced Greyhounds in the 1920s. His father, E.L. (Skinny) Beckner, continued the tradition. Ron Beckner was first put in charge of a kennel at the age of sixteen, filling in for his father when he made trips. Beckner got his trainer's licence at the age of nineteen, lying about his age. Littermates All-America Blendway and Wonderland Derby winner, Bartie (Perceive – Buzz Off), earned over 450,000 dollars for his kennel. In 1993 the Beckner kennel earned seven stake victories through the first ten months of the year: Kansas Bred Holiday Sprint at The Woodlands (Breakdown Albert), Hollywood Distance Classic (By Tar), Wonderland Derby (Be Alive), Woodlands Sprint (By Tar), Tampa Distance Classic (Beige Ace), and the Kansas Bred Top Dog Sprint (Breakdown Albert).

PAUL WHEELER

The Bale kennel was founded thirty years ago by Paul's father, Allen, who died in 1987. In this time the kennel has been responsible for countless thousands of winners, including almost every feature race in Australia. In recent years Paul Wheeler, vice president of the United Greyhound Association, has a record two 100,000 dollar Supercoat Petcoat wins at Dapto from only four runnings of the feature race.

Paul Wheeler with Yay Bee Bale, winner of the Dapto Supercoat final in March 1994.

Q. WHAT ARE YOUR FACILITIES LIKE, AND HOW MANY GREYHOUNDS DO YOU ACCOMMODATE?

MULLINS (Britain): "The kennels at Manningtree, Essex, are set in nine and a half acres of land. We have seven large paddocks – the largest is a five-acre meadow, the smallest is three-quarters of an acre. There is no schooling track, but we use one of our fields as a gallop which is 250 yards long. We have a 'machine room' – a treatment room with all the latest technology to get injured racers back to the track as quickly as possible.

"I have about one hundred Greyhounds in my care at present, of which sixty to sixty-five are available for racing. On average, we usually have about fifteen Greyhounds trialling, and between five and ten Greyhounds who are lame or injured. I have twelve retired Greyhounds, and a few brood bitches. I try to breed two litters every year.

"Most of my dogs are kennelled in twos, although we have one or two awkward characters who need separate kennels. But on the whole, Greyhounds do like company."

DE MULDER (Britain): "I have twenty-one acres set aside for the Greyhounds. This includes a gallop which is 382m (400 yards) in length. It is a good gallop with an uphill climb, and it has certainly seen some great Greyhounds over the years. The surface is grass, which is well-watered and generally well-maintained.

I can kennel forty Greyhounds, but I do not keep that number these days. At the moment I have fifteen racing Greyhounds and six puppies that have just been schooled. I have not kept graded runners for over two years, as I like to concentrate on the open race scene. I only breed one litter a year. You can kennel a dog and a bitch together, but I prefer to keep them separate."

O'SULLIVAN (Ireland): "My kennels occupy about twelve acres in Balingarry. I started off with redundancy money from a local joinery firm, and I have built up the kennel making full provision for around sixteen race dogs, twenty saplings, six brood bitches,

The schooling track at Geoff de Mulder's Redlum kennels.

and three stud dogs. The stud dogs – Greenpark Fox, Manx Treasure and Slaneyside Hare – are probably the busiest stud dogs in Ireland. I have an all-weather 400-yard gallop, plus all the latest technology for treating injured Greyhounds.

"I always kennel two dogs together with muzzles on. Bitches are kept separate, usually with pups that are schooling. I find that when a dog and a bitch are together, the dog is distracted – always wanting to smell the bitch's urine, for example. My race dogs are kept separate from the puppies and the stud dogs."

KOERNER (USA): "I race at Dairyland in Kenosha, Wisconsin, and Mile High in Denver, Colorado. We have sixty crates at each kennel and that is how many pups I have. However, race tracks in Colorado or Arizona allow the Greyhounds to be kennelled off-track on the farm. In every other state it is mandatory that the dogs be kennelled at the track. The facilities now at the new tracks in the United States are real good. When Texas, Wisconsin and Kansas came along (approving pari-mutuel wagering), the breeders were involved in the legislation and we have some real nice facilities.

I raise all my own Greyhounds, which works out at around 250 to 300 a year. Ninety per cent of the kennels lease their Greyhounds from farmers that are not at the race track. They then pay a percentage of the purse to the owners. Usually the deal is 65 per cent to the kennel and 35 per cent to the owner. Sometimes they (the owners) will receive 40 per cent, but most lease agreements are 35-65, which is a good percentage. I built my farm on 35 per cent. My farm is fairly typical of the larger Greyhound operation in America. It sits on a 33 acre site near Hays, Kansas. I have twenty-five 300ft runs for the young pups, and one whelping kennel with five stalls. There are two kennel buildings, each holding between 60-70 Greyhounds in training. After weaning, the young pups go to the runs until they are thirteen or fourteen months old. Then they move into the kennels for training. I also have a facility which houses seven stud dogs. They are kept in individual pens with their own runs. To run the operation, I employ a full-time staff of five, plus four part-time younger students to lead the young pups."

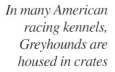

In many American racing kennels, Greyhounds are housed in crates

BECKNER (USA): "I race at three tracks, Tampa-St. Pete, Southland and The Woodlands, and I have roughly sixty pups in each kennel. Right now I probably have 500 head on the farm, which sits on forty-six acres in Lee, Florida. We are not the biggest, but we are right there in the top percentage in amount of dogs. The farm consists of eighty runs, ranging in size from 300ft to 600ft. There are two kennels, one housing eighty-six pups, the other accommodates some forty-four dogs. I have two whelping houses, and my seven stud dogs stay in the kennel. After weaning, the young pups move from the whelping house to the long runs. They stay there until they are fourteen months of age, when they move into the kennel buildings. The pups are finished in a quarter-mile training track, located on another eighteen acres adjacent to the farm."

WHEELER (Australia): "We have between 100 to 150 greyhounds on our eleven-hectare property, which has been developed into one of the best kennel complexes in the world. It includes a loam training track, which is almost an exact replica of Wentworth Park. We kennel in banks of six, which can be locked for security."

Q. WHEN DO YOU START SCHOOLING? WHAT METHODS DO YOU USE?

MULLINS: "As I have no schooling track here, I send my dogs away to be schooled when they are twelve months old. I believe the change of scene is good for them, and they gain invaluable experience at their schooling track. We have found that twelve months is the best age, as it gives plenty of time for training. If we wait until the dogs are fourteen months old, they are likely to be a bit backward, and it will take them longer to reach the track.

"Obviously, while they are at Manningtree we encourage the youngsters to chase and run. They have plenty of room – the pups are housed in a big paddock and let out into the five-acre meadow for a hour's exercise, three times a day. We provide old sheets and jumpers so that the puppies can play around, having tugs-of-war etc. This is all part of growing up and helps to develop their strength and their mental attitude.

"Schooling takes about six weeks, and then the Greyhounds come back and start preparing for their trials. The dogs are schooled behind a whirligig. They are also taken to other schooling tracks so that they gain experience of other hare systems, and this also gets them used to travelling in a van, which is an important part of the learning process."

DE MULDER: "When the pups are being reared, they must have complete freedom. They have to get used to going out in big spaces – ten to fifteen acres – you cannot rear Greyhounds in a small paddock. If you attempted to rear puppies in a small paddock, 100 yards long and 30 yards wide, with four puppies in one paddock, and four puppies in an adjoining paddock, the dogs will spend all day running up and down, driving each other mad. Puppies that are reared in these conditions – eating and sleeping in a confined area – become bored with their surroundings. They literally know every square inch of it. Their galloping is restricted to 90 yards, and once you restrict a Greyhound to that space, it will tell when it comes to the race track. That is why the Irish always score with their open system of rearing.

"The Irish rear their greyhounds on farms out on the mountains, and they are given as much freedom as possible. They are allowed to roam around, investigating their surroundings, playing with each other, jumping over walls. There is a handful of breeders in England who can match the Irish at their own game. But if your pup does not have the space to gallop, there is no possible chance of rearing a Champion. I encourage my youngsters to chase by putting a couple of dog-squeakers inside a rabbit skin and sewing it up tightly. If you put this out in the field with the dogs they have a lot of fun with it. They believe it is alive – and this is important, as it is essential to arouse their natural hunting instinct.We get them used to collars and leads at six months, and I put youngsters through the boxes when they are about eight months old. This may seem early compared with some trainers, but it is all part of educating the dogs. When they are twelve months of age, I start schooling behind the drag lure. I treat dogs and bitches exactly the same."

O'SULLIVAN: "In order to get a youngster chasing, I would take him out on the farm at twelve months of age to have a go at catching live rabbits. At the track, I would put a youngster through the traps with the front open. I would do this two or three times, treating the dog very gently. The first time the dog is expected to chase, I would handslip him through the open traps."

SCHOOLING

All trainers have slightly different methods of schooling Greyhounds for the track. But the basic principles are widely applicable. This is the method used by Nick Savva at his Westmead Kennels.

The novice Greyhound is introduced to the lure. In this case it is a racoon-skin.

The Greyhound quickly gets the idea of going after the lure and, at this stage, is allowed to grab it.

The racoon skin is propelled forward on the whirlygig, and the Greyhound is hand-slipped. The dog's chasing instinct is keen and he is quick to set off in pursuit.

The Greyhound must learn to go into the starting box.

To begin with the Greyhound is put into the starting box and encouraged to walk out at the front.

The next stage is to entice the Greyhound out of the starting box by dragging the racoon-skin in front.

This Greyhound is quick to respond to the lure and has no hesitation in coming out of the box.

Now the racoon-skin goes back on the whirlygig, and the Greyhound is encouraged to chase the lure from the starting box.

Again, the Greyhound is quick to respond.

The reward is catching hold of the lure.

This Greyhound has shown that he is keen to chase using the whirlygig. The next step is to use the lure on the rail at ground level. The dog is hand-slipped to give maximum visibility of the lure.

It is now time to try the Greyhound from the starting box.

Success! The Greyhound comes cleanly from the traps and sets off in pursuit of the lure.

KOERNER: "I start schooling a little later than a lot of people. We start our training at about 13 to 14 months. We start the dogs on a drag lure. We pull a coyote hide approximately 1200 to 1400 feet. That is the key: the distance. You have to pull the lure long enough. A lot of these artificial lures are not long enough and they really don't get a dog excited. Then, at the end of the race, we use a predator call.

"Some dogs take a little more than others. We usually give six to seven drag lures and then we go to the whirligig, which is an arm and a rail. We tie an artificial lure on the end of the arm. What we are doing here is familiarising the dog with the turns. A Greyhound is bred to sight, chase and kill. That is on a straight run on the ground. With the whirligig, the Greyhound gets used to chasing something off the ground, and he gets use to the rail. This is the step before he goes to the race track.

"We usually whirligig two or times, then we go to the race track. At my training track we do not school as much as a lot of people, but we usually do ten to fifteen schoolings. Next the pup goes to an official race track. There he is schooled unofficially ten to fifteen times, depending on the Greyhound. Some dogs need a little more than this. From the start, we would give extra training for those that are not chasing good.

"After that the Greyhound is ready to go on to official schooling and racing. A Greyhound will get a start every fourth day. That's an ideal racing schedule: every four or five days. But when a kennel gets short of dogs, a pup may get only two days in between racing, but that's not good. They should have at least three days between racing."

Linda Mullins is well-known for her success with hurdlers. Here she shows how she starts schooling over the hurdles with an easy obstacle to give the dog confidence.

When the Greyhound has learnt to clear the obstacle, he can graduate to chasing the lure over hurdles.

BECKNER: "We begin schooling at roughly twelve to thirteen months of age. We use an Australian lure that sounds like a jackrabbit. Dogs seem to really like the sound of it. It keeps their attention. We school twice a week on a training track. This goes on from the time they hit the training track for three months."

WHEELER: "I start schooling between the ages of twelve to fifteen months. We have a whirligig track, which is a push-around set up, approximately twelve metres across, with a small set of starting traps. We pre-educate all our young ones here, so they learn to chase and to use the boxes before progressing to a full-sized track."

Q. HOW DO YOU ASSESS A GREYHOUND'S IDEAL RACING DISTANCE?

MULLINS: "Personally, I like to wait and see how a Greyhound performs on the track before assessing its proper distance. You arc not guaranteed to get what you want when breeding Greyhounds. It is completely different from breeding race horses, where you know even before they reach the track what distance they will be effective over.

In Greyhound racing you can have a sprinter, a middle distance runner, and a stayer all in the same litter. If I want to try a Greyhound over a longer trip to find out whether it will become a marathon racer, I do this gradually by stepping the dog up to 640m, then perhaps 750m, and then on to 800m plus."

The Greyhound will need to be muzzled for official trials, and for every race thereafter.

The secret is to fasten the muzzle so that it is comfortable for the dog but there is no risk of it coming off in the course of a race

DE MULDER: "The distance a Greyhound races over is in the breeding – a sprinter is a sprinter, a middle distance dog is a middle distance dog, and a stayer is a stayer. For example, Greenpark Fox is a top sprinter, yet he throws up some good middle distance dogs. That is because the bitches that are sent to him are usually able to stay 550 yards or 600 yards. I have seen plenty of Greyhounds run on really strong to the pick-up, looking as though they needed six bends. yet, when they were tried over that distance their engine burns out. I would only step up a dog in distance gradually. For example, if he was running on over 475m, I would then try him at Perry Barr (500m), Hove (515m), Stainforth (495m), Shawfield (500m) or Hackney (523m)."

O'SULLIVAN: "The first thing I do is look at the dog's breeding and his dam's breeding in particular. After that, you learn to evaluate a dog on experience – you get to know which distance a dog is likely to prefer.

"I would never switch a dog that stays well over 525 yards to 700 yards in one go. I would put him up to 575 yards, then 600 yards, and so on."

KOERNER: "If a dog has a strong backside run but levels off in the stretch, he usually won't go a distance. A dog that will run a 3/8 is a dog that will start to make his move up the stretch, or at the 3/8 box, and he just keeps coming. We start our pups in sprints, and then assess which distance they will run. We look to see if a dog shows real early how far he will run. A dog will show me at home on my training track how far he can run, and then we know what will suit him at the race track."

Performance on the track depends on receiving a well-balanced diet, and the skilful trainer works out the individual requirements of the dogs in their charge.

The racing Greyhound is prepared for the track with a programme of walking and gallops.

BECKNER: "In my opinion, most Greyhounds are just 5/16 dogs. That is their top distance. There is a small percentage of 3/8 Greyhounds and an extreme small percentage of marathon Greyhounds. Greyhounds are not horses. They are not bred to run marathon races. I am opposed to marathon races and I think it's cruel for some of the tracks to force the kennels to have marathon dogs. A lot of tracks think that any dog you have can run 3/8. But that is not true. If you run a dog further than he is capable of going, you can destroy the dog. You won't kill him but the dog will never be the same.

"Sometimes it's just guesswork when you are trying to judge if a dog can run distance. If we see a dog that looks like he's not getting tired and he's not getting caught, we might try the dog at 3/8. If we see a dog that goes to the front and then it is all he can do to just barely hold on in a 5/16 race, he's not going to run 3/8. Sometimes a dog will fool you. Some dogs have a lot of kick in a 5/16 and you would think this dog can go 3/8, but he cannot.

"It seems to be true that many of the 3/8 stake races are being won by basically sprinters. It's like anything else. A dog that goes to the front has a big advantage. I just don't think there are many true 3/8 dogs in the country. Over the years I think most breeding programs bred distance out.

"Blendway and Bartie were basically 5/16 dogs, but I won a 3/8 stake with Bartie (Wonderland Derby), and I ran second with Blendway in the Sunflower Stake. They could run 3/8 but they were not the type of dogs that you could just put in 3/8 and forget about them, start after start. You could get by with many four in a row, three eliminations and the final, but you could not leave them over there ten, eleven times."

WHEELER: "I assess the correct distance for a Greyhound by watching him run. If a slow beginner is running home strong, I increase the distance."

Q. HOW DO YOU COPE WITH PROBLEM DOGS – BAD TRAVELLERS, DOGS THAT TURN IN THE TRAPS, POOR CHASERS, ETC. ?

MULLINS: "We have not had much trouble with bad travellers, but bad kennellers are a common complaint. Unfortunately, there is no hard and fast solution. We have used a radio in the kennel, we have chained the Greyhound up, and we have even put a broom upsidedown to make out that someone is in the kennel. However, each Greyhound has his own reason why he frets in the kennel. It would be better if all track kennels were built to the same design. The kennels at Hove and Sunderland are the best. They are two-tiered, open-cage style, and they face each other so the Greyhounds can hear and see everything that is going on. This means the dogs do not feel so claustrophobic. Security with open-caged kennels is paramount, but Hove and Sunderland have shown that it works, and I believe that other tracks should follow suit.

"If we start having problems with a Greyhound that turns in the trap we send him away for re-schooling. They use a half-trap which is narrower than a normal box, so the Greyhound does not have the opportunity to turn. After six trials in the half-trip, the Greyhound is usually cured of the problem. The best solution for poor chasers is to put the dog behind a different hare system. If a Greyhound will not chase a Sumner hare I try him on a McGee, and vice versa. It is not fair to the owners to try and race a Greyhound behind a hare that does not suit. For fighters and dogs who will not go by, we usually try them over hurdles. This helps to freshen a dog up, and will keep his mind on the job."

DE MULDER: "I have a special herbal remedy which I use on bad travellers. I have been using it for years, and I find it very effective. It is made from six different flowers, and it seems to keep the dog calm. With a bad kenneller, I would gallop the dog on the morning of the race, just to take the steam out of him. I would chain up the dog in the kennel, and I have found that playing a radio often works. The sound of music and voices seems to be soothing. Another tip is to wear your work coat on the way to the kennels, and then take it off and leave it in the kennel. The Greyhound can smell your scent, and he will be reassured that you are around.

"For dogs that turn in the traps I use a special trap that is is constructed with a piece of timber so that it narrows the space inside. I find that when a Greyhound is tried in this a few times, they kick the habit. Another method is to put your dog in the trap and stand in front, calling the dog's name to keep his attention. You can also try handslipping another dog just in front of your problem dog, before the trap opens. This gives the dog plenty of encouragement to face the right way as the lure goes past. If a Greyhound turns his head, there may be a reason for it. It could be that the dog is feeling off-colour, or it could be because the dog was badly bumped at the first bend and is trying to get his own back on a rival. In this sort of situation, the Greyhound is unlikely to repeat the offence. I call Greyhounds who will not go past 'nappers', and, funnily enough, I don't mind them. They have ability, but will not always show it. You can sometimes kid this type of Greyhound by taking him to a new track without a trial – and you may well find that the dog wins first time out."

O'SULLIVAN: "If I have a bad traveller, I try to have someone who will travel in the back of the van with the dog. With a bad kenneller, I put cotton-wool in the dog's ears to stop him getting excited by the noise. I have found that if you give this type of Greyhound more attention at home, it helps to build up his confidence. I also move the dog around to different kennels until he learns to settle. If I have a dog that turns in the traps, I put a collar on with a piece of string as a lead. The string passes out the front of the traps, and you can keep the dog facing forwards until the lids open, and then quickly release the string. I would do this three times before trying the dog on his own. I have only had one failure with this method. Obviously it is best to put a stop to trap-turning as soon as possible – the younger the better.

"For a Greyhound that is a poor chaser, I would freshen him up by taking him out into the fields to run after rabbits, or I might take him coursing. The only real solution for fighters is to put them over hurdles, but I find this only works in about twenty per cent of cases. If a dog will not go by, I handslip him with dogs of lower ability so he has to go by. I then gradually increase the ability of the opposition as the dog gains confidence."

KOERNER: "You can use tranquillizers when travelling, but usually this type are also bad kennel dogs. We call them fretters – and they are not good track dogs. They are nervous and they usually run their race in the paddock before the race. There is not much you can do.

"If we have a dog that turns in the traps we work on that at home on the farm, so that it does not happen at the race track. If a dog turns in the box he's not even going to make the race track. We familiarize our dogs with the box when they are young. When we put them in the box we make sure that there is a good opening in the front of the box so the Greyhound sees the daylight and doesn't get in the habit of turning around.

"If a Greyhound is not chasing the lure, he will not make the race track. He will be ruled out at the schooling stage. If a dog shows a tendency to fight it means that he is not chasing the lure. He is interfering with the other dogs racing and he will get ruled off. There are some dogs that will not pass. They are not really chasing the lure, but they will not interfere with the race. Some of these dogs will make a lot of money that way. They will take a lot of seconds, but they are not chasing the lure. If you break a dog right, you will eliminate a lot of these problems. On our farm we start at an early age. Every pup is lead-broke by the time he is four months old. We lead-break them, we handle them. Then, when we are ready for training, the pup is mentally prepared. His mind is 100 per cent on what he is trying to do. If you do things right with a dog at home on the farm, it definitely reflects as to what kind of a racer he is going to be. Bad habits will not occur if you start off the right way."

BECKNER: "If you have a bad traveller, we try to ride him by himself. You don't want to double up a bad traveller. Sometimes you might have to fly on, but a bad traveller – you have to make sure he has water in his crate. With an extra bad traveller, you have to make sure the dog has kidney pills if needed, and that you walk him periodically. If I have a Greyhound that turns in the starting box, I would take him out and put him right back in. Keep doing it. As soon as you get him facing straight, open the box. Most Greyhounds will get the hang of it right away. I don't think there is a lot you can do with poor chasers or fighters. I don't think you can straighten a fighter out. I have seen people that think they can, but once a dog gets it in his head he wants to fight, he may not do it for a few starts, but eventually it's going to come back out in him. I don't like fighters. A Greyhound who will not go by, a pacer, will make you a lot of money. They will run in the money a lot, but they will not win very often. I would rather not have a pacer, but it's surprising how much money a pacer will make for you – and that is the bottom line to this business."

WHEELER: "Greyhounds that turn in the traps, poor chasers and fighters are usually barred from racing. Dogs that will not go by sometimes pace themselves, so increasing the distance they race over sometimes helps."

Q. WHAT DO YOU FEED YOUR RACING DOGS?

MULLINS: "My Greyhounds are fed twice daily. We give them a breakfast of milk and cereal early in the morning. The afternoon feed is the main meal, which includes Wafcol, some Respond mixed with meat, plus vitamins or iron supplements. On a race day, the Greyhounds do not get a main meal, but they have a half-breakfast which includes 1/4lb of meat, cereal and soup all mixed together. When they arrive home from racing they get their main meal. It is important to bear in mind that what you put in you get out, so I feed my Greyhounds the best. Their stomachs and their feet are the most important parts of their bodies."

DE MULDER: "Modern trainers use complete diets such as Purina, Kasco or Red Mills. These feeds are all balanced with vitamins, and, strictly speaking, you should not add meat to this type of diet. However, I think that if you did not add meat, the Greyhounds would not stand up to the racing schedule that is demanded of them. A complete diet without supplements is OK for a domestic dog – but not for a racing Greyhound.

"I like to give a bit of variation in the diet, and so red meat and chicken is often mixed up with the Purina. It is important to get the balance right. There has to be an even balance between the protein and the carbohydrates. The old method was to use bread, but I cannot get the type of bread that I want, and so I use the modern foodstuffs. Vegetables can be used, but I do not think that Greyhounds can digest carrots. Greyhounds do not need salt, because they do not sweat like a race horse. Greyhounds sweat through their pads, tongues and ears."

O'SULLIVAN: "For breakfast I feed brown bread with a small amount of tripe or chicken, and a cup of half-tea, half-milk. For the main meal I feed brown bread with beef and raw vegetables, e.g.

carrots, turnips, potatoes. On one day a week the beef is replaced by chicken, and on one other day I feed fish. The supplements I use are cod-liver oil capsules, iron, and vitamins E and C are very important. The raw vegetables supply the rest."

KOERNER: "Like most American breeders, I feed a mixture of meat, high-protein meal, and vitamin supplement. The young pups are fed raw milk until they are thirteen to fourteen months old when they are moved to the kennel buildings."

BECKNER: "We use a beef for a base. We then use a mixture of high-protein meal and we use milk. I think dogs also need vitamins. We cook fresh stew for them four days a week, sometimes five days a week. I believe that the feed bowl helps you win races. Everybody's going to be different. There are no two people who feed exactly alike. If it works, that's fine. You have great athletes from all over the world and they have different diets."

WHEELER: "For breakfast we feed one cup of milk (powdered), half a teaspoon of calcium, half a teaspoon of vitamin E supplement, one teaspoon of glucose, one teaspoon of neutraline, plus biscuit. For the main meal we feed dogs 1lb 14oz meat (bitches: 1lb 10oz) and 8-10oz kibble (bitches: 6-8oz) mixed with the same amount of water, half a teaspoon of iron and one teaspoon of Feramo D."

Q. HOW MUCH EXERCISE DO YOU GIVE YOUR RACING DOGS?

MULLINS: "I believe galloping Greyhounds is far more important than just walking them, but with the heavy schedule of the racing Greyhounds these days, there is a fine balance in preparing them for the track. Sprinters can run off their beds, but stayers need a lot more work and must be kept running to keep on improving."

DE MULDER: "At fifteen months a Greyhound pup will be schooled. I believe that if you have reared a Greyhound in complete freedom, and then you start to walk him, and stop giving him his freedom, then he will be prone to lameness. It is unhealthy to keep a Greyhound locked in a kennel twenty-two hours a day. However, if you take a Greyhound out and train him in complete freedom – in exactly the same way as you have reared him – it has got to lessen the chance of lameness because the limbs and muscles are being fully exercised every day.

"When a Greyhound has been off the track, you should prepare him with a gallop before attempting to trial him. A Greyhound that has been resting and eating well, will not be physically ready to stand up to the track. His heart and his lungs must be exercised first."

O'SULLIVAN: "Dogs that are preparing to race will be walked one mile in the morning. They are then taken out for ten minutes at dinner-time to empty, and then walked a further two miles in the evening. In addition to this, they will be galloped over 300 yards, three times a week. The only difference in exercise routine for a dog that is already racing is that he would only receive one gallop a week."

KOERNER: "If a pup is racing every four or five days we usually get them out one time for a sprint, or we take them for a good walk."

BECKNER: "When our Greyhounds get to the track they still run twice a week, whether they draw in an official race or are being schooled unofficially."

WHEELER: "Our trainers are in banks of six. We free-run them twice daily, every day. They are kept on a lead for forty-eight hours before they race."

Q. WHAT IS YOUR GROOMING/CARE ROUTINE FOR YOUR RACING DOGS?

MULLINS: "We do not massage all the Greyhounds every day, but dogs and bitches that cramp or have a tendency to tighten up are massaged with oils to make their muscles more supple. Greyhounds run on their feet, so it it essential that they are kept in tip-top condition. Feet should be clean, and well-maintained."

GROOMING AND MASSAGE
Demonstrated by Linda Mullins

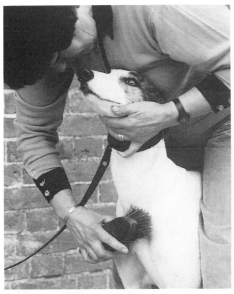

Linda starts off by grooming with a hard bristle brush.

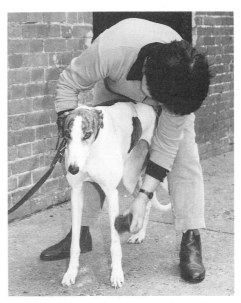

She begins at the front, working down to the legs.

The whole body needs to be brushed, ending up with the hindquarters.

For the next stage Linda uses a grooming pad, which helps to tone up the Greyhound's muscles. Again, she starts from the front.

The hindquarters, the powerhouse of the Greyhound, are worked on.

The process continues right down the hindlegs.

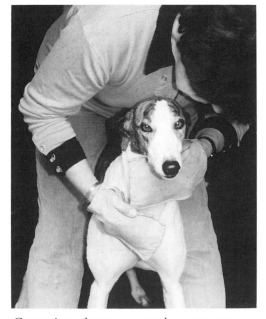

Grooming gloves are used to massage the Greyhound.

Linda works on the body.

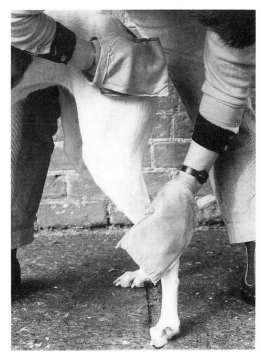

The hindlegs are given attention.

The tail, a vital aid to balance, is also massaged.

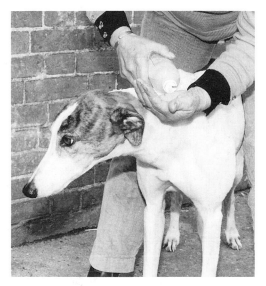

The final stage of the grooming process is to apply an embrocation and massage it into the Greyhound's body.

It is essential that the embrocation is worked into all the muscles, and so most trainers follow a set routine, working from the front of the dog.

Continuing down to the front legs.

Massaging along the the body.

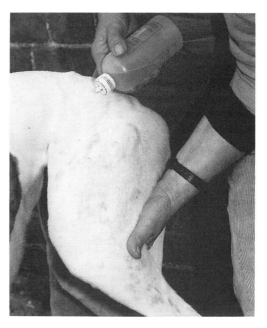

Finishing with the hindquarters.

Teeth should be brushed as part of the grooming routine in order to keep them free of tartar.

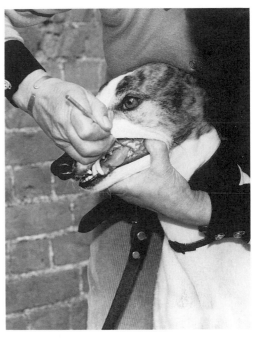

If tartar accumulates, it will need to be removed with a tooth-scaler.

A racing Greyhound risks injuring its feet in the rigours of a race. This risk is minimised if the nails are clipped regularly.

DE MULDER: "Since we are, in general, racing on sand, I think the most important parts of the Greyhound's anatomy are the shoulders, wrists, gracilis muscles, the whip muscles and the tendons. These should be rubbed down with a little bit of linament to create some heat. This helps the blood circulate around the body, and it increases the suppleness of the muscles. I usually do this on the morning of a race. Make sure you muzzle your Greyhound so he does not lick himself – otherwise you may have trouble with your urine samples at the race track.

"I would rub a dog down all over when he's had a gallop, a trial, or a race, but at any other time I would just groom the dog, using a brush and comb. I also use a grooming glove and a towel to improve the Greyhound's coat and condition. A dog's backside should be washed regularly, and his ears and teeth should be kept clean. A Greyhound's pads should be checked regularly to make sure there are no cracks. If you find any cracks, these should be treated. There are a number of products on the market; they are like Vaseline, and help to keep the pads clean, strong and healthy."

O'SULLIVAN: "Every day all the dogs are checked over, paying particular attention to toes, shoulders, tendons, wrists, hocks and muscles. This only takes about ten minutes. The dogs are groomed and have their teeth cleaned. The only variation to this routine is on race days, when the dogs would be massaged."

KOERNER: "On race days we usually brace a dog out with Absorbine. We rub the dog down and give his muscles a good rub down with our hands before we weight him in. When a dog comes off, you have to be sure to check for soreness and get right on the soreness so you can get that out of him before his next start. To do this, we use ultra-sound machines or a whirlpool to keep the soreness out. I have a walker at every one of my kennels, and we walk the dogs between starts."

BECKNER: "On race days and the day after they run, all of our dogs go on a grooming bench. They are checked over for any possible nicks or ailments. We comb and brush our dogs every time they are in; we always check their toes and nails. On non-racing days, we mostly allow the dogs to lay, unless they have an injury – then we treat them. We use the ultra-magnetic boxes for treatment."

WHEELER: "We check every dog thoroughly after racing, and then again four days before racing. Soreness or injuries are treated with ultra-sound and hydro-bathing."

Q. WHAT IS YOUR ROUTINE ON A RACE DAY?

MULLINS: "If the Greyhounds are running that night, they never come off the lead. They are gently walked first thing in the morning, and again after breakfast and after dinner."

DE MULDER: "My racing dogs get a short walk in the fields first thing in the morning, which lasts for twenty to thirty minutes. However, if you are racing twice a week, you could get away with allowing the dog to exercise in a decent-sized paddock. After exercise, we feed breakfast, and after a short break, the dogs are given a massage."

O'SULLIVAN: "On race days the dogs have a one-mile walk in the morning, then they have a light breakfast. At 11am we groom and massage all the racing dogs, and at 2pm they are let out to empty. At 3pm we give a racing feed, which consists of 4oz of meat and some glucose. The dogs are then left until it is time to leave for the track, when we give them ten minutes to empty before loading them up."

KOERNER: "We turn out by 6-6.30am. At this time we get all the beds and kennels cleaned up. Then we go over all of the Greyhounds that are going to race that day. We work the dogs that have been injured and are coming back. We do all of the sprinting, walking and unofficial schooling at this time. Some kennels feed in the morning, around 10-11am. Some kennels will feed in the afternoon, but most kennels today are feeding the dogs that are not in for that day in the morning.

"We leave the kennel around 11am or midday so the dogs can rest. Our next turn-out is 3pm or 4pm, and when we turn out at 4 o'clock in the afternoon, we make sure it isn't five minutes before or five minutes after. You wouldn't want to turn out one day at 3pm and the next day at 4pm. A Greyhound will set his schedule on your turn-outs, so you really don't want to have your turn-outs at different times. We are consistent and don't want to vary turn-out times over ten minutes either way. Next we get the dogs ready for the weigh-in at night. We put them on the bench and brace them all down. Then we weigh them in, usually between 6 and 6.30pm. The Greyhounds are kept in a pre-race lockout before the races, which usually begin at 8pm. The rule is they have to be weighed in two hours before their first performance. The last turn-out at night is usually 10pm."

BECKNER: "We start at 5.30am with our first turn-out. As soon as we turn-out we shake all of the beds. I'm a firm believer in paper for bedding as compared to carpet, which most people seem to use. I like it because the dogs can move the paper around and create their own cushion. On carpet they just lay on it. They get rug burns on their elbows, and if they get cold they cannot get under it. With paper, a greyhound can work his way under it if he gets cold, and if he gets hot, he can slide the paper back and lay on the floor which is cooler.

"The next job is to start benching and weighing all the dogs that are in that day. Normally, by the time you get through with that it's time to feed the dogs and make your second turn-out. We feed roughly around 8 o'clock in the morning, unless it's a schooling morning which throws us off later. Basically, your morning's complete by 9.30am. Then you are off until the afternoon – or if you have a matinee you have to come back earlier, depending on what time weigh-in is – when you start getting the dogs ready for the races."

WHEELER: "On race days we let the dogs out in the morning just to empty. Then they are fed a light breakfast."

Q. HOW DO YOU BUILD UP TO A COMPETITION (STAKE RACE) AND KEEP A DOG GOING THROUGH SEVERAL ROUNDS?

MULLINS: "It really depends on the dog and on the track as to whether we trial beforehand. For example, the St Leger is run at Wembley and that is an easy track for most Greyhounds. I would not expect a Greyhound to need a trial before competing there.

"If you have a Greyhound starting off in a competition, and you have doubts about their stamina, you must make sure the dog is 100 per cent for the first round. You cannot take any chances, hoping for an easy first round draw. Most of my Greyhounds will be galloped in-between rounds, but again, it depends on the individual. There are some who are lazy when they are released in the paddock. They just fiddle about, and therefore, if they need the extra work, I have no hesitation in giving it to them. However, when the youngsters are let loose, they run and run. Their exuberance means there would be no need to gallop them as well."

DE MULDER: "I would never go into a forty-eight dog stake unless my dog was 100 per cent fit. I would have ear-marked him for the competition some three months before the start of the event. You have to build up a dog gradually in single races, perhaps two in ten days. When you get close to a competition you should speed him up – perhaps three races after every six days. You know by then that you have your Greyhound in good form. Give him a solo trial seven days before the competition starts and then keep him sweet until the tournament begins.

"The Greyhound Derby is a different race altogether. I have been to fifteen finals and have won the Derby twice. To have a dog for the Derby you need a Greyhound with a touch of class. To prepare for the Derby, a Greyhound must have a winter's rest. When he comes back, you clean him out and worm him, and then give him a few gallops. I try to get the dog ready for a few trials in March. By mid-April, he would have had one race and a few trials, and five races – though probably not in a competition – before the Derby begins in May.

"Before the Derby begins, I would let the dog down slightly to make sure he doesn't go over the top during the competition. I would change the diet slightly, and make sure the dog is not too highly-fed, although he must be looking well. In the Greyhound Derby you can keep a dog one pound or one and a half pounds above his racing weight, leaving a bit of room to work on for the latter part of the competition.

"Wimbledon (the host track for the Derby) is a track in itself. If you don't have the dog – don't go. Your Greyhound needs to have experienced the track before the start of the competition with at least a couple of trials. The circuit is a law unto itself."

O'SULLIVAN: "Three weeks before a competition, the dog will be given three gallops a week, and then a sprint a week before the race. Two or three days before the race, the dog will be given a hard gallop. This should ensure that the dog is eighty-five per cent right for the first round. I would then give the dog a 300-yard gallop midweek throughout the competition, but this varies from dog to dog. If I feel a dog is peaking too soon, then I wouldn't gallop him. If the dog was not quite right, he might be given two gallops – it all depends on the individual dog's fitness."

KOERNER: "In the United States we have such a heavy schedule of racing there isn't a lot you can do differently to prepare for a stake race. If it is a 3/8 stake you can take a dog out of that distance and run him in some 5/16 races to let him rest. If it is a type of dog that can't run a sprint race, you can cut back to racing, say once a week, to give him a rest. You keep him legged up by sprinting and walking him. We want to go into a competition with a Greyhound as fresh as it can be. I also like to go into a stake race with a Greyhound that is a little heavy. We like to do well the first couple of rounds. It's nice when you can win the first round: that way you can back off him if he makes it into the finals so he's really in top shape. I don't change the feed for a stake race. We feed the same diet for a stake dog as we do a regular dog. We feed a mixture of meat and meal and a vitamin supplement. You don't want to change anything."

BECKNER: "I don't think there is any secret in a stake race. We just hope we have a good enough dog, and a little luck to go with it. There's no need to change your routine in a stake race. What works with this dog year-round will work in a stake race if the dog is good enough. I have seen a lot of people change their routine. I have seen people bracing dogs down, putting blankets on them, stuff that they don't do normally. To me you can over-tune a dog. Dogs get into a set routine. They know your routine. When you start changing it, sometimes they don't perform as well. You should turn out the same time every day. You should go over dogs the same time every day, and feed approximately the same time every day, and the dogs know what to expect. When you change the routine – for example, some trainers will take a dog out because he's in a stake race and rub him down or put this blanket on him – he knows this isn't done to him normally."

WHEELER: "I start running the Greyhound with a 300m circle and straight tracks, and then, when the dog is coping, I progress to 400m circle and then a 500m circle. Detecting injuries is very important. If an injury is detected early enough, it can be treated and there is a good chance of preventing it from becoming a serious injury."

Q. HOW LONG DO YOU KEEP A DOG IN TRAINING WITHOUT GIVING HIM A REST?

MULLINS: "There are some stayers that need very little rest, and they may only have two or three weeks rest in between competitions. Again, it is horses for courses. I have raced sprinters straight from their bed after three weeks, and they have shown their best form. With a stayer or a marathon-type dog, a gallop, a trial, and then perhaps a pipe-opener over a shorter distance, will help the dog to gain in strength before your intended target."

DE MULDER: "I recommend keeping a dog in training for three to four months, and then resting him for four weeks. You need to let a dog down and give him a different diet. This may surprise you, but I believe that a dog must be let off the lead, despite being rested – not every day, but perhaps two or three times a week. A Greyhound is made to run. He will then come back much quicker than if he had been left on the lead all the time. If you have a Greyhound running well, my advice is to leave him alone."

O'SULLIVAN: "I race my dogs for ten to twelve weeks at a time, followed by three to four weeks rest."

KOERNER: "It depends on the Greyhound. Some Greyhounds can take more than others. But as soon as we see that Greyhound starting to tire, we take a 3/8 or 7/16 dog and drop him back into a sprint. Or, if he's a dog that can't sprint or primarily runs 5/16, we take him off and let him miss a start. It is important to keep a Greyhound as fresh as possible.
    "We have a real tough schedule here. In Ireland, England and Australia they race primarily weekends. They don't race the schedule we race. An overseas dog's lifetime starts won't be as many as one of our dogs in one year. With year-round racing, some dogs get one to one-and-a-half starts a week. We race fifty week, so that's fifty to seventy-five starts a year."

BECKNER: "Normally we don't give dogs that much of a rest once they are at the race track, unless they stale off and are not racing up to their potential. As long as they can hold their grade we don't rest them unless they come up with an injury."

WHEELER: "I keep a Greyhound going for as long as he is competing without problems, which may be due to injury or failure to keep his grade."

Q. WHAT IS THE PERFECT TEMPERAMENT AND BUILD OF A RACING DOG?

MULLINS: "Everyone likes a Greyhound who lies on his bed and takes everything in his stride, rather than the one that is jumping up all the time. However, all Greyhounds have different personalities. I do not mind nervous types, as long as they do not start shaking the moment they walk on to the track. As for conformation, you can get some really illogical results. For example, you could have a 76lbs dog who goes round the rails at Romford, while a really small bitch might run wide around a big galloping track like Wembley."

DE MULDER: "The temperament of a Greyhound is important. I prefer Greyhounds that are laid back, with a nice, kind head on them. This is the type of Greyhound that you can kennel anywhere and who eats well. You do not really want a Greyhound that is jumping about, edgy and highly strung. Contrary to popular belief, build does not often affect the running ability of a Greyhound. For example, there have been plenty of small bitches and dogs that have won great races. Lacca Champion was only 61.5lbs, Spanish Battleship was only 63lbs – and they were both world beaters in their time. It is not the size that counts, it is what is inside them. The conformation of a good Greyhound is one that stands up well on his feet, with good straight legs, good quarters, a deep chest, good brown eyes, and a wide skull (not too narrowly featured). The dog should not be too tall, with a bit of length to him, and a long tail. All these things go to making a good Greyhound."

O'SULLIVAN: "This is a difficult question to answer because every dog has a different temperament, and some dogs that look like Champions are far from it in reality. I like a dog that doesn't get excited and jump all over you – the type that is laid-back in the kennel, but is aware of what is going on around him, returning the affection you give.

"On weight, a bitch should be somewhere between 54 and 70lbs and a dog should be 64 to 77lbs, ideally 70 to 72lbs."

KOERNER: "Most people like to see a big 80lb Greyhound, but that is too big. There is too much pressure on his pressure points – on his shoulders and ankles. An ideal build for the race track is probably a nice leggy, good-balanced dog. For a male, his weight should be 68-72lbs; a female should weigh 65-68lbs. As far as temperament is concerned, you want a good, quiet individual – one that is not nervous and excitable. I don't like to have a Greyhound that wants you to play with him and that jumps around. You just want a real quiet Greyhound with a good temperament that can take a lot of stress.

"Your best Greyhounds are intelligent, they know how to race. The best Greyhound I've ever been around is Dutch Bahama. His mother and his grandmother were both intelligent Greyhounds. They just knew how to race. Those are your good ones. And this is the reason Bahama was such a good stud dog – he was so intelligent."

BECKNER: "The better dogs will be very calm – you will hardly know they are in the kennel. If you get a high-strung dog that is continuously raising Cain, wanting to get into a fight, these are not your better dogs. Ninety-nine per cent of the time they will not be your stake calibre dog, although they may be useful dogs. There's something special about the stake dogs."

WHEELER: "I do not like my Greyhounds to be nervy with people or timid. Equally, it is not good to have a crazy Greyhound who drags you to the boxes, as he could spend himself before racing. I suppose you want a Greyhound that is in-between the two extremes. In my years in greyhound racing, I have never been influenced by the way a Greyhound is built, as long as he can perform on the track."

Q. NAME THE BEST GREYHOUND YOU HAVE TRAINED?

MULLINS: "We have been lucky enough to be responsible for some outstanding greyhounds, and I do not like comparing them. However, I do admit to having a soft spot for Deerpark Jim. I fell in love with him as soon as he walked into the yard. It was just the way he looked at you and the way he walked, he was a real individual.

"Pantile was a real cuddly bear. We have some mischievous ones too. Supa Trip is the current rebel of the kennel. He will not allow himself to be caught when we let him loose in the field – he loves the game, and is always wagging his tail. The other day he hid his bowl by covering it up in his kennel. The next day we could not find it – it turned out he was lying on it! He's a real character and he knows it."

Track record-breaking hurdler Deerpark Jim: A great favourite with Linda Mullins.

DE MULDER: "Obviously my two Derby winners, Jimsun and Sarah's Bunny, have a soft spot in my heart. However, I have had some great dogs through my hands, including Desert Pilot, Pat Seamur, Fearless Champ, Fearless Action, Fearless Mustang, Dale Lad, John Silver, Clohast Rebel, Fionntra Frolic and Foxy Copper are just a few. One thing I do regret is that I never tried Manderlay King over 825 yards. He recorded 39.57 at Wembley, without a trial, in preparation for the St Leger. But he picked up a shoulder injury. I suppose I did not try him over a marathon distance because I thought too much of him."

O'SULLIVAN: "Manx Treasure, my Irish Derby winner, is certainly my best Greyhound. I believe the Irish Derby is the true test of a Greyhound, and Manx Treasure lived up to that, injuries and all. You would be accused of dreaming if you took a dog from an unraced stake straight into the Derby – and you cannot afford to dream in Greyhound racing. But Manx Treasure did that and won."

KOERNER: "For me, it is obviously Dutch Bahama, two-time All-American, Flashy Sir Award winner and inductee to the Greyhound Hall of Fame. Dutch Delusion, an All-American. Dutch D West is a another good dog, as was Dutch Dugan, winner of the Irish American. I have had a number of nice Greyhounds. Everything I have, I have to attribute to my Greyhounds. They have been very, very good to me."

BECKNER: "I believe the best dog we ever trained was By Tar. He's the best dog in the country, in my opinion. He's a dominating type dog. Having a brood matron like Buzz Off, has been one of my major successes of all times. Not only has she thrown all these stake dogs, but her offspring are starting to look like they are throwing some stake dogs.

"You have to surround yourself with good people – the best people you can find. I am very lucky. I have great farm people. I believe that most of a dog's ability is created on the farm. You need good trainers on the race track, but a trainer can only get out what a dog has in him. The trainer gets all the glory, but it's the farm people that do all the work preparing the dog for the trainer."

WHEELER: "Kylie Bale must rate as my number one Greyhound. My greatest achievement has been training two A$100,000 winners in the last four years."

Q. WHAT IS YOUR AMBITION?

MULLINS: "I would love to win a Greyhound Derby. I was involved when my husband, Pat, won with Lacca Champion, but I would like to have the honour myself. That also applies to the St Leger – a competition we have never won. The Irish Derby would also be special, if I could win it with one of our home-bred Greyhounds. I would also like to see my family follow in my footsteps and become even more successful in Greyhound racing."

DE MULDER: "I have had a quiet time recently, and I have kept a low profile for personal reasons. However, I have always said that I would win the Greyhound Derby three times – I just need one more."

O'SULLIVAN: "Having won the Irish Derby, I would love to win the English Derby or the Oaks."

KOERNER: "I would like to see our industry get more solvent. I am going to do everything I can to make it better. Our industry is at a low, right now. I love what I am doing. I love to race Greyhounds and I am going to continue racing. I just hate to see the industry at the point it is right now. It's going to get better and I'm going to do anything I can to make it better."

BECKNER: "Right now, it is to continue to try to maintain my current level as long as possible. I have been around long enough to know that one of these days it's going to come to an end. When that day comes, we will just have to hang on until we can get it turned back round. Nobody can dream of winning seven stake races or running out $350,000 in stake money. You just don't plan for it. You don't think it's possible. It's great while it lasts. But I've seen so many cases when a kennel gets on a roll – it lasts so long and then they come back down to earth."

WHEELER: "To continue to produce successful racing Greyhounds, as in the past few years, and to win a major training premiership."

Chapter Ten

ADOPTING A RACING GREYHOUND

GREYHOUNDS WHO NEED REHOMING

Greyhounds have a marvellous, placid temperament, and they make ideal family pets. However, the numbers of Greyhounds who are bought as puppies to be companions are very small.; The great majority of Greyhounds are bred to race, and it is when their racing days are finished, that they need a home to go to. Many owners and trainers take responsibility for their charges when this point is reached, but the sheer number of Greyhounds needing rehoming is daunting.

The principal Greyhound racing countries have all set up rehoming schemes on a national basis, and there are many dedicated volunteers who run local schemes. In Britain the Retired Greyhound Trust (which is run by the National Greyhound Racing Club) rehomes 700 Greyhounds every year. In the USA there are some thirty organisations that find homes for retired racing Greyhounds, but the problem is immense. Approximately 15,000 Greyhounds are adopted every year, which speaks volumes for the work of the Greyhound rehoming schemes, but, tragically, another 30-40,000 ex-racers are destroyed.The Greyhound has always had its champions, and, fortunately, there are many individuals who spend their time and money finding homes for those dogs who have reached the end of the road as far as the track is concerned but still have many years of healthy, active life ahead. In Britain, Johanna Beumer has worked as a homefinder for the Retired Greyhound Trust for many years, and has written a book called *The Sporting Life Guide To Owning A Racing Greyhound*. In the USA Cynthia Branigan is President of Make Peace with Animals, an animal protection group, with a special interest in Greyhound rescue and placement. She has also written a book, *Adopting The Racing Greyhound*, published by Howell Book House. Both Cynthia Branigan and Johanna Beumer have tremendous experience of rehoming Greyhounds, and they have a great deal of useful advice to offer the owner of a newly-adopted GreyhoundIn most cases, a Greyhound will have come straight out of racing kennels, where he will have spent the majority of his life. Many ex-racers have never been inside a house, and so there will be a lot of things for the new arrival to adapt to. The Greyhound is used to the routine of the kennels and the race track, and it has to literally learn how to become a family pet. With love and a little patience, this is not hard to accomplish, but the new owner will certainly benefit from making the right start with regard to training, socialising and generally caring for their new pets. Cynthia Branigan and Johanna Beumer have each answered a series of questions, based on the queries and problems they most commonly deal with when new owners ask for advice.

IF I HOUSE MY GREYHOUND OUTSIDE, WHAT SIZE KENNEL WILL HE REQUIRE?
JOHANNA BEUMER: "Most Greyhounds are used to company and prefer to be indoors. However, if this is impractical, you must ensure the kennel is large and airy. It must be free from draughts

Greyhounds love a little luxury, and a soft bed located in the house is the ideal arrangement.

and kept warm in the winter. The ideal size for a single Greyhound is 6ft by 4ft (the size of an average garden shed). The bed must be raised from the floor, and I would suggest that straw or paper bedding is used. This should be changed regularly, and the kennel should be cleaned and disinfected daily."

CYNTHIA BRANIGAN: "It is not recommended that Greyhounds be kept as outdoor dogs. They have insufficient body fat and too sparse a coat. Additionally, they do not adapt well to extreme heat or cold. (In the US most racing kennels are kept at 72 degrees Fahrenheit year-round.)"

IF I KEEP MY GREYHOUND IN THE HOUSE, WHAT SORT OF BEDDING IS MOST SUITABLE?

BEUMER: "Greyhounds love their comfort, and I would recommend a duvet, a large bean-bag, or an old eiderdown. Most Greyhounds also appreciate a blanket to snuggle into. Again, the bed must be located somewhere warm and draught-free."

Cynthia Branigan: "Greyhounds are prone to develop pressure sores on their hips and elbows, so you must ensure that your dog has a soft blanket or cushion in his bed."

DO I NEED ANY OTHER EQUIPMENT?

BEUMER: "Your Greyhound will need a fish-tail or straight leather collar, and this must be fastened close behind the ears, not halfway down the neck. Greyhounds have a great habit of slipping their heads backwards and coming out of their collars, so make sure the collar will not go over your Greyhound's ears. The best test to check that the collar is tight enough – but not so tight as to choke your dog – is if you can slip one finger between the neck and the collar.

"I would recommend a fairly long lead (approx 6ft), and this can be made of leather or nylon. I do not think that choke-chains are suitable for Greyhounds. A lightweight muzzle is useful when you are de-training your Greyhound (getting him to accept cats, small dogs, hamsters, etc.), and you must ensure this is the correct size for your dog in order to prevent accidents."

BRANIGAN: "I strongly recommend that all Greyhounds wear a safety collar. The width of a greyhound's head is not much greater than the width of his neck, so it is very easy for a Greyhound to slip a conventional buckle collar. A Greyhound should wear a flat, nylon half-choke collar. These are also known as martingale collars.

"A lightweight plastic muzzle is useful when introducing your Greyhound to cats or to small dogs in his new family. Once your greyhound has settled into his new family, the muzzle will not be necessary. "

IF MY GREYHOUND HAS COME STRAIGHT FROM RACING KENNELS, WHAT IS THE BEST WAY OF TEACHING HIM TO BE CLEAN IN THE HOUSE?

BEUMER: "Most Greyhounds are clean in their racing kennels – a dog is always loath to soil his sleeping quarters – and so if you take your Greyhound out regularly, he will soon learn that he must not mess in the house. Greyhounds are most regular in their habits, and if you adopt a routine of taking your dog out at set times of the day, your Greyhound will soon learn what is expected. If your dog lifts his leg indoors, tell him "No" very firmly (with a tap on the behind) and take him straight into the garden. Your Greyhound will want to please you, and he will quickly understand that this behaviour is not acceptable."

BRANIGAN: "In the US, Greyhounds at the race track are kept in large individual crates (cages) most of the day. Generally, they are let out to stretch their legs and relieve themselves four times a day – first thing in the morning, noon, around 5pm, and last thing in the day. Most Greyhounds do not soil their crates, and so are used to waiting to be let out.

"In a home it is best, in the beginning at least, to use a crate. Not only will it help with house-breaking, but it will also prevent your dog from chewing or damaging your property. Since Greyhounds are used to the four-times-a-day routine, it is best to approximate that schedule when your Greyhound arrives in his new home. Most people find, to start with, that their Greyhound needs to go out more frequently, and this is probably a combination of nerves and a change in water and food.

"Since I recommend feeding a Greyhound twice daily (as they do at the track), a typical day might be trips out at 7am, immediately after breakfast, around noon, immediately after dinner, and just before bed. In addition, if you see a dog pacing around in corners, take him out straightaway. If your Greyhound has an accident in the house, scold the animal gently. Greyhounds have a very sensitive nature and are easily overwhelmed by criticism. A firm "No" is usually sufficient.

"In the first few weeks after your Greyhound arrives in his new home, I suggest that you continue to use a crate until you are sure your dog is house-trained. Some owners then discard the crate, but Greyhounds like to have a place to retreat to, and if the crate-door is left open, this can be a perfect place of refuge."

WHAT SHOULD I FEED MY GREYHOUND?

BEUMER: "Although Greyhounds look thin, even when retired, they are quite a 'power-pack' and require two good meals a day. Avoid canned food, as racing Greyhounds are not used to it, and it generally causes an upset stomach. This also applies to feeding liver.

"I suggest using minced beef or packets of meat pieces and then casserole the meat. Allow to cool, and then you can remove the fat from the surface. make some gravy and mix this with the meat and some bread or dog food mixer to make the food into a porridge-like substance.

Greyhounds require two meals a day.

Vegetables can also be added. The main meal of the day should be fed in the morning, and a lighter meal in the late afternoon, early evening. The time can be adjusted to suit the family's routine, but once you have set a routine, mealtimes should be kept as regular as possible. Always make sure that fresh water is available, located where your Greyhound knows where to find it."

BRANIGAN: "I would suggest you feed your Greyhound four to six cups of a dry premium dog food. We recommend brands such as Purina, pro Plan, Iams, Nutro Max or any other high-quality dry food. Avoid 'supermarket' brands or the semi-moist foods, which tend to be rich for a Greyhound and can cause gas or diarrhoea. If you wish, you may add cooked vegetables to the diet. Racing Greyhounds are used to getting these and they love them. Retired racers *do not* need high-protein dog food, so make sure you get a diet for regular adult maintenance. Boiled white rice added to the food can help to control loose stools."

WHAT ROUTINE SHOULD I ADOPT IN ORDER TO KEEP MY GREYHOUND WELL GROOMED?

BEUMER: "A quick brush and comb every day will keep your dog in good condition, and check that he has not come into contact with any fleas. I find that if you rub a little olive-oil into the palm of your hands and then rub it into your dog's coat, it helps to maintain condition. Remember, good feeding is always reflected in a healthy coat. Teeth should be brushed at least once a week using a stiff toothbrush and any brand of toothpaste. Your Greyhound will be used to this from kennels. Nails grow quickly and they do need clipping back. This can be done quite easily using the guillotine type of nail-clippers. You must ensure that you do not cut into the quick of the nail, as this can be very painful and will cause the nail to bleed. If you are not confident, your vet will do it for you."

BRANIGAN: "Greyhounds should be brushed with a hound glove (preferably sisal) or with a rubber grooming glove that can be used to remove excess hair when you are bathing your dog.
  "It is possible to purchase special toothbrushes for dogs, and if you are gentle and persistent, you can brush your dog's teeth once a week or so. Since Greyhounds have a soft diet at the race track, they often have severe tartar build-up. If this is the case with your dog, you may need to ask your vet to clean the teeth under general anaesthesia. After that, you can usually care for the teeth by regular brushing and by giving your dog rawhide and crunchy biscuits. Toenails can be clipped every three to four weeks."

HOW MUCH EXERCISE DOES MY GREYHOUND NEED? IS IT SAFE TO ALLOW MY DOG TO RUN FREE?

BEUMER: "Greyhounds love to run freely, but you must keep your dog on a lead to begin with. Even a 'non-chaser' – a Greyhound lacking the instinct to chase moving objects – has to learn who his new owner is, and to respond to his name when he is being called. Do not let your Greyhound off the lead until you are quite sure that he is safe with other dogs. Try to find an enclosed space, with only one gate which you can shut, before you venture into public woods or the park. Remember, your Greyhound was only used to running free at the track or in the paddock, and he may take off when he first experiences freedom. It is therefore essential not to rush things. Do not allow your Greyhound to run free until you are confident that he will return to you. A flexi-lead can prove useful, as you can retain control while giving your Greyhound the freedom to roam."

BRANIGAN: "Retired racers do not have exceptional exercise requirements. In fact, the most common myth concerning the breed is that a former racing dog is going to need huge amounts of exercise. What makes Greyhounds different, however, is that it is unsafe to allow them to run unleashed, unless you are in a fully fenced area. This is because Greyhounds are sighthounds as opposed to scenthounds, and so they hunt by sight rather than by scent. As such, they naturally pursue what they see. No human being can out-run or even keep up with a sighthound who is in full gallop. Greyhounds, the fastest of all the sighthounds, have been clocked at speeds of over 42mph. A Greyhound in pursuit does not respond to commands.

"In this instance, we are not talking about just any Greyhound, but former racing Greyhounds. Practically from the moment of birth, their running/chasing instinct has been enforced. In addition, ex-racers are uneducated about things in the real world, such as cars, plate-glass windows, etc. – so many hazards await a Greyhound in full flight.

"Former racers should be walked on a lead, and released *only* in conditions which are totally safe. If you do not have a fenced yard, you can find a tennis court, a baseball field, or even a playground to exercise your Greyhound. Fences should be at least four feet high – Greyhounds are capable of jumping over fences, although the majority of them do not show any great desire to do this."

I AM WORRIED ABOUT MY GREYHOUND CHASING CATS AND SMALL DOGS. WHAT IS THE BEST WAY OF INTRODUCING MY DOG TO OTHER ANIMALS, AND HOW CAN I CURB THE CHASING INSTINCT?

BEUMER: "Some Greyhounds are 'non-chasers'. They have never raced, and they will go straight into homes with cats, rabbits, hamsters etc. Some ex-racers are 'de-trained' and can safely go with small animals; other racers only chase on the track and have no interest in small, furry animals in a different environment. However, there are many former racers who remain 'keen', and any small furry animal will remind them of the 'hare' at the track. It makes no difference whether this type of Greyhound is a male or a female – keen is keen!

"For these Greyhounds, you must use a muzzle, ensuring it is the correct size to avoid accidents. You can de-train a keen Greyhound so that he gets used to other animals, but it takes time and patience. On the plus side, your Greyhound is intelligent and eager to please, and he will soon learn that you are displeased if he tries to pull on the lead and chase other dogs. If your Greyhound starts pulling on the lead, tug him back, and say "No" in a firm voice. If necessary, correct your Greyhound by giving him a tap on the nose.

The former racing Greyhound will live peaceably with cats and other small animals, but it is important to work on a de-training programme.

"One of the hardest things to establish in a Greyhound's mind is that other four-legged dogs of different breeds are indeed dogs. Former racers have lived exclusively with Greyhounds, and therefore they only recognise other Greyhounds as dogs. Once your Greyhound has had a chance to meet other dogs under controlled circumstances (with his lead on), he will, hopefully realise that the four-legged animals he meets in the park, are not there to be chased. For your first few encounters, pick a reasonable size of dog, such as a Labrador Retriever, and then as your Greyhound becomes more settled you can introduce him to smaller dogs. Try to meet up with a friend who has another breed of dog and go out for walks together.

"If you have a keen Greyhound, it can take from three weeks to three months before you can trust him with a cat. Introduce your Greyhound to that cat indoors, keeping your dog muzzled and on a tight collar and lead. Let the cat stay in the same room, and every time your Greyhound pulls towards the cat, pull him back sharply and say "No, Leave" in a very firm voice. The next step is to get your Greyhound to lie down close to the cat.

"When you think you are making progress, take away the muzzle, keep the tight collar and lead on, and feed your Greyhound and the cat together. The reason for this is so that the two animals are alongside each other but do not have their minds on each other. Gradually move the feeding bowls closer together, and allow your Greyhound to sniff the cat. When you are feeling more confident, replace the muzzle and take away the collar and lead. In time, the muzzle can also be removed.

"Your Greyhound will get used to your own cat and accept it as a member of the family, but cats outside the home will still be regarded as 'fair game' for a chase. All dogs chase cats, but Greyhounds are so much faster, they stand a far greater chance of catching them."

BRANIGAN: "I have found that ex-racing Greyhounds generally fall into one of four categories when it comes to chasing cats or small dogs:
1. Not interested.
2. Mildly interested, but timid.
3. Interested, wants to play.
4. Extremely interested, wants to lunge.

"An approximate breakdown of these categories is that seventy per cent of ex-racers are types One and Two, twenty per cent are Type Three, and ten per cent are Type Four. Males and females are represented equally in all types. Types One and Two do not present any problems. Type Three

To begin with, the ex-racer may be suspicious of other breeds of dogs, but most problems will be overcome if you supervise the introductory period.

Greyhounds enjoy human company, and, in general, they are very tolerant with children.

just needs correcting with a gentle tug on the collar and a firm "No". It has been my experience that Type Four cannot be retrained. It is very laborious to try to correct this type of behaviour, and in ninety-nine per cent of cases, it is a wasted effort. Why try and force a square peg into a round hole? However, these Greyhounds can still make excellent pets, as long as they are placed in homes without cats or small dogs.

"All Greyhounds should wear a muzzle when first introduced to a cat. Do not hold the cat above your dog's head, and do not allow your dog off the lead. Do not leave your Greyhound alone with a cat in the initial stages. In order to distinguish between curiosity and a more dangerous intent, check your dog's tail. If it is up and wagging, your Greyhound is friendly and curious. However, if the tail is either stiff and held straight out, or held between the legs, this indicates that your Greyhound is interested, but not friendly. An unfriendly Greyhounf will either lunge immediately, or become rigid with a transfixed stare."

WHAT IS THE AVERAGE LIFE EXPECTANCY OF A GREYHOUND?

BEUMER: "Vets usually reckon that a Greyhound lives to eleven years of age, but the average life-span of those I have homed is twelve to thirteen years old. My own 'Foxy' is currently fourteen years young!"

BRANIGAN: "The average life expectancy of a Greyhound is twelve to fourteen years old. This is considered a good life-span for a large dog – but Greyhound owners will assure you it is not nearly long enough!"

Despite the initial time and trouble that is needed to acclimatise an ex-racer to his new home, all those who have adopted Greyhounds have found them the most loving and rewarding of canine companions. According to Cynthia Branigan, the most important part of Greyhound adoption is recognising the adjustment period and managing it successfully.

She says: "It must be remembered that being a companion instead of a racer involves a dramatic change in your dog's routine, and he must be given time to adjust to his new surroundings. In this regard, a quiet Greyhound may become fretful, a good eater may be reluctant to eat, a clean dog may have an 'accident'. Your love, patience and understanding will help your Greyhound through this adjustment period, which may last from a few days to a few weeks."

Both Cynthia Branigan and Johanna Beumer can relate numerous success stories that have inspired them to continue their work of helping ex-racers to start a new life. There are a couple of case histories which stand out, illustrating the remarkable temperament of the Greyhound.

BEUMER: "I remember a large white and black Greyhound who was rescued after being badly ill-treated. He was rehomed by a family in London and settled down well with his new family. One day 'Hoopy' was being taken out for a walk, and on the way home an elderly gentleman was knocked down and badly injured.

"Hoopy lay down in the road next to the old man, with his owner's coat over the two of them. He stayed there, calm and comforting, until the ambulance arrived. The next day the police came to visit Hoopy, bringing a large bone for the hero who had saved the old man's life.

" 'Bill' was a large fawn-and-white Grehound who had won many races at Walthamstow. When he reached retirement age, he was passed round to a number of racing homes. His condition deteriorated until a trainer finally took pity on him and bought him because he felt so sorry for him. I cried when I first saw Bill. He had been scalded right down the side of his face and neck, and he was incredibly thin. His back legs were so weak, he looked as though he had rickets.

"En route home I stopped at a newsagents, where, six months earlier, I had homed 'Byron', a fine, strapping ex-racer. Mr and Mrs Carter and their five sons lived above the shop, and when I called in, Mrs Carter was clearly upset when she saw Bill. She asked her husband to carry him upstairs, and Bill stood shakily in the sitting-room. Byron came over to him, and then led him to his own bed. He then disappeared into the kitchen and returned with a large marrow bone, which he lay down in front of Bill. The pair were inseparable from that moment onwards, and they spent many happy years together.

" 'Snowy' was left in a coal-bunker when her owners went back to Ireland. She was rescued

It will not be long before the ex-racer becomes a much-loved member of the family.

when neighbours heard her pitiful cries. She was treated by a vet, as she had eaten coal to stay alive, and she had a terrible infection in her pads from trying to scrape her way out. Once she was cleaned up, she was a white Greyhound with a few black markings. But she had a funny, fat face and a turned-up nose, and none of the grace and style you expect to see in a Greyhound.

"Several visitors came to the rescue kennels, but she was always turned down. I am sure this was because of her looks, as she had a lovely nature. Then a family in South London applied to rehome a Greyhound, and as they had no transport, they asked the kennel staff to select a suitable bitch, with a nice temperament, who would be good with children. I took a chance on Snowy. I took her into the lounge, and the mother knelt down in front of Snowy, saying: 'Aren't you beautiful, we are going to love you.' I don't think she could understand my tears of happiness!"

BRANIGAN: "One of the most interesting case histories that comes to mind involves my own first adoptee – 'King'. King was a Grade A racer and had won hundreds of thousands of dollars during his career. While on the track he was taken to Mexico to race. On the way back to the United States the truck driver abandoned the truck, which was carrying King and three other Greyhounds. King was the sole survivor, although the dehydration and starvation he suffered almost certainly shortened his racing career.

"At the age of five and a half years King was retired. His original owner had been approached with offers to buy him as a stud dog, but she declined because she felt he had earned the right to a life in a home. His first adoptive home was to a man who wanted him as a guard dog. King was extremely mild-mannerd (as is suggested by his racing name, Low Key Two), and so he was not up to the job. He was returned to the adoption agency.

"King's second home came six months later, and this family cared for him very much. Unfortunately, the couple divorced and King was made homeless again. Just a year after being in his new home he was returned to the adoption agency. King's third home came six months later – and this also met a bad end. He was adopted by a single man who later married. His new wife was not a dog-lover, and she insisted that King must live in the basement of the house. To make matters worse, the man's work schedule changed so he was rarely home at all. He finally notified the adoption agency that King needed another home.

"It was a lucky day for King and for me when I met an acquaintance who adopted ex-racers. When she learned that my previous dog, a Border Collie, had just died, she told me of King's plight. She added that since King was now nine years old, he would be destroyed unless a new home was found for him. Needless to say, I picked him up the very next day.

"King's adjustment to my home was a slow process. Probably because of his age and the many homes he had before mine, he had lost his interest in everything. He was alternately afraid and depressed. He certainly had no interest in me – and yet he didn't want to be left alone. The first time I let him run loose in a fenced area, he just stood there. When I raised a stick above my head to throw it for him, he hit the ground and quivered. This went on for several months.

"Finally, one night, when I had just about given up on having a relationship with King (and was about to settle for just being glad that I had given him a home), he gave life one last try. It was after supper and we were sitting on the sofa – but not close together, King always kept a good eight inches between us – and I was reading a book. Suddenly I was aware of King staring at me – something he had never done before. I returned his gaze, and began to talk to him softly. Without breaking his stare, King extended his paw and placed it on top of my hand. We stayed like that for some minutes – and ever since that moment King and I have been inseparable.

"King's gentle and dignified manner made him an excellent ambassador for former racers, and he has accompanied me to innumerable functions and fundraising events. King has not only inspired countless people to adopt a Greyhound, but the story of how he regained his trust has proved to be uplifting to many people as well."

Chapter Eleven

THE SHOW GREYHOUND

THE EARLY DAYS

Although no Greyhound appeared at the world's first dog show, held in Newcastle, England in 1859, this was because the show was restricted to Pointers and Setters. In fact, the breed was one of the first to make its mark in the show ring. The catalogue of America's first Westminster Show, held in 1877, shows an entry of eighteen Greyhounds, and ever since then, the Greyhound, a member of the Hound Group, has been extremely well represented at all major dog shows around the world. In 1873 the English Kennel Club was founded, followed by the establishment of the American Kennel Club in 1884. Both organisations laid down a set of rules governing dog shows and also set up a system of recording and registering dogs and recording their wins.

Breed Standards were formulated and written down, and these were soon accepted as the standard of excellence by which dogs should be judged in the ring. Thus, for the first time, it became necessary to judge a Greyhound on the basis of its looks, rather than on how it performed in the field. However, the two were not entirely unrelated, since the Standard was drawn up with a view to describing a dog which was ideally built for hare coursing, combining speed, power, agility and stamina. The Greyhound, with its thousands of years of careful selective breeding for this specific purpose was clearly a prime candidate for the show ring, as it was an impressive, sound, even-tempered dog with few vices, and one which reproduced itself to a fairly standard type.

Of course, there were some slight regional variations in type and size resulting from the demands of the vastly varying terrain over which the dogs coursed. The fairly primitive transportation available until the late nineteenth century meant that people in the more outlying areas tended to use only those dogs which were available locally for breeding, and this helped to perpetuate these regional variations. To some extent this can still be seen in the so-called Cornish type of show Greyhound we see today.

THE FIRST EXHIBITORS

The early exhibitors of Greyhounds were often coursing men. Indeed, some of the earliest show winners were none other than the Waterloo Cup Winners of 1855 (Judge), 1861 (Canaradzo) and 1885 (Bit O' Fashion). Some exhibitors were quick to realise that in order to win in the show ring it was necessary to produce dogs which closely matched the Standard, irrespective of whether or not they were actually capable of coursing. Perhaps not surprisingly, it did not take long before this led to a split in the breed between the coursing and showing fraternities, a split which exists to the present day in England.

The coursing breeders resented their dogs being beaten by dogs which were inferior in the field, or, even worse, by dogs which made no pretence to compete in the field on equal terms, and which were kept by their owners purely as show dogs. Many of the early exhibitors, who were primarily coursing enthusiasts, became disillusioned and dropped out of the show scene, preferring to have their dogs' abilities judged on their performance in the field rather than on some theoretical standard for excellence which could be subject to the whims of fashion as well as the personal, and possibly biased, opinion of the judge.

Presentation and some superficial points such as smooth glossy coats, dark eyes, clean teeth and well-trimmed nails became important, as they were easily seen by the judge. At the same time extra elegance was sought, even though this has never been one of the major points required by the Breed Standard, and this led to dogs with finer skulls, longer, more arched necks, cleaner, less muscled shoulders, longer tails, proportionately longer legs, as well as more compact and neater feet. Other points were also exaggerated to put emphasis on them, such as greater angulation of front and rear quarters, greater depth of brisket and increased overall size.

While all this was happening, it was also realised that much cleaner lines could be presented if the dogs had flatter (or less) muscle, and so exercise was reduced as a result of the desire to "improve" the looks of the breed. In many cases, gallops became a thing of the past and controlled short walks became the only form of exercise, for fear of producing loaded shoulders. Movement of the show dog is only ever assessed at a collected trot, and so it became merely a matter of opinion as to what effects these changes had on the function of the dog as a hunting animal.

In the early days of the development of the breed as a show animal, transportation by rail and motor car was rapidly improving. As a result, enthusiasts of the breed became more aware of the stock being exhibited in other areas, and hence of the opportunity to improve their own lines by the introduction of fresh blood, previously unavailable to them.

THE GREYHOUND DEVELOPS

All this did not happen overnight, but by the late 1920s a distinct type of dog had been developed specifically for the show ring – to quote the English Kennel Club Standard: "an upstanding dog of generous proportions", which was generally bigger, but with less bulky muscle, more angulated and more elegant than the coursing stock from which it was descended.

Unfortunately, good-quality, reliable pictures of the dogs of the last quarter of the nineteenth century and the first quarter of the twentieth Century are extremely difficult to come by. Photography was in its infancy, and the artists of the day tended to represent the dogs as their owners wished to see them, rather than how they actually looked. However, many of the dogs depicted in the early coursing prints would not look too out of place in today's show ring, while some of the photographs of the early show winners bear little resemblance to the modern show dogs.

It must be said at this stage that although the show dog has developed along different lines from the coursing dog, it is still much closer in looks to the coursing dog of today than it is to the average racing dog, the branch of the breed with which the general public is now most familiar. The racing dog has been selectively bred purely for speed over a flat, oval circuit of relatively short distance. Looks play absolutely no part in the breeding of the racer, and although there are some very handsome racers on the tracks, most bear little resemblance to the modern show Greyhound. The racing dog tends to be much smaller, more heavily-muscled, shallower in brisket, more upright in shoulder and straighter in stifle – to mention but a few of the differences.

AMERICAN IMPORTS

Much has been written on the history and development of the breed in the inter-war years (1918-

1939), and very exciting times they must have been – on both sides of the Atlantic. Many large kennels were founded in the USA, based mainly on stock imported from England, and particularly from Cornwall, which had long been, and still is, a stonghold of the breed.

Just before and following the First World War, Ben Lewis Snr (who emigrated from Wales to the USA) and his son Ben Jnr began a trend of importing some of the best English Greyhounds into America – a trend which has continued to the present day. Among these were Am. Ch. Lansdowne Liskeard Fortunatus (registered as Rosemont Liskeard Fortunatus), who was bred by Harry Peake in Cornwall. In his day, this dog was the top-winning male in the breed in the USA with seventeen Best in Show wins to his credit. Other Lewis imports from Cornwall included Am. Ch. Lansdowne Sunflower (North Road Spinner – Fleet), bred by F. Gilbert in 1915, and Ch. Butcher Boy (Red Minnick King – Water Lily II, whelped 1907), who was to become an extremely influential stud dog.

Probably the best known of Butcher Boy's offspring was Am. Ch. Master Butcher (out of Butcher's Queen, whelped in 1913), the illustrious stud dog of the Gamecock kennels, owned by Mr and Mrs West, who bred and showed their Greyhounds with considerable success from the 1920s through to the l950s. Many of today's winners in America can trace their pedigrees back to the early Gamecock hounds, and thus to the old Cornish coursing stock.

In the late 1920s and early 1930s the Windholme Greyhound kennels, owned by Harry T. Peters, became well established in America, again largely through the import of dogs from England combined with dogs bought from the Gamecock kennels of the Wests, which were, in turn, descended from the English dogs mentioned above.

Another rich and famous Greyhound fancier in the USA, who imported dogs from Cornwall a few years later, was Mrs Geraldine Rockefeller Dodge. One of her best-known imports was Am. Ch. Giralda's White Knight (Ch. King of Trevarth – Penley Patience, whelped 1938). This dog later went to Mr and Mrs William Bagshaw and was an extremely influential dog in the foundation of their Canyon Crest kennels. Also imported from England was Am. Ch. Giralda's Cornish Man (King Kenall – Queen Kenall, whelped 1938) bred by J.B. Cole.

The list of owners who imported dogs from England into the USA during the period just before and after the Second World War is too long to detail here, but there are a number who deserve a special mention, as they imported dogs who were to be a great influence on the future of the breed. Mr and Mrs Anderson (Mardormere) imported a dog, Parcancady Cherry, who sired several Champions including Specialty winners. The Farrells (Foxden) imported Carnlanga Pirate (renamed Foxden Flamingo), another important stud dog, and much later they imported Ch. Shalfleet Starlight of Foxden from Barbara Wilton-Clark (Odell). Mrs Mason (Little Andely's), imported from Bill Boggia, Eng. Ch. Boughton Blue Lad (bred by Peter George), who was to have a tremendous influence on the future breeding programme of many leading kennels in America. Peggy Newcombe (Pennyworth) imported the littermates Parcancady Leader and Eng. Ch. Seagift Parcancady Heatherbell. These two Greyhounds came from Dorothy Whitwell, who, by the early l950s, had become one of the leading breeders and exhibitors of Greyhounds in the UK. Then, from Judy de Casembroot's Treetops line came the black Treetops Raven of Pennyworth, followed by Eng. Am. Ch. Carnlanga Caramel of Pennyworth, Ch. Treetops Penguin, and Pennyworth Sensation from the Parsons.

THE BRITISH INFLUENCE

It must seem from reading the above that there were no Greyhounds left in England by the time the 1950s came around! This was not so, of course, but with the depression of the twenties and early thirties and the war looming in the late thirties, the money offered for top-quality stock must

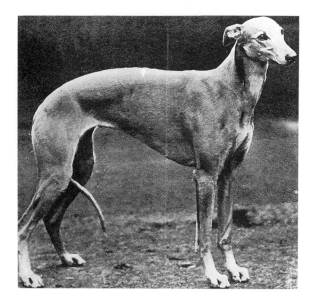

Primley Sceptre:
Best in Show, Crufts
1928.

Southball
Moonstone: Best in
Show, Crufts 1934 –
later an American
Champion.

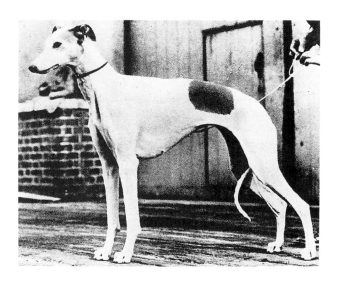

have been extremely tempting for the English breeders of the time, who were, for most part, far from wealthy.

A look at the old KC Stud Books of the era reveals the considerable success of many English kennels whose prefixes appear many, many generations back in today's winners around the world – the Boveways of Harry Peake, Jimmy Berryman's Butcher's dogs, the Canfields of Mr Benetto, The Primleys of Mr Whitley, Jack Searle's Ventons, Jesse Prowse's Carnlangas, Peter George's Parcancadys, and the Matthews Bros' Viverdons – to name but a few.

During this period two Greyhounds won what is considered by many to be the ultimate prize in the dog showing world, Best In Show at Crufts. They were Primley Sceptre in 1928 and Southball

Moonstone in 1934. This feat has been achieved only once in the last sixty years by a Greyhound –
Treetops Golden Falcon, in 1956.

BRITISH KENNELS

By the late 1940s the English show scene had begun to take shape again. With food becoming
more readily available for both humans and dogs, Greyhound owners were beginning to put
together their breeding programmes which had, in many cases, been severely curtailed for six
years or more. However, it was not until 1948 that the first post-war English Greyhound
Champions were made up. These were Boughton Blue Lad (owned by A.G. Boggia), Fleet of
Trevore (J. Phillips) and Carnlanga Corsair (Jesse Prowse).

The period immediately following the war was dominated by a handful of very influential
kennels. By far the most important were the Cornish kennels of Jesse Prowse (Carnlanga) and
Peter George (Parcancady), both of whose lines were already well established before the war.
Among the major winners bred by Jesse Prowse were the Champions Carnlanga Corsair,
Carnlanga Caramel and Carnlanga Prelude. Peter George bred Ch. Parcancady Lancer (Barum
Carnlanga Conquest – Parcancady Lady), the sire of the great Ch. Treetops Hawk, who was to
become indisputably the most important stud dog of all time in the breed. The littermates Ch.
Seagift Parcancady Bluebell and Royaltan, both of which were exported to America, were bred by
Peter George. They were sired by Ch. Treetops Hawk out of Carnlanga Topaz, a bitch who was on
loan from Jesse Prowse.

*Ch. Seagift
Parcancady
Bluebell with her
sire, Ch. Treetops
Hawk. Bluebell
was later exported
to the USA.*

This period of Cornish dominance was followed by the era of Dorothy Whitwell's Seagift
hounds (some in partnership with Peter George) and Judy de Casembroot's Treetops dogs, in the
1950s and early 1960s.

TREETOPS

Judy de Casembroot's Treetops line was founded on a mating of Ch. Parcancady Lancer to
Treetops Flicka of Canfield. This litter produced eight puppies, four of which were culled on the
advice of experienced breeders, who told Judy that it would be unwise to try to raise more than
four puppies as a first time-breeder of Greyhounds. One of the survivors was a brindle dog called
Treetops Hawk. Although he did not win at his early shows, Judy persevered and he went on to
become a Champion, winning fourteen CCs, including Crufts in 1953 and 1955, as well as

Ch. Treetops Hawk: the greatest stud dog of all time in the breed.

Ch. Treetops Golden Falcon: Best in Show, Crufts 1956 – the most famous son of Ch. Treetops Hawk.

winning eight Best in Show awards. Judy considered his greatest triumph to be winning over fifty-three Champions at the British Breeds Show.

As well as being a great show dog of beautiful type, Hawk proved himself to be the greatest stud dog of all time in the breed, siring some thirty Champions in England and not far off the same number overseas. His most famous son (out of his half-sister, Treetops Penelope of Canfield) was Ch. Treetops Golden Falcon, the Best in Show winner at Crufts in 1956. Such was Hawk's influence on the breed that it would be extremely difficult to find a top winner anywhere in the world which does not have at least one line back to him. Most successful lines today are line-bred back to Hawk several times over.

SEAGIFT

The other large, successful kennel of the 1950s and early 1960s was the Yorkshire-based Seagift kennel, owned by Dorothy Whitwell. Dorothy had been involved in both coursing and showing the breed before the war, owning, amongst others, Ch. Leading Lady. In the late 1940s Dorothy managed to purchase from Peter George three littermates, all of whom became Champions. They were Ch. Parcancady Banker, Ch. Seagift Parcancady Stella and Ch. Seagift Perran Polar Queen.

Dorothy bred or owned many more Champions, some in partnership with Peter George. She exported to the USA the extremely important littermates Chs. Seagift Parcancady Bluebell and Royaltan, who had a tremendous influence on the breed in the United States. It seems only appropriate that, when she finally gave up the Greyhounds, some of her dogs, including the very influential stud dog, Ch. Seagift Sheriff, found their way back to the land of their ancestors in Cornwall with Paul Talling.

Ch. Treetops Ringdove: Foundation of the Shalfleet kennel.

SHALFLEET
The late 1950s and early 1960s saw the beginning of the most influential of modern English Greyhound kennels, which was to dominate the show scene for the next twenty-five years. The story of this kennel's development, establishing the Shalfleet line, is featured in Chapter Five: *Breeding Greyhounds*.

RP

This kennel is based in Cornwall, owned by Ralph and Barbara Parsons, and in more recent times in partnership with their daughter, Kay Chapman. The RP kennel has been active in the breed with considerable success for almost fifty years, and is the proud holder of the current breed record for CCs won for both dogs and bitches. Ch. Royal Portrait (Ch. Gaysyde White Christmas – Ch. Ro Poth) has won thirty-three CCs and four best in Show awards, and was top Greyhound in 1988, 1989, 1990 and 1991; while her grandsire, Ch. Rych Pyscador, won twenty-one CCs and one Best in Show, and was Pup of The Year in 1981. There have been numerous RP Champions over the years, and the old Cornish lines are well represented around the world through the influence of the exported RP stock.

SOLSTRAND

Dagmar Kenis-Pordham's Solstrand Greyhounds represent a truly international mixture of bloodlines. Her dogs go back to the Swedish and American lines she brought with her when she moved to England from California in the early 1970s, combined with the old English lines to which she has bred. The most famous Solstrand dog was Ch. Solstrand Double Diamond (Ch. Shaunvalley Cavalier – Am. Ch. Solstrand Bossa Nova), who was, in his day, the top-winning sight hound of all time at Group level, having won around twelve Hound Groups as well as five Best in Show awards, and Veteran of the Year 1982. Other big winning Solstrands were Chs. Solstrand Leading Lady, Solstrand Pall Mall of Exhurst, Singing the Blues at Solstrand, and many more too numerous to mention.

The Solstrand influence is strongly

Ch. Rych Pyscador: A Best in Show winner with a tally of twenty-one CCs.

Ch. Royal Portrait: Winner of thirty-three CCs, Top Greyhound of the Year in 1988, 1989, 1990 and 1991.

Ch. Solstrand Double Diamond: Winner of five Best in Show awards.

felt all around the world. In Scandinavia, Knut Blutecher's Showline kennel was founded on two very nice Solstrand bitches – Blues Image and Autumn Leaves – while the beautiful brindle, Diamond Lil, did a tremendous amount of winning in Australia.

GAYSYDE
Brenda and Jim Rowe (Gaysyde) have had a long run of success as exhibitors, stud dog owners and breeders. Their stud dog, Ch. Starbolt Cetus, produced many winners in the 1970s, and Ch. Gaysyde White Christmas has been the leading stud dog in the breed in the late 1980s and early 1990s. Among his offspring are the current breed record holder Ch. Royal Portrait and her brothers, Ch. Relentless Pursuit and Am. Ch. Rich Pickings, and also Ch. Repeat Performance (as

Ch. Gaysyde White Christmas: Leading stud dog in the breed in the late 1980s and early 1990s.

Sally Anne Thompson.

Ch. Snow Queen of Windspiel: Top CC winning bitch in the UK in 1993.

his name suggests, from a repeat mating to Ch. Ro Poth) and Ch. Regency Picture (out of Rynyow Pokkyl). Next came the all CC-winning litter out of the Top Brood Bitch of 1993, Ch. Windspiel Northern Style: Ch. Gaysyde Christmas Cracker, Ch. Gaysyde Christmas Carol, Ch. Snow Queen of Windspiel and Special Style at Windspiel.

OTHER LEADING KENNELS

Other kennels of note are Daphne Gilpin's Wenonah kennel, which produced the previous breed record holder, the late Eve Young's Ch. Wenonah Goosander (Ch. Shaunvalley Cavalier – Padneyhill Philomel), winner of twenty-nine CCs as well as being a multiple Best in Show winner. Unfortunately, she was never bred from. Daphne also had the courage to import dogs from Scandinavia to try to strengthen her lines with new blood. Her dogs, Hawk Lines Ferrari of Wenonah and Jets Oscar de la Renta, have produced some useful winners including several Champions and other winners, notably from the Rondelin kennel of Edna Hibbs. Frank Brown's Shaunvalleys, June Minns' Exhursts and Cynthia Boissevain's Branwens have also produced several Champions in recent years. If other influential kennels or individual dogs have been missed it is through lack of space rather than by intent, and I hope breeders will forgive me.

AMERICAN KENNELS

As can be seen from the history of the breed, there has been an almost constant flow of the best of the English bloodlines across the Atlantic and the North Sea. While the loss of England's top winners of the past is mourned by today's breeders and exhibitors in the UK, this movement of stock has resulted in the strengthening of many of the foreign lines, and many of the following kennels are ample proof of this.

CANYON CREST

Mention has already been made of the Canyon Crest line, owned by the Bagshaws in California. Although they imported few dogs, three of their biggest winners came from England, namely their first Champion, Am. Ch. Giralda's White Knight (via Mrs Dodge and Percy Roberts), Am. Ch. Viverdon Stafarella, and much later, Am. Ch. Barmaud Starbolt Europa. In between times they produced countless winners under the Canyon Crest name, including the foundation bitch of

Stanley Petter's very successful Hewly line, Am. Ch. Canyon Crest's Coronation.

This bitch had the distinction of also becoming a Champion in France when she accompanied Mr Petter there during his military service in the late 1950s. On his return home, Mr Petter bred and exhibited his Hewly Greyhounds with considerable success, as he does to this day. The most recent wins for the line came at the Greyhound Club of America's 1993 Eastern Specialty Show, with BOB going to Hewly Hit The Roof, and BOS to her sire, Ch. Hewly Hispanic II, who himself has been a BOB at previous GCA Specialties.

Mr Petter, a thoroughbred horse breeder, has paid frequent visits to the UK, and these visits have often resulted in the movement of an English Greyhound back to America. His imports include: Am. Ch. Hewly Red Plume, Eng. Am. Ch. Seagift Parcancady Bluebell, and Pennyworth Sensation. Bluebell's litter brother, Royaltan, also spent his later years with the Petters.

RUDEL
The Rudel's kennel, owned by Elsie and Rudolph Neustadt, has produced many outstanding dogs for around forty years, as well as successfully showing dogs bought in from other lines. Outstanding dogs included: Ch. Rudel's Firefly, the top-winning Greyhound of all time (until Ch. Aroi Talk of the Blues came along), Ch. Argus Of Greywitch (who was, until very recently, the top-producing sire of all time in America), and the top-winning Greyhound dog, Ch. Suntiger Traveler.

I recently read a short article by Elsie Neustadt in which she gave very short shrift to the theory that the Standard is merely a loose guideline which gives judges almost total freedom to interpret as they wish. She is a very firm believer that there is only one "type" of Greyhound, that which most closely fits the written Standard as a whole, not just the bits of it which an individual thinks to be most important. To this end, a careful line breeding programme was followed, always with an eye on the dogs behind the pedigree of potential matings. Over the years, the proof of her intention – to produce balanced dogs which fit the Standard – has been there for all to see. Many could follow this example to their own – and the breed's – advantage.

AROI
The Aroi kennel of Georgianna Mueller in California produced a string of winners from around 1960 to the mid-1980s. The most outstanding was the top-winning Greyhound of all time, the

Aroi Blue Tiger Blues: A fine representative of the Aroi kennel.

immortal 'Punky', Am. Ch. Aroi Talk of the Blues (Ch. Aroi Blue Tiger Blues – Ch. Aroi Talk of the Town), who was owned by Nat and Gloria Reese and handled for them by Corky Vroom. This blue brindle bitch's record was phenomenal by any standard: No 1. Greyhound in America 1975, 1976, 1977, sixty-eight all breed BISs, five GCA Specialty BOBs, including one as a nine-year-old veteran; 165 Group wins, including Westminster twice, and Top Dog all breeds 1976. She was very closely line-bred to Hawk (who appears four times in the pedigree, four generations back) through Royaltan, Golden Falcon, Ringdove and Wicked William.

HUZZAH

It would take a page just to list the number of Champions produced by the Huzzah kennel of Don and Pat Ide in California. There must have been somewhere around one hundred all over the world by now, including several BIS and Specialty winners. A few of these top winners were the Chs. Huzzah The Drumbeat, Jungle Rhythm, Pursuit of Happiness, Stars 'n Stripes, and Mad Hattie. Ch. Huzzah The Voyageur has had a tremendous influence on the breed in Australia in recent years. Many of the Huzzah Greyhounds have been brindles of a very distinctive, elegant type, with tremendous reach of neck and covering lots of ground.

Huzzah Midnight Sun: A representative of the successful Huzzah kennel.

KINGSMARK

The Kingsmark Greyhounds of Judith and Richard Donaldson in Illinois have certainly made their mark over the past twenty years or so with a whole host of Champions, BIS and Specialty Winners. Ch. Kingsmark Lalique (Ch. Hero Kingsmark – Ch. Kingsmark Lady Chatterley) was top Greyhound in America in 1988 as well as being a Specialty and BIS winner.

SUNTIGER

Gail Burnham's Suntiger dogs are a major force in America, mainly through the fantastically successful stud dog Am. Ch. Suntiger Traveler (Am. Ch. Midnight Shadow Traveler – Am. Eng. Ch. Shalfleet Stop The World), who now holds the record for the number of Champions sired – forty-six to date. The previous record holder was his grandsire, Ch. Argus of Greywitch, and so he is, like so many others, line-bred to Hawk. Gail also imported Eng. Ch. Shalfleet Shirley Ann from England and campaigned her to her American title, as well as breeding several Champion offspring from her. Traveler, mated to Eng. Am. Ch. Shalfleet Socialite, produced twenty-one Champion offspring in three separate litters, thus making Socialite the top-producing bitch of all time in America.

Eng. and Am. Ch. Shalfleet Shirley Ann: Imported from the UK and campaigned to her American title.

Hewly Hit The Roof: Best of Breed at the Greyhound Club of America Specialty, 1993.

OTHER LEADING KENNELS

Some of the other kennels consistently producing and showing major winners in America are: Another Episode (Ann and Lisa Tater), Heathero (Jean Metzler and Linda Transchel), Hewly (Stanley D. Pretter Jr.), Iveragh (Deborah Littleton), Lochinvar (Robert and Maureen Lucas), Ryal (Sue and Grant Cassem) and Tre Kronor (Jim and Judy Elmquist). Apologies to those not included due to lack of space.

SCANDINAVIAN KENNELS

Again, it is impossible to do justice to the Greyhounds of Scandanavia in the space available here, but to fail to mention them at all would be doing a terrible disservice to an area where the breed is among the strongest in the world and the enthusiasm and knowledge of the breeders is second to none. The Guld kennel, owned by Ann Gustafsson in Sweden, has consistently produced typical, quality hounds for over twenty years. The best-known include Int. Chs. Guld, Gulds Beauty Belinda, Golden Geisha, Rare Rachel (a liver brindle), and the studs, Billy The Kid and Tawny Topstar. Many top winners around the world go back to the Gulds line.

The long-established Sobers kennel of Astrid Jonsson and Bitte Ahrens has produced many winners, and the Solstrands of Dagmar Kenis can trace their lines back to the Sobers dogs. Greyhound of the Year in Sweden in 1992 was Goran Bodegard's Ch. Magna Charta, the result of eight generations of carefully line-bred Greyhounds from this kennel, which goes back to the original Guld Champion, Int. Ch. Guld.

Swed., Ch. Magna Charta: Sweden's Greyhound of the Year in 1992.

Other famous Greyhounds from this kennel were the prepotent sire Ch. Psykotic, whose influence is seen in England through Daphne Gilpin's import, Hawk Lines Ferrari of Wenonah, and Ch. Markurell, whose descendants are having quite an influence in the USA.

In Norway, two kennels have dominated the breed for some twenty to thirty years: the Jet's of Kari Nylen and her son Espen Engh, and the Showline Greyhounds of Knut and Cecile Fr Blutecher. Both have consistently produced many typical winners, far too numerous to list here. The latest in this seemingly endless supply of Champions is Jet's Headed Like A Snake and Showline Summer Light. Both kennels have exported throughout Scandinavia, Europe and beyond, and their influence on Greyhounds around the world will be felt for generations to come.

Finland now has a number of top-winning Greyhounds, mainly imported from the other Scandinavian countries, and it will be interesting to observe the progress of the Finnish dogs over the next few years.

Chapter Twelve

THE BREED STANDARDS

THE PURPOSE

I have titled this section 'The Breed Standards' since it is worth noting that there is more than one written Standard to describe the breed. However, for this purpose I shall refer to the two main Standards currently in use throughout the world when judging the breed in the show ring, namely those of the Kennel Clubs in the UK and the USA. Both these Standards have been developed over a considerable number of years to become what they are today – a fairly concise but general description of the ideal show Greyhound.

It is often said that the Breed Standard is a blueprint which specifies exactly how the ideal Greyhound should look and move. However, this statement does not stand up to close examination, since a blueprint (along with a materials specification) lays down the exact dimensions, weight, shape, colour, constituency etc. of an inanimate object. It should be possible for any number of manufacturers, with the correct tools and skills, to reproduce exactly the same object by using the blueprint and specification. How many artists, who had never previously seen a

Ch. Flyalong Non: This outstanding bitch is the only Greyhound to win Best in Show at a General Championship Show in Britain, in 1993.

Greyhound, would come up with a picture even resembling the breed, never mind one looking like the ideal Greyhound? The chances of any two such artists coming up with pictures of a similar dog are even more remote.

The Breed Standards are, of necessity, concise, but the aim is to lay down the essentials of the breed, particularly those points which differentiate the breed from any other. It is clear, however, that some prior knowledge of the breed and dogs in general is necessary before the reader can understand the Standard and envisage a mental picture of the ideal dog .

THE BRITISH STANDARD

All English KC Standards were rewritten in the early 1980s with a view to using a standard form of words across all breeds in order to eradicate misunderstandings in terminology between the various breeds. The Kennel Club consulted the various breed clubs – fortunately there is only one for Greyhounds in the UK, namely The Greyhound Club. The fact that very few alterations were found to be necessary is perhaps proof not only that the then existing Standard was reasonably well written, but also that breed type had been maintained over the years.

The only two slightly contentious issues I can recall in the Greyhound Club Committee discussions at the time were eye

Huzzah Tiger Doll winning Best of Breed at Westminster, 1985.

colour and the ideal size of the dogs. On eye colour it was agreed that introduction of "preferably dark" eyes, compared with the 1982 Standard, which did not mention colour at all, or the "dark in colour" of the previous Standard, was an improvement, although this still did not specifically take into account the difficulty with the dilute colours, with their (almost inevitably) lighter eye colour. Perhaps it would have been better to have added a sentence to the effect that lighter eyes matching the coat colour are acceptable in the lighter (dilute) coloured dogs. This is certainly a view taken by most UK judges. On the question of the ideal size, there was some feeling that, as most of the dogs then being shown were somewhere near or above the maximum size (30ins) laid down in the Standard, it should be increased to take account of this fact. It was argued that improved feeding and better stock management would inevitably lead to increased size in the breed. However, the argument that an increase in size would result in an untypical dog – no longer capable of fulfilling its original purpose (coursing) – won the day, although there was a view held by some that the purpose of a show Greyhound is to win in the show ring and not to chase the hare.

THE BRITISH BREED STANDARD

GENERAL APPEARANCE
Strongly built, upstanding, of generous proportions, muscular power and symmetrical formation, with long head and neck, clean well laid shoulders, deep chest, capacious body, arched loin, powerful quarters, sound legs and feet, and a suppleness of limb, which emphasise in a marked degree its distinctive type and quality.

CHARACTERISTICS
Possessing remarkable stamina and endurance.

TEMPERAMENT
Intelligent, gentle affectionate and even-tempered.

HEAD AND SKULL
Long, moderate width, flat skull, slight stop. Jaws powerful and well chiselled.

EYES
Bright, intelligent, oval and obliquely set. Preferably dark.

EARS
Small, rose-shape, of fine texture.

MOUTH
Jaws strong with a perfect, regular and complete scissor bite, i.e. upper teeth closely overlapping lower teeth and set square to the jaws.

NECK
Long and muscular, elegantly arched, well let into shoulders.

FOREQUARTERS
Shoulders oblique, well set back, muscular without being loaded, narrow and cleanly defined at top. Forelegs, long and straight, bone of good substance and quality. Elbows free and well set under shoulders. Pasterns moderate length, slightly sprung. Elbows, pasterns and toes inclining neither in nor out.

BODY
Chest deep and capacious, providing adequate heart room. Ribs deep, well sprung and carried well back. Flanks well cut up. Back rather long, broad and square. Loin powerful, slightly arched.

HINDQUARTERS
Thighs and second thighs wide and muscular, showing great propelling power. Stifles well bent. Hocks well let down, inclining neither in nor out. Body and hindquarters, features of ample proportions and well coupled, enabling adequate ground to be covered when standing.

FEET
Moderate length, with compact, well knuckled toes and strong pads.

TAIL
Long, set on rather low, strong at root, tapering to point, carried low, slightly curved.

GAIT/MOVEMENT
Straight, low reaching, free stride enabling the ground to be covered at great speed. Hindlegs coming well under body giving great propulsion.

COAT
Fine and close.

COLOUR
Black, white, red, blue, fawn, fallow, brindle or any of these colours broken with white.

SIZE
Ideal height: dogs 71-76 cms (28-30 ins); bitches: 68-71 cms (27-28 ins).

FAULTS
Any departure from the foregoing points should be considered a fault and the seriousness with which the fault should be regarded should be in exact proportion to its degree.

NOTE: Male animals should have two apparently normal testicles fully descended into the scrotum.
Reproduced by kind permission of the English Kennel Club.

THE AMERICAN BREED STANDARD

HEAD – Long and narrow, fairly wide between the ears, scarcely perceptible stop, little or no development of nasal sinuses, good length of muzzle, which should be powerful without coarseness. Teeth very strong and even in front. Ears – Small and fine in texture, thrown back and folded, except when excited, when they are semipricked. Eyes – Dark, bright, intelligent, indicating spirit.

NECK – Long, muscular, without throatiness, slightly arched, and widening gradually into the shoulder.

SHOULDERS – Placed as obliquely as possible, muscular, without being loaded.

FORELEGS – Perfectly straight, set well into the shoulders, neither turned in nor out, pasterns strong.

CHEST – Deep, and as wide as consistent with speed, fairly well-sprung ribs.

BACK – Muscular and broad.

LOINS – Good depth of muscle, well arched, well cut up in the flanks.

HINDQUARTERS – Long, very muscular and powerful, wide and well let-down, well-bent stifles. Hocks well bent and rather close to ground, wide but straight fore and aft.

FEET – Hard and close, rather more hare-than cat-feet, well knuckled up with good strong claws.

TAIL – Long, fine and tapering with a slight upward curve.

COAT– Short, smooth and firm in texture.

COLOR – Immaterial.

WEIGHT – Dogs, 65 to 70 pounds, bitches 60 to 65 pounds.

SCALE OF POINTS
General symmetry and quality: 10
Head and neck: 20
Chest and shoulders: 20
Back: 10
Quarters: 20
Legs and feet: 20
TOTAL: 100
Reproduced by kind permission of the American Kennel Club.

INTERPRETATION

The following analysis of the Standards is intended to clarify the the written points. It is, of course, a personal analysis drawn up from my own picture of the ideal Greyhound and should be treated as such. Different people will inevitably have a slightly different picture in their mind, and thus will put more or less emphasis on various parts of the Standard. It is these slight variations in personal interpretation of the Standard which result in the fact that the same dogs do not win all the time.

That is not to say that the Standard is merely a very loose guide which may be interpreted so freely that it is possible to justify any placings, however divergent from the norm. A dog which closely fits the Standard should invariably be somewhere near the head of the line, and a dog which is lacking in many breed characteristics, and thus breed type, should always be well down the line.

In the following analysis I have used the British Standard, which is much more comprehensive, and have commented on the American Standard only when there are significant differences.

GENERAL APPEARANCE

This is probably the most quoted part of the UK Standard, and it sums up many of the essential elements which go towards describing what makes the Greyhound a distinctive breed, and not just any old mongrel. It describes very clearly what is required of a dog to be the correct "type", and thus, unmistakably, a Greyhound. The AKC Standard does not have such a general description of the appearance of the Greyhound, and in my view it suffers as a result. However, the AKC Standard does have a Scale of Points, which indicates the relative values which should be placed on the various sections of the dog's anatomy, theoretically, limiting the amount of emphasis put on individual faults or virtues by a judge.

"Strongly built, upstanding, of generous proportions" are key elements of this section of the Standard. A Greyhound must never be flimsy, weak or delicate. It must have good strong bone with no sign of weakness. To be upstanding, I see a Greyhound as having a certain proud bearing and a presence which commands the attention of those around it. It does this without any sign of aggression to other dogs or to people, its physical presence – whether standing or moving – being quite sufficient. With the term "generous proportions", I picture a well-covered, muscular dog, standing over lots of ground. A big, well-muscled dog with no spare flesh, rather like a well-trained modern athlete. Bitches will, of course, be smaller and more feminine than dogs, but they must never be weak, over-elegant or too fine.

This section of the Standard also describes the general features which come together to give an overall picture of the breed. "Muscular power" is obviously necessary if the dog is to be able to run at very high speeds, and to possess the ability to twist and turn after its prey. Any dog without this musculature is to me untypical of the breed. The dog must have "symmetrical formation". To me, this means that the dog must be balanced, possessing the necessary symmetry to give

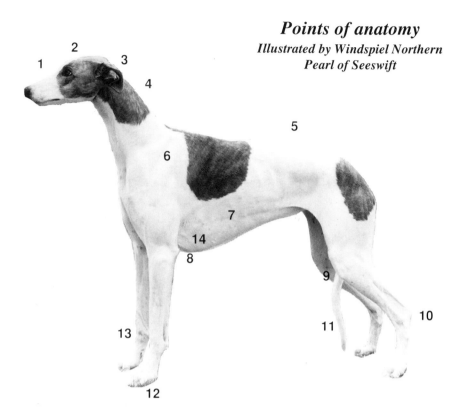

Points of anatomy
Illustrated by Windspiel Northern
Pearl of Seeswift

1. *Stop: slight.*
2. *Skull: flat.*
3. *Ears: small, rose-shaped.*
4. *Neck: long, muscular, elegantly arched.*
5. *Loin: powerful, slightly arched.*
6. *Shoulders: well set back, muscular.*
7. *Ribs: deep, well-sprung.*
8. *Elbows: well set under shoulders.*
9. *Stifles: well bent.*
10. *Hocks: well let down.*
11. *Tail: long, set rather low.*
12. *Feet: compact, well-knuckled toes.*
13. *Pasterns: moderate length.*
14. *Chest: deep and capacious.*

controlled power and suppleness, speed and stamina. It must not be too heavy or light at the front or back. Nor must it be too angulated or too straight in shoulder or stifle. It must be neither too short, too deep, too shallow, too long or too tall. Balance is all-important, and without balance and symmetry the dog cannot possess type.

The remainder of this section gives a general description of those parts of the dog which are described in detail later in the Standard, but phrased in such a way as to give a very good impression of a distinctive breed which is capable of great speed and suppleness. When I read this section, I picture a beautifully curved, powerful outline, with absolutely no sharp angles and few straight lines, other than the front legs. For those who find it difficult to memorise things, if you remember only this section of the Standard you should have a fairly clear picture of what is required in the breed.

CHARACTERISTICS

"Possessing remarkable stamina and endurance." Although this may be a most desirable characteristic, I see no way in which this can be assessed in the show ring. Perhaps we should all take our dogs out coursing after the completion of judging in order to ascertain their staying power. Or maybe we should charge around the ring until either handler or dog falls to the ground through fatigue. I think more handlers than dogs would be found wanting!

TEMPERAMENT

Intelligence is a requirement, but it is not defined. Intelligence in a sighthound is sometimes confused with the basic instinct to chase and kill small game – an instinct which has been selectively bred for over thousands of years in our breed. Although the Greyhound is not generally used for other types of work where it may demonstrate its intelligence in the same way as gundogs or herding dogs, for example, I have seen some quite impressive displays of both Obedience and Agility from the breed at the Greyhound Club of America Specialty shows. This is something rarely seen from the breed in the UK.

The Greyhound certainly demonstrates the other requirements of gentleness (once out of the wild puppyhood stages), affection and even temper. It is rare to see a vicious or bad-tempered dog either with people or other dogs, and I would regard any sign of this as a serious fault. It is equally rare to see a dog who is shy or frightened, or one who refuses to be handled in the ring. They may not always be the most enthusiastic of showmen, but rarely do they exhibit any vices. Strangely, the AKC Standard makes no mention of temperament.

HEAD AND SKULL

The description here is self-explanatory. The whole head is long, the skull flat and of only moderate width, and with only slight stop, giving the impression of being stream-lined yet powerful, but with no sign of heaviness or coarseness. The jaws must be powerful and well-chiselled, capable of picking up and despatching a hare at full speed. There should be no weakness, particularly of the underjaw.

While the head is an important part of the dog in completing the overall picture, it should not be regarded as its major attribute and many excellent dogs in all other respects have possessed rather plain heads. It should be borne in mind, when judging, that the breed is not a 'head breed' like, for example, the Bulldog. Very fine, long, over-refined, weak heads are no more typical than short, broad heavy heads.

The Greyhound's head should be long, moderate in width, with a flat skull. The expression should be one of gentleness and intelligence.

EYES

The Standards state that eyes should be bright, intelligent, oval (not round and bulging or small and pig-like) and obliquely set (not set square in the skull and looking straight forward), and this really describes all that is necessary. I have commented earlier on the failure of the Standard to address the problem of light eyes in dilute colour dogs. The Standard prefers a dark eye, and so light eyes, particularly in the non-dilute coloured dogs, must be regarded as a fault. The colour of the eye has no effect on its efficiency, and dogs with light eyes see just as well as those with dark ones. The Standard here is based purely on aesthetic considerations and not on functional ones. It should be remembered that light eyes in puppies often darken somewhat with age. Although there is no mention of it in the Standard, I always prefer to see a soft, kind eye, rather than a hard, staring expression.

EARS

Ears should be a tight rose shape, small and fine. Big, floppy ears are untypical and spoil the expression of the animal. The American Standard allows ears to be semi-pricked when excited.

MOUTH

The jaws and teeth must be strong and the bite should be a scissor bite, with the top teeth overlapping, but touching the bottom teeth. Overshot mouths crop up from time to time in the breed, where the top teeth overlap the bottom ones excessively and do not make contact with them. I have never seen an undershot mouth in a show Greyhound, although I know people who have. Given that a good mouth and strong jaws are essential to the original purpose of the breed, I regard any mouth faults as being quite serious, although I am not fanatical about counting pre-molars as are some European judges.

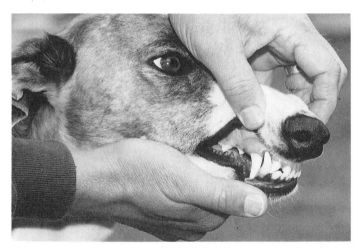

The teeth should meet in a scissor bite, with the top teeth overlapping, but touching, the bottom teeth.

NECK

The neck should be long and muscular. Remember a hound running flat out has to reach down to pick up the hare, which is no lightweight animal itself. Excessively long necks with little muscle, which often go with extremely fine heads, may look very elegant, but they are hardly functional for the breed and are incorrect in the show Greyhound. The required elegant arch of the neck, which gives those possessing it such a look of quality, results from the correct muscle attachment between vertebrae and skull. A long neck usually goes with well-laid shoulders. The two, together with the slight arch to the upper neck, result in lovely flowing curved lines from the skull right down to the withers, with no sharp angles to be seen anywhere.

FOREQUARTERS

Shoulders must be oblique and well laid back if front movement is to be of the true, long-reaching, low "daisy-cutting" style. Upright shoulders severely restrict the ability of the dog to reach forward, either trotting or galloping, and result in a short, choppy terrier-type action, or even worse, a hackney action which is totally untypical. Shoulders should be well-muscled but not over-loaded and bulky. There should be sufficient space between the tops of the blades to allow the dog to lower its head without the blades touching. The days when some judges used to push down the dog's head almost to the ground while at the same time trying to get two fingers between the top of the blades, fortunately, seem to be behind us.

Although upper arm is not mentioned in the Standard, it is essential that it is of a similar length to the shoulder blade, and at a reasonable angle with it, so as to give the desired unrestricted front reach. It is this angle between the shoulder blade and the upper arm to which we refer when we talk about 'front angulation'. Books of the past have often said the ideal angle is around 90 degrees, but this is clearly not so – unless of course you want your Greyhounds to have fronts like Dachshunds. The correct angle is probably somewhere between 120 and 130 degrees.

The bone of the front legs should be long, straight, strong and of good substance and quality. Although the Greyhound is a long dog in comparison with its height, to me, a dog with short legs is unbalanced and thus untypical. Ideally, the elbows should be directly below the top of the shoulder blade for perfect balance in the well-angulated dog. Unfortunately, this is rarely seen, which accounts for some of the poor front movement evident in today's dogs. Elbows should be free and not tied. A tied elbow severely restricts front movement and gives a most ungainly impression when movement is viewed either from front or side.

Pasterns should be of moderate length and slightly sprung. Some over-long pasterns, with their consequent weakness, are occasionally seen, but I think the vertical pastern with absolutely no spring is a far worse fault. This often goes with over-knuckled toes and extremely tight feet. I cannot see how such a pastern and foot could ever be functional, particularly over rough ground. Elbows, pasterns and toes should turn neither in nor out.

BODY

The description of the body is based upon the fact that there must be sufficient capacity to contain a large heart and enormous lungs, while at the same time providing the muscular power to allow the tremendous flexing of the whole body in order to achieve very high speeds.

The chest must be deep, the ribcage reaching down to the level of the elbows in the adult dog. The ribs must be well-sprung without being barrel-shaped, which would interfere with elbow movement. The ribs must also be carried well back to maximise the chest capacity.

Flanks must be well cut up, and it is this tuck-up which gives the Greyhound its unique outline. Again, this tuck-up should be a nice smooth curve, and not an abrupt sharp line, which results from a short keel, or saggy, as seen in an overweight animal.

The back of the Greyhound is long, but in no way weak. It should be rather broad and square, with the loin slightly arched and very powerful. This arch must be over the loin, and not over the whole length of the back, which gives a roached look – a serious fault which seems to be creeping into the breed in some areas. The arch in the loin results from a very slight curve in the spine in this area, along with extremely well-developed muscles. It is this construction which allows the dog to flex and extend its whole body when galloping. The whole of the back should be firm and well-muscled. The croup should curve gently down to the powerful hindquarters, with no sharp cut away – another fault which seems to be creeping into the breed.

HINDQUARTERS

The description here is one of muscular power and propulsion. Thighs and second thighs must have both depth and width of muscle if they are to give the tremendous drive from behind which is required in the breed. The well-bent stifle refers to the angle between the thigh (femur) and the second thigh (fibula and tibia). This should be approximately the same angle as that seen in the forequarters, if the dog is to look balanced. The muscular development of the thighs smooths out the angle into a nice continuous curve down to the hock. Over-angulation of the hindquarters gives the dog a look of crouching, or almost of kneeling in extreme cases.

The distance from the hock joint to the foot is relatively short when compared with the long, sweeping lines of the hip to hock. The hocks should be vertical and incline neither in nor out. The feet should be placed well back when standing (but never over-stretched) and this, combined with the ample proportions of the body and quarters, allows the dog to stand over a tremendous amount of ground.

FEET

The feet should be of moderate length and well-knuckled, but definitely not so short in toe as to be almost knuckled over. The American Standard states rather more hare- than cat-footed. Pads should be rather thick and strong for cushioning when running. Feet should not be flat, splayed or thin-padded. Nails should be kept well trimmed.

TAIL

The description in the Standard sums it up perfectly. Long, set on rather low, tapering, carried low and slightly curved. Short tails set on high, as well as being untypical are not functional. Anyone who has watched a Greyhound running free will know just how much the dog uses its tail as a rudder, almost pressing down on the ground with it to assist in turning.

GAIT/MOVEMENT

The Standard describes the movement as straight, low reaching and free striding, which, to me, seems an adequate description for the show ring. However, it then goes on to mention the ability to cover the ground at great speed and to say that the hindlegs come under the body to give great propulsion. This is somewhat more difficult to assess in the ring.

COAT

Close and fine. The coat is very short, soft, shining, and almost velvety smooth to the touch in a well-conditioned and groomed dog.

COLOUR

Whereas the UK Standard specifies black, white, red, blue, fawn, fallow (described in my dictionary as pale-brown or reddish-yellow), brindle, or any of these colours broken with white, the AKC says colour is immaterial.

There has been some debate on the acceptability of the liver and liver-brindle, neither of which I have ever seen in the UK, but which have occurred in both Scandinavia and the USA. Like other

The Greyhound should be free striding, with the ability to cover the ground at great speed.

dilute colours, the livers often have light eyes, but unlike most of the others, they also sometimes have liver-coloured noses and lighter body pigmentation. This is not something I would personally like to see in our dogs, and, strictly speaking, the colour is not acceptable according to the UK Standard, but where a Standard permits all colours then there can surely be no objection.

SIZE

In the UK Standard the ideal heights are dogs 28-30ins, bitches 27-28ins, with no mention of weight. The American Standard calls for dogs of 65-70lbs and bitches of 60-65lbs, with no mention of height.

Having seen dogs on both sides of the Atlantic as well as in Scandinavia, I have not noticed any great differences in either height or weight between the countries and can only conclude that there is something amiss with the Standards. Certainly a 28 inch dog would look small in the ring in the UK, as would a 65lb dog in the USA; and I hate to picture a 30 inch dog weighing only 65lbs, an acceptable specimen if you combine the extremes of the Standards.

While there is no functional advantage to be gained by increasing the size of the breed, some of the bigger dogs undoubtedly look very impressive in the ring, and providing a big dog loses none of the other essentials of the breed, including sound movement, it should not be penalised too heavily on size alone. Far better a slightly big dog than a weak, undersized one, but better still is one of the correct size.

FAULTS

Faults should be judged in accordance with their degree. There are no absolute disqualifying faults, not even the lack of a normally descended testicle in male animals.

Chapter Thirteen

THE SHOW RING

SELECTION OF STOCK

It is perhaps stating the obvious, but most people who enter the world of dog showing do so with some hope of success. It is surprising, therefore, how haphazard is the selection of the stock which they intend to show. There is not space here to go into all the aspects of picking a potential winner, but the following brief guidelines should help to avoid some of the potential disasters.

Firstly, make sure you actually like the breed and can live with it. Remember show Greyhounds are large dogs with big appetites, they need lots of room and exercise and demand lots of care and attention. They can also go through an incredibly naughty puppy stage during which your property may be wrecked through sheer clumsiness when running around, rather than through any malice. Attend a few shows, take a good look at the breed, talk to owners and breeders and find out all you can about the breed in general before you even contemplate buying one. Only if you are completely satisfied that you and a Greyhound would be compatible should you move on to the next stage, that of selecting your own dog.

Obviously the easiest way to pick a winner is to buy an adult with a proven record in the ring, but this can be very expensive and most people prefer to buy a puppy who can grow up with them and who they can train in their own way. While this is unquestionably more fun, it does have the drawback that you may not be successful in selecting a potential winner. Even the most experienced in the breed make mistakes in selecting a puppy.

Before dashing off to look at puppies, read the Breed Standard and make sure you understand it. Look at what is winning in the show ring and decide which lines seem to win most consistently under a wide variety of judges, and then decide if this type fits your own picture of the Standard. Do not be frightened to ask questions. Most exhibitors and breeders will be only too pleased to help, but remember they may be biased in favour of their own stock or against that of their rivals. Once you have decided on the breeding you fancy, wait until something suitable is available. It is pointless taking the trouble to find out what you like and what you think you can win with, and then becoming impatient and buying the first puppy advertised in the dog Press. Keep your ear to the ground and be aware of the litters being planned by the breeders whose stock you most admire, and let them know of your interest, if you want to avoid disappointment. You may have to wait some time as the breed is not numerically strong – there are probably less than a dozen litters a year whelped in the UK.

ASSESSING PUPPIES

Many breeders who know their own lines, maintain that they can pick the best puppy in the litter at birth. Most people who are buying a puppy do not have this advantage, so once the pups are born,

Treetops puppies: Sound construction and a sound temperament are essential attributes to look for when assessing Greyhound puppies.

arrange with the breeder to see them when they are around six weeks old. This is probably the earliest age at which any reasonable assessment of potential can be made. Ask the opinion of the breeder on the attributes of the puppies. Most will point out their virtues, even if some of the faults may not be highlighted! Have a particular look at those points not mentioned by the breeder, as well as the ones which are.

If you have not seen puppy Greyhounds before, you may be shocked at their appearance, for they bear little resemblance to their parents or to any other Greyhound, often looking, to the uninitiated, more like Staffordshire Bull Terriers or Labradors. They are often not even the same colour as either parent. It is not unusual to have whites, solid colours, parti-colours and brindles all in the same litter.

The same principles apply when picking a Greyhound puppy as for any other breed. Avoid any pup who has obvious faults either in structure or temperament. Never pick a small, weak-looking puppy, as substance is extremely important in the finished dog. Pick a dog with good heavy bone – it always fines down as they grow on. Dogs which look over-long at this age often finish up looking balanced when mature. Indeed, many people specifically look for a long puppy, on the basis that puppies which look balanced often finish up being a shade short-coupled when maturity is reached. Feet should be large, with thick pads and well-knuckled toes. Poor feet at this stage rarely improve with time.

The overall Greyhound shape should be evident, with some depth of brisket and some spring of rib (although this develops with age) and the ribs should go well back. Good sloping shoulders and angulation should be apparent from an early age. The tail should be long, often touching the ground, and should be set on fairly low and not carried gaily. Heads are almost impossible to assess at this age, but avoid thick, very large, floppy ears, and those that are obviously very short-muzzled, broad-skulled, and heavy-headed, as they usually finish by being rather coarse. Mouths should be correct at this age. Light eyes often darken with age, but this cannot be guaranteed. Dogs may not have both testicles descended at this age, but these often appear later. If you pick a dog which is not entire, make sure you have an agreement with the breeder as to what happens if the testicles do not subsequently appear.

If there is a puppy which you like, come to an agreement with the breeder and arrange to see the dog again in a couple of weeks, on the understanding that if you are still happy you will then buy the dog. Somewhere between eight and ten weeks is probably the ideal age at which to take the puppy home. Always obtain a full diet sheet from the breeder, and get advice on feeding and care right through to adulthood. Greyhounds are not the easiest of breeds to raise and great care should be taken with both diet and exercise as well as with housing.

The Greyhound is a very slow breed to mature and it goes through some very rapid periods of growth, during which it may look anything but the world-beater you thought you had selected. Do not despair: a dog which looked right at six weeks will usually look the part again by the time it is around a year old, however ugly it looks in between times. A Greyhound should never be rushed into the show ring before it is ready. It is much better at home getting the food, exercise and rest it needs, rather than being dragged around the country to shows before it is ready. If you have had the patience to wait to select the right dog, then be patient again and wait until it is ready to show.

FEEDING

Feeding is very much down to the individual preference of the owner and the dog. An eight-week-old puppy will generally require five or six meals a day, spread out reasonably evenly from around 6am to 10pm. Three or four of these meals will be based on a variety of minced or finely chopped meats, plus good-quality biscuit meal, and the others will be milk-based, possibly with egg or cereal. Alternatively, there are many excellent complete meals available, some of which are specially formulated for puppies. The number of meals is gradually reduced and the quantities per meal increased until the dog is down to two meals a day at around a year old. Many dogs are best kept on two meals a day for the rest of their lives and some are better on just one meal.

Calcium, phosphorus and other minerals are essential to good growth, along with the correct balance of vitamins, particularly D, E and B. These are available either as supplements or naturally in some foods. Great care should be taken not to overdose vitamins and minerals as this may cause severe problems. Take the advice of the breeder and your vet, and remember that many of the complete meals are already balanced and no extras are required.

HOUSING

Housing is also very much a matter of personal preference. The show Greyhound will live quite happily in the house or in a kennel. Whichever is chosen, it is essential that the dog feels it has its own place and that this is warm, comfortable and draught-free. While adult Greyhounds make wonderful house companions and pets, they can be absolutely unbearable adolescents who charge around almost aimlessly, bumping into everything and everybody.

Good rearing is essential if Greyhound pups like these, pictured at four weeks, are to fulfil their potential in the show ring or, like those below, on the race track

GREYHOUND MOVEMENT

Through selection over thousands of years the Greyhound has been moulded into a superb athlete.

The long limbs are designed for biomechanical stride length.

The strong upper body muscles provide propulsion power.

Larger lungs and heart deliver blood and oxygen.

The back arches prominently when galloping, and the long tail provides balance.

The slimline shapes gives a high power to weight ratio which is the most efficient design for a four-legged sprint athlete.

LEFT: Greyhounds must be regularly exercised and fed a well-balanced diet, suitable to their needs, in order to remain in peak condition.

BELOW: They're off! Greyhounds are bred to chase, and with careful training, they quickly adapt to chasing the artificial lure.

FACING PAGE: Hewly Hit The Road and Hewly Hit The Roof: The show Greyhound must maintain a racing build, even if it is not required to fulfil this function.

RACING AMERICAN STYLE

ABOVE: Track heroes Oshkosh Juliet (left) and the incomparable Dutch Bahama.

BELOW: Derby Lane, St Petersburg: Greyhound racing is big business and purpose-built stadia accommodate the spectators in comfort.

RACING BRITISH STYLE

ABOVE: Action all the way as a trio of Greyhounds take a bend almost together.

LEFT: 1992 English Derby winner Farloe Melody.

ONE MAN AND HIS DOG: World record holder Ballyregan Bob, pictured with his trainer George Curtis.

I prefer my puppies to spend most of their time in outside kennels which have free access to outside runs, with a little time each day spent in the house and several gallops round the garden or a field in between times. An almost miraculous transformation seems to take place once a Greyhound reaches full adulthood – their behaviour in the house suddenly seems to become perfect, as though they had spent all their lives inside. The difficulty then is in prising them out of your armchair to get them outside, particularly if it is cold or raining!

I find that the best floor inside the kennels is fairly smooth concrete, which is easily cleaned. A liberal covering of sawdust or wood-shavings helps keep things clean, and also assists in keeping the kennel warm. The floor should always be kept dry. A great deal has been written and said about the best surface for outside runs. Obviously, concrete is easiest to keep clean, but many people believe that smooth concrete results in flat, splayed, unsightly feet. I feel that this is probably true if it is too smooth and if it often gets wet and slippery, since this causes the dogs to spread their toes to try to obtain some extra purchase. I have found no problems with a lightly tamped concrete surface, which offers a good grip. The other options which are said to produce good feet are sharp sand, pea gravel or shingle, but all are difficult to keep clean. Muddy, slippery surfaces should be avoided. A good variety of surfaces on which the dogs can walk and run is probably best.

I find the best kennel bedding to be a good thick layer of soft shredded paper in a wooden bed, which is raised slightly off the floor and is free from draughts. This type of bedding is warm, clean, free from parasites, and easily disposed of.

EXERCISE

Opinions on the correct exercise for a show Greyhound vary almost as much as those on feeding and rearing. The opinion of the breeder should be sought, as he or she will be most familiar with what suits their particular line. However, as a golden rule, do not over-exercise youngsters, and always build up exercise very gradually over a period of time. Too much exercise does much more harm than good.

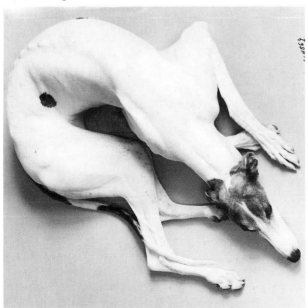

Am. Ch. Talos Dear Abby: This interesting shot of a Greyhound in repose shows that although this breed should be slimline, it should still give an impression of muscular strength.

John L. Ashby.

Walking, other than the very short socialising walks, should not start until five or six months, and even then it should be of very short duration – no more than about half a mile at any one time. During this early period youngsters will exercise themselves sufficiently if they have a reasonable-sized outside run or access to the garden. Distances walked can be increased to around a mile at nine months, and to two miles at around a year or so. It is essential, if a dog is to fully develop, that some free running is also available, preferably once or twice daily for five or ten minutes at a time.

The exercise programme of the mature adult will depend on the individual, but somewhere between two and four miles brisk walking, and ten or fifteen minutes free running a day would not be unusual for a fit-looking, well-muscled show dog. Too much running is said to lead to heavy shoulders. Too little exercise may result in a dog of generous proportions, but this will be soft fat and not the required hard muscle.

TRAINING

In the UK most dogs share their owners' homes and are handled in the ring by their owners. To some extent, this makes training easier than in those countries where the professional handler is the norm. Five minutes can be spent two or three times a day in training the dog, or it can be done whenever the owner has some spare time. The professional handler's training cannot be done in this way, since the dog is often adult before the handler ever sees it, and it may live with the handler only for short periods during the show season. I will deal here only with the dog handled by its owner.

Before starting to train a Greyhound for the show ring, it is well worth reading and making sure that you understand the Breed Standard in order to have a picture in your mind of the ideal Greyhound. If you do not know what a Greyhound should look like, how can you possibly train it and show it off to its best advantage?

Informal training actually starts at a very early age when you should get your puppy used to being handled by playing with it. The more people who play with it and handle it, the better. If it enjoys playing with people it should never be nervous or aggressive in the ring. During this period tidbits, given from the hand, should ensure you do not have problems when it comes to the judge examining teeth later on. Once the puppy has been vaccinated it can go for very short walks for further socialisation, and this also helps it get used to traffic and all the other strange noises and objects in the big world outside. Do not over-exercise the young puppy. These first trips out are for socialisation only. It is essential that the dog is confident in strange situations if it is to be a successful show dog. However, before doing this it will be necessary to lead train the dog.

I have never found Greyhounds to be too difficult in this respect, and some have happily accepted a collar and lead with no training at all. The ones which object will usually be perfectly behaved with a little perseverance, and will usually be fine if they are walked next to a well-behaved adult dog which is used to the lead. It often helps to put a collar on for a few minutes at a time to let the dog get used to the feel of it, before attempting to attach the lead.

RING TRAINING

When the dog is accustomed to walking on the lead in a reasonable manner, training can begin in earnest. The Greyhound is not a difficult dog to train for the show ring, provided it is started early in life and not overdone. A few minutes at home in the garden each day, from around three or four months of age, is usually quite sufficient. Always try to make it enjoyable for the dog, giving praise whenever it does what is required, and not being too harsh when things do not go quite to plan.

Start by moving the dog around in a large anti-clockwise circle on a loose lead, trying to keep the head up and forward. A gentle hand under the chin will discourage sniffing along the ground. When the dog is used to doing the circuits without too much trouble, move on to more complicated patterns, such as triangles and straight lines up and back. The dog will quickly get the idea, particularly if praise is lavished whenever the exercise is correctly completed. Concentrate on getting the head up, but not too high like an Afghan, and making sure the dog is moving straight and not crabbing. Do not expect the perfectly sound, straight-through movement you would see in an adult – the dog's skeleton and muscle will not have developed sufficiently to achieve this. Never carry on until the puppy becomes bored or tired, or if you become bad-tempered when things are not going exactly to plan.

In between each circuit or triangle get your dog to stand in a show pose, at the same time giving the firm command "Stand". Gently place the feet where they should be to show the dog off to advantage, but never try to over-stretch a young puppy. Make sure the head is held fairly high. If the head and feet are in the correct place, everything else should naturally be in the right place. Assistance may be required at this stage, as it is not the easiest thing in the world to see just how the dog is standing when you are directly above, trying to place four feet where the dog does not want to put them, at the same time ensuring that the dog keeps its head off the ground!

Video cameras can help enormously in showing not only a dog's faults, but also how the handler may improve the look of the dog by the use of better handling techniques. Patience is definitely required before any measure of success or improvement is evident in this area. With luck, training and the correct, mature structure of the dog, this will eventually come right, although it may appear most unlikely for quite some time.

When the dog is confident standing, the next step is to get someone to go over the dog, looking and feeling all over the dog's anatomy, including the mouth. It is best if this is first done by people the dog knows and trusts. Once this has been achieved without too much fidgeting, then the dog should be gone over by other people it does not know.

TRAINING CLASSES
I have never found training classes to be particularly useful from a technical handling point of view, other than to socialise a dog and to get it used to being handled by strangers and meeting other dogs. Far too much time is spent waiting your turn, and too little on being handled or moved to derive great benefit. However, some people swear by the benefits of the training class, so it is all a matter of opinion. Whichever way you choose to train your dog, once you have mastered the basics, you are ready for you first show.

GROOMING
Being a short-coated breed, the Greyhound's grooming presents few problems. A daily brush with a hound-glove will remove dead hair and keep the coat in shining condition. A bath before the major shows, particularly for white dogs, is advisable. A few years ago it was normal to trim the long face whiskers, but this practice now seems to have disappeared without detriment to the look of the breed. The longer hairs on the back of the thighs and on the underline on the flanks and tuck-up are often trimmed to give a smoother outline. Some people trim the long hair on the underside of the tail, but I prefer the tail to have all the protection it can get in view of the frequency of injuries to this area.

Nails should be kept short by clipping about once every two weeks. Long nails not only look unsightly, but are prone to injury when the dog runs free. Show Greyhounds normally have dewclaws removed as young puppies. Teeth should be checked regularly to make sure they are clean and white. Canine toothpaste is now available for this purpose. Beef marrow bones, rawhide bones, and hard biscuits do some good in keeping teeth clean, but for some reason Greyhounds as a breed seem to build up tartar very quickly if it is not kept in check. My vet is of the opinion that this is caused by excessive acidity in the salivary fluids which the dogs produce.

SHOWING YOUR GREYHOUND

Unless you are very experienced and have an outstanding puppy, the best place to first show your dog is at a small local show and not at a major Championship show several hundred miles away from home. This gives both owner and dog a chance to make mistakes where it does not really matter and where people generally are not too concerned about winning, but are more intent on having an hour or two of fun. Even more important, it means the dog is not over-tired and away from its food and rest for too long. Greyhound puppies should not be overshown. Most are still growing until they are over a year old, and they will become bored with showing long before they reach their physical peak if they are over-exposed as youngsters.

Once the basics of handling have been mastered at small shows and the dog is mature enough to travel, it should be ready to graduate to the bigger show, where it will be competing against other

SHOW TRAINING
Demonstrated by Ian Bond and Windspiel Northern Pearl of Seeswift

The head should be held proudly; the topline should be arched slightly over the loin, and the underline neatly tucked up.

The Greyhound should be encouraged to stand with the front feet directly below the top of shoulders, and the legs, when viewed from the front, should be parallel.

The back feet should be positioned well back so that the dog covers a fair amount of ground.

When training your Greyhound for the show ring, start by encouraging your dog to move with a smooth, free-flowing action.

Greyhounds for the first time. It is from this point that the handler must make sure of getting the best out of the dog, both when moving and standing, by emphasising the points required in the Breed Standard. The perfect Greyhound has not yet been born, but clever handling can make some fairly average dogs look pretty good, just as bad handling can ruin a good dog's chances.

It should be remembered that the dog must have a smooth, free-flowing action, with long, low-reaching strides at the front and a powerful thrusting action from behind. The dog best achieves this at a steady controlled trot on a loose lead, at a pace at which the dog feels comfortable, neither pulling back or forward or to the side. Dogs which are strung up like terriers when they move, with their front feet barely touching the ground, will shorten their stride and look very choppy in front, not to mention struggling to get their heads down and almost choking in the process. Dogs which have not been encouraged to keep their heads off the ground may go round the ring like a Bloodhound following a scent, of which there are usually plenty at the show ground.

When standing the Greyhound the front feet should be placed in a line directly below the top of the shoulders, pointing straight forward, and the legs when viewed from the front should be parallel. The back feet should be positioned well back so that the dog covers a fair amount of ground, avoiding overstretching, which causes the topline to flatten and, if done to the extreme, to slope down to the croup in a long straight line. The topline should be arched slightly over the loin and the underline neatly tucked up. This is only possible if the dog stands naturally over lots of ground without being stretched out too much, when it will look more like a rocking horse than a Greyhound.

The head should be held proudly atop a slightly arched neck, and this may be achieved either by gently putting a hand under the chin or holding it up with the aid of the lead well up under the chin. Some handlers get the head up by using a little liver to attract the dog's attention. I hate to see dogs tightly held up by the end of the muzzle, as is practised by some handlers. It looks most unnatural and uncomfortable for the dog as well as hiding the face of the dog, which could well be one of its main attributes. Of course, if the handler is really lucky and the dog is well constructed and well trained, it may do all this quite naturally. The rest is entirely in the hands of the judge.

JUDGING
So what does the judge look for when judging the Greyhound? In a nutshell, he or she should be looking for the dog which most closely fits the Breed Standard, but this is an over-simplification, as many people will interpret the Standard in slightly different ways, putting different emphasis on different points, as mentioned earlier in the analysis of the Standard. Briefly, however, what all judges should be looking for when making a decision are: type, temperament, style, quality, and soundness.

TYPE
Of these, type is by far the most important. It is type which differentiates the dog as being unmistakably a Greyhound and nothing else. If a dog is not of the correct type it should not be considered for a major award. If a dog is totally lacking in type, it is not a true Greyhound. Quite

HANDLING FAULTS

This Greyhound is being strung up on the lead, which inhibits the dog from moving with a free-flowing stride.

The front feet have been placed too far apart, which ruins the smooth flowing line from shoulder to leg.

A typical 'rocking horse' position caused by over-stretching the Greyhound.

The hindlegs are too wide apart, which throws the whole body out of balance.

Practise makes perfect: This Greyhound has been trained to show off all its attributes in a stylish show pose.

The judge is looking for style, quality and soundness, and he assesses each Greyhound by how closely they conform to the Breed Standard.

simply, type means closely fitting the Standard in all aspects – fitting that picture which all judges must have in their minds of a well-balanced, upstanding dog of generous proportions, with beautiful, clean curved lines, well-muscled and free-moving, with a look of speed, power and elegance.

TEMPERAMENT

The Greyhound is a gentle dog and should show no sign of aggression or nervousness. Like most sighthounds, it may not be the most enthusiastic show dog and may be somewhat reserved with strangers; but poor temperament, particularly viciousness should be heavily penalised.

STYLE

Style is not easy to define, but if a dog is to go to the top he must have some style and showmanship. After all, we are talking about a show dog, and as such he must be prepared to show himself off a bit, if he expects to win.

QUALITY

Quality is the blend of all the requirements of type, style, soundness and temperament put together to produce a dog which is ideally fitted for the purpose to which we are putting it, namely the show ring. Quality is often used to mean fine as opposed to heavy and coarse, but this is not a definition with which I agree.

SOUNDNESS

Although important, this is not breed specific. Any dog, a mongrel or a pedigree, can be sound. It merely means that it possesses no structural malformations or injuries which prevent it from physically functioning correctly. A dog lacking breed type should never be put above a more typical example of the breed on soundness alone.

Chapter Fourteen

GENERAL HEALTH CARE

The Greyhound is a relatively easy breed to care for with its short coat and athletic physique. Inevitably, racing and coursing Greyhounds are exposed to the risk of suffering injuries, and the stress of being in training imposes strain on the metabolism which can result in stress-related problems. However, once the Greyhound has retired from racing, the owner will have little trouble keeping their dog in good condition, and most Greyhounds can look forward to a life expectancy of some twelve to fourteen years. Those who keep Greyhounds as show dogs will benefit from having a breed that has few inherited problems and needs very little grooming care to look its best.

In order to keep your Greyhound fit and healthy, it is important to adopt a regime of good diet and regular exercise, and to provide suitable draught-free accommodation. You will also need to adhere to a vaccination policy and follow a programme of parasite control.

FINDING A VET
It is important to establish a good relationship with your vet, so that you feel you have someone you can trust if your dog should become ill. If you own a racing dog, you will probably require the services of a vet who specialises in racing Greyhounds, with extensive knowledge of treating racing injuries. However, if you own a retired Greyhound, a vet who has a small animal practice will be perfectly suitable for treating the normal range of canine ailments. If you are lucky, you will find a vet who has some experience in treating Greyhounds – for there is no doubt that familiarity with a breed helps with both diagnosis and treatment.

ROUTINE CARE

TAKING YOUR DOG'S TEMPERATURE
If your Greyhound is off-colour, it may be useful to take a temperature reading in order to find out more about your dog's condition. You will need a round-ended thermometer, suitable for rectal insertion. You may find it helpful to have an assistant to hold your Greyhound steady when you take the temperature. The best procedure is to lubricate the end of the thermometer with a little Vaseline, and then insert it about two inches into the dog's rectum. Hold the dog steady and wait for two minutes before withdrawing the thermometer and taking a reading. The normal temperature for a dog is 101.5 degrees Fahrenheit (38.5 degrees Centigrade). You should inform your vet if the temperature shows a rise of two degrees Fahrenheit.

GIVING MEDICINES
The easiest way to administer liquid medicines is with a syringe. Your vet will supply you with

The Greyhound is a hardy animal, and regular exercise, a well-balanced diet, and attention to general health matters will ensure that your dog stays fit and well.

one, on request. When you have sucked up the correct dose of medicine by withdrawing the plunger, open your Greyhound's mouth and gently drip the medicine between the lips. Make sure the dog's head is tilted upwards and gently stroke the throat, encouraging the dog to swallow.

GIVING TABLETS

If you need to give your Greyhound a tablet, you must make sure you insert the pill well to the back of the tongue. If you get the pill to the side of the tongue, the dog will be able to work it forward and spit it out. Close the dog's mouth and hold it shut, stroking the throat until the dog swallows.

Most dogs cannot resist cheese, and if you wrap the tablet in a cheese 'sausage' you will usually find that the dog is only too happy to co-operate and will swallow the tablet down with the cheese treat.

VACCINATIONS

All dogs are vulnerable to a number of infectious diseases, and your dog will need regular vaccinations throughout its life in order to be protected from contracting the major known diseases. These include parvovirus, distemper, hepatitis, and leptospirosis. In the US vets give a DHLP vaccination, which includes parainflueunza. In most cases, a puppy will be vaccinated at about three months, with a second injection two weeks later. The vaccination programme may vary, depending on the incidence of disease in a particular locality. In the US, the parvo vaccine is given every six months.

Your puppy should not come into contact with other dogs until the vaccination programme has been completed, and you should not allow your puppy to sniff around areas where other dogs exercise until your dog has received complete protection. From then onwards your Greyhound will require an annual booster injection, and you should keep a record of all vaccinations, as boarding kennels will require this if you need to leave your dog at any time.

Most boarding kennels also stipulate that your dog should be vaccinated against kennel cough. This is rarely a killer disease, except where the particularly vulnerable are concerned, such as puppies and elderly dogs. In most cases antibiotic treatment is effective, but affected dogs should not mix with other dogs for at least six weeks. If you vaccinate your dog against kennel cough, a booster is usually required after six to nine months.

Depending on where you live, your dog may also need to be protected against rabies. In the US dogs must be vaccinated against rabies. Boosters can be given annually, or there is a vaccine which affords protection for three years.

ECTOPARASITES

These refer to parasites that live on the dog's skin.

THE FLEA

Regular grooming will reduce the incidence of flea infestation, but it is a problem that nearly all dog owners have to cope with at some time, particularly if your dog regularly comes into contact with other dogs. Warm weather aids the flea's life cycle, and so infestation is more likely to occur in the summer months, although central heating in houses tends to make this a year-round problem. It is hard to actually see fleas on your dog, but the fleas' droppings – which look like black grains of sand – are readily visible.

The flea lays its eggs on the dog's bedding or in carpets, so that it is essential to treat the furnishing at the same time as you treat your dog. An insecticidal bath will cure the problem, but it is useful to adopt a preventative policy and either spray your dog regularly with anti-parasitic aerosol, or ensure that your dog wears a flea collar at all times. However, in the US all flea collars are sold with a warning stating that they are not suitable for Greyhounds or Whippets because of their extreme sensitivity to the chemicals in them. There is a flea collar, made in France, which is specifically for Greyhounds, and this is marketed in the US. Another solution is to use two cat flea collars (ensuring that these fit a Greyhound's neck), as the chemicals are milder than in the dog flea collar.

TICKS
Dogs are likely to pick up ticks in areas where sheep or deer graze. The tick attaches itself to the dog by its head and feeds on the dog's blood. Eventually it becomes so engorged it may resemble a bean in size and shape. You must never attempt to pull the tick off, as the head will remain attached to the dog and could cause an abscess. The best policy is to drench the tick, using a piece of cotton-wool soaked in surgical spirit. The tick will then loosen its hold, and you can ease the head out of the dog's skin.

   Lyme Disease, associated with infection by the tick-borne spirochaete, Borrelia burgdorferi, is a growing problem in North America, although it is rare in the UK. Affected dogs may have a fever and enlarged lymph nodes, but the main clinical feature is lameness in one or more limbs. The lameness may occur weeks or even months after exposure to a tick. The condition must be treated with antibiotics, prescribed by a vet, and in most cases this has proved to be successful.

MANGE
DEMODECTIC
This condition is caused by a tiny mite, the demodex canis, which is too small to be seen without a microscope. The signs are hair loss, but the dog may not scratch. This starts in a localised form – with hair loss around the eyelids, the lips, the corners of the mouth and the front legs – and unless treated it may become generalised, spreading to all areas of the body. It is not contagious between dogs and cannot spread to man. Most dogs carry small numbers of demodex mites which they acquire as puppies when suckling. The dog's immune system usually stops the multiplication of the parasites. If the condition occurs it is usually in puppies and young adults. The treatment for localised demodectic mange is available from your vet, and is usually very effective. The treatment for generalised demodectic mange is prolonged and the response is much slower.

SARCOPTIC
This type of mange is highly contagious, either from direct contact with other dogs or from grooming equipment, as the parasite can survive off the host for two or three days. Dogs affected with sarcoptic mange will scratch excessively, often causing self-mutilation. Treatment is simple and effective, and your vet will prescribe an anti-parasitic shampoo or dip.

ENDOPARASITES
These refer to parasites that live within the dog's body.

ROUNDWORMS
Most puppies carry a burden of roundworms because they are born with larvae passed to them from their mother while in the uterus. By two weeks old, these have developed into mature worms, which will go on to lay eggs in the intestine. Responsible breeders will usually start a worming programme at an early stage, which can be when the puppies are two weeks old. There are

worming pastes available from the vet which are easy to administer. Treatments must be repeated on a regular basis during puppyhood, and then twice yearly as part of a routine worming programme. A puppy that is infested with worms will look pot-bellied and will appear out of condition with a dry, staring coat. The worms will appear in the motions, and in severe cases the puppy may vomit and you will see evidence of roundworms, which look like strands of spaghetti.

TAPEWORMS
The flea acts an intermediate host of the tapeworm: the flea swallows eggs passed from the dog, and if a dog inadvertently swallows a flea, the worm larvae will mature into adults in the dog's intestine. The tapeworm is segmented and can measure up to two feet in length. The head of the worm attaches itself to the wall of the intestine, and each segment of the body contains eggs. When these segments are excreted by the dog they look like small grains of rice and can be seen around the dog's anus.

A dog suffering from tapeworm infestation will lose condition very rapidly. Treatment is simple and effective, and it is wise to worm for tapeworm on a twice-yearly routine basis. It is also a good preventative measure to keep your Greyhound free from fleas.

HEARTWORM
This is a parasite of tropical and sub-tropical regions, and the mosquito is an intermediate host. It does not occur in Britain, but is of major importance in parts of the USA and Australia. The heartworm is a large worm, and is usually located in the right ventricle of the heart and adjacent blood vessels. A dog infested with heartworm will suffer from heartworm disease, and it is essential to follow a rigorous preventative programme if you live in an area where mosquitoes breed. Before starting a preventative programme, a blood sample from your dog must be analysed to make sure it is free from the disease. From then onwards, you must dose your dog with a tablet once a month for at least half a year in cool sections, and year-round in very warm or mosquito-infested areas.

HOOKWORM
Adult worms are found in the small intestine of the dog and produce eggs which are passed out with the stools. These microscopic eggs hatch larvae while on the ground, and so the majority are taken in by the mouth. Dogs exercised in grass runs are most frequently affected, and regular dosing plus strict adherence to hygiene is required.

WHIPWORM
This type of worm has the appearance of a stockwhip, and measures up to three inches in length. Infestation is most likely to occur in ground that has been contaminated by eggs. It is therefore more likely to occur in kennel dogs who are exercised in grass runs. A dog infested with whipworms will lose weight and will frequently suffer from diarrhoea. A number of preparations are available for treating dogs with whipworms. But hygiene in the grass runs – picking up stools at least twice daily – is an essential preventative measure.

CANINE AILMENTS AND CONDITIONS

ANAL GLANDS
The dog has two anal sacs located on either side of the anus. These are sometimes referred to as scent glands, and they are used for marking territory and as a means of individual recognition. The

glands usually empty themselves as a result of rectal pressure when the dog defecates. However, in some cases the glands become too full, and they will need to be emptied manually to avoid impactation. This simple procedure can be carried out by your vet. It is thought that lack of roughage can be a cause of this problem, and so a change in diet may alleviate the condition.

BAD BREATH

If your dog suffers from this anti-social problem, it may well be that the teeth are in need of attention. Regular cleaning of the teeth with a toothbrush and a canine toothpaste prevents the accumulation of tartar. If the teeth are very dirty, you may need to descale them with a tooth scaler. If you are worried about doing this, your vet will advise. In severe cases, the dog may be given a general anaesthetic in order that the teeth can be cleaned thoroughly.

Sometimes the teeth may appear to be clean, but bacteria causing bad breath can accumulate around the teeth/gum margins. In this case, it is advisable to swab the teeth/gum margins with a cotton-bud dipped in 50/50 hydrogen peroxide and water. This can be repeated daily for two or three days, and it will kill off the harmful bacteria that lead to bad breath. Dental health is aided by providing roughage in the diet, and by giving your dog a bone to chew on. This must always be a marrow bone, and should always be given when the dog is being supervised. Never give your dog cooked bones or poultry bones, which can splinter with disastrous results.

Bad breath may also be the result of a low-grade gut irritation, in which case the dog may also try to vomit itself. In this situation, you should ask the vet to give your dog a thorough check-up. Some Greyhounds are sensitive to red meat in their diet, and if you are feeding red meat, it may be worth changing to chicken or fish for a week or two, to see if this helps digestion.

BALDNESS

It is a fact that many Greyhounds suffer loss of hair over the thighs and tail area due to the stress of repeated racing. This is thought to be the result of a thyroid deficiency which prevents normal hair regrowth. In this case, the skin is usually shiny, and there is no evidence of fine hair on the skin. A course of thyroid tablets from the vet may help to stimulate hair growth. Hair loss can also be caused by the dog wearing the hair off on its bedding. In this instance, you will see some evidence of the hair attempting to regrow. Your best course of action is to change your dog's bedding – shredded paper has been found to be useful in correcting this condition.

CANKER

Ear mite infestation is usually the cause of an ear discharge, commonly referred to as canker. The first signs of this are the dog shaking its head, and the inside of the ear will appear red and inflamed. This will be followed by a dark, waxy discharge, which is often foul-smelling. The vet will prescribe a suitable treatment, and the condition usually clears up in a few days. The best preventative measure is to clean the ears on a regular basis, making sure that you do not probe too deeply into the ear canal.

COPROPHAGIA

The habit of eating stools sometimes occurs in dogs that have been kennelled. It can also be due to lack of fibre in the diet. Prevention is the best cure, and so it is important to 'clean up' after your dog, never leaving stools lying around. You can ask your vet to give your dog a course of Vitamin B12 injections, as it has been found that manure eating is connected with those dogs that cannot absorb B12 from their own bowels. Another 'cure' is to dose your dog with a substance which will make the stools unattractive. In the US a commercial product is available, which is sold in pet stores, and this can be mixed with your dog's food to discourage it from eating stools. Sprinkling Tabasco or a strong pepper on the stools will also discourage this unwanted behaviour.

DIARRHOEA

In most cases, diarrhoea is the result of a straightforward stomach upset. The best policy is to starve your Greyhound for twenty-four hours in order to give the stomach a chance to recover. It is important to ensure that your dog has access to a supply of fresh drinking water. When you start feeding your dog again, it is sensible to reduce the rations and to offer something which is easy to digest like boiled fish and rice, or cooked chicken and rice. Hopefully, this will cure the problem. However, if your dog continues to suffer from diarrhoea, you should ask your vet for advice. It may be that a course of antibiotics is needed. If at any time you detect blood in your dog's motions, you should contact your vet immediately.

GASTRIC TORSION (BLOAT)

This is one of the few emergency situations you may encounter, and it is essential to get your dog to the vet immediately. This condition can be fatal. It is caused by fermenting food and an accumulation of gas in the stomach. The stomach may twist (torsion), and if this happens, both the entrance and exit are blocked, preventing evacuation. Immediate surgery can save the dog's life, but the condition has been known to recur.

HEATSTROKE

The racing Greyhound may suffer from this condition following excessive exertion in race. But for most pet owners, it is far more likely to occur if a dog is confined in an enclosed space, such as a car, with limited ventilation. In this situation the temperature builds up to an excessive degree in a very short space of time, so no dog should ever be left in a car, even on a moderately warm day.

   If your Greyhound should suffer from heatstroke, the immediate first aid measure is to bring the temperature down as quickly as possible. This can be done by immersing the dog in cold water, spraying the dog with water from a hose, or packing frozen foods round the dog. Unless the temperature can be reduced rapidly, the result can be fatal.

ANAESTHESIA PROBLEMS

All anaesthesia, whether for dogs or for humans, caries some risk. However, Greyhounds are particularly sensitive to anaesthesia, and you must ensure that your vet is aware of this before you agree to its use. The reason for this is that a Greyhound's liver metabolises drugs more slowly than is the case in other breeds of dog. Another factor is the Greyhound's low percentage of body fat proportionate to its size. On average, Greyhounds have sixteen per cent bodyweight of fat, compared with thirty-five per cent bodyweight of fat in mixed breed dogs of similar weight.

   This does not mean that you should avoid the use of anaesthetics, if required. But there are some types which are more suitable for the Greyhound. Discuss this with your vet, and you can then be confident that the risk involved is minimised.

Chapter Fifteen

TREATING RACING INJURIES

The racing Greyhound is prone to a number of common injuries and problems. Whilst the majority are a result of the physical stress of fast, high-intensity exercise and repeated racing, in some cases the risk is increased by lack of an adequate and balanced diet or poor preparation and conditioning for racing. These common problems can be classified into three main groups.

1. Musculo-skeletal stress injuries.
2. Nutritional imbalances/inadequacies.
3. Problems of metabolic origin.

Although performance standards have not increased significantly over the past two decades, there is now much more stress associated with competition and racing on a regular basis, especially in large commercial kennels. By far the most common problems are related to stress and strain on the musculo-skeletal system, accounting for up to 85 per cent of downtime from racing.

MUSCULO-SKELETAL INJURIES

Most racing Greyhounds suffer some type of muscle injury or damage during their racing career. In fact, it is common for Greyhounds to sustain minor 'wear and tear' injuries every time they gallop. Muscle injuries are the most common cause, not only of lost training days, but more significantly, of reduced opportunity to compete for prize money in racing Greyhounds.

Although many trainers are skilled in recognising the more serious types of injuries that cause lameness and pain, the lower grade injuries often go unnoticed. However, even mild injuries cause a subtle change in efficiency of the gallop, and hence the Greyhound's ultimate performance. If not detected, minor injuries can be aggravated by galloping and result in more serious and long-term injuries to muscles and bony structures.

PREDISPOSING CAUSES

Greyhounds have a high power to weight ratio, and when galloping exert tremendous pressure on their muscles, bones and joints, which is increased by the centrifugal forces of cornering on a circle track. Greyhounds can rapidly accelerate from a virtual standing start, often without an adequate warm-up prior to a race. The overall incidence of muscle-related problems, including tears, strains and rupture, as well as cramping, are influenced by the fitness of the Greyhound for the distance of the race, the age and bodyweight of the animal, and the ambient temperature at the time of the race.

Accelerating into the first bend of a circle track at speed increases the stress forces on the muscles and bones. Centrifugal forces (or 'G' forces) are increased as the Greyhound leans into the corner at speed, greatly magnifying the stress load on bones, tendons, and toes. The high cornering stress loads are the underlying cause of metacarpal (shin) soreness in young Greyhounds whose bones have not had sufficient time, or step-wise increases in speed to adapt their metacarpal bones to the increased loading forces. In older, heavier male dogs running on tight, heavily banked corners, a syndrome termed radial stress fracture of the forearm bone, with fatigue-like cracks into the bone surface at a particular point down the inside of the radius bone of the right leg, has been recently documented. Relative risk of these types of injury is directly related to the degree of banking on the curves or crossfall on the track, the type of track surface, the individual animal's speed and the length of the initial straight for the animals to attain their maximum speed.

Most of the knocks, collisions and strain of altering direction at speed occur on the first bend, when Greyhounds are cornering in a group. In the later stages of a race, when the Greyhounds are spaced out more, the risk of interference is reduced. Other factors such as too much bodyweight, particularly in larger male Greyhounds, inadequate fitness and poor conformation in the front legs in particular, can cause a Greyhound to throw a leg resulting in imbalance of the gallop or the risk of knocking itself when racing. Sudden overload or strain of muscles can result in tearing of the muscle itself, or in serious cases detachment of the muscle from its anchorage points on bone. Down time from racing must be avoided, as ideally Greyhounds should race as often as possible when conditioned and fit for racing.

GRADING OF MUSCLE INJURIES
Muscle injuries can be categorised into four basic types. The major classes of muscle injury, graded on severity, are summarised in the table below.

TYPES OF MUSCLE INJURY

TYPE	SIGNS	DETECTION	TREATMENT	MANAGEMENT
1	SORENESS & STIFFNESS Minor reduction in form. Obvious signs of soreness may not be exhibited even on examination.	Careful examination of individual muscles by an experienced person or a veterinary surgeon will detect small changes in muscle consistency and feel. Hard to detect immediately after racing - examine once dog has cooled down.	Early detection and treatment is absolutely essential to avoid more serious muscle damage if dogs are allowed to race. Every dog should be examined after racing. Physiotherapy, by deep seated massage with MR Iodised Oil twice daily for 3-5 days will stimulate the blood supply and help healing. Twice daily application of warm fomentations, or pulsed hydrotherapy, and magnetic field therapy may be beneficial. Ultrasonic therapy, 0.5-1.0 watt/sp.cm. for 3-4 mins twice daily for 3-5 days aids muscle healing. Consult a veterinary surgeon for advice.	Reduce exercise to walking only for 3-4 days. Do not allow to gallop on track. Walking machines are helpful in providing graded controlled exercise. Exercise at speeds of up to 15-20 km/hr. Free galloping over 300-400 metres (straight track or even field surface) is also helpful after 3-4 days initial treatment to aid muscle repair and return to strength. Do **not** use pain-killing drugs if free galloping is given as they may mask symptoms and risk more serious muscle damage. Consult a veterinary surgeon for further advice.
2	PAIN, HEAT, CORDING AND SWELLING OF MUSCLE AREA. Usually some reduction in form.	External pressure on examination of injured area will normally cause obvious discomfort, particularly the day following the initial injury. Swelling and heat will also be more easily detected.		
3	PAIN, SWELLING, HAEMORRHAGE AND RUPTURE OF SOME MUSCLE FIBRES. TEAR IN MUSCLE SHEATH. Reduction in form, discomfort and lameness when cooled down	Localised areas of swelling and heat are apparent on external palpation within a few hours with painful reaction. Severely damaged areas will have a squelchy texture (haemorrhage) and a loss of muscle tone.	**First Aid:** Apply cold packs to injured area. Treatment under supervision of a veterinary surgeon is necessary, as the damage is serious and more sophisticated medications are required.	Rest with graded walking exercise as advised by veterinary surgeon. Do not use ultrasound therapy where haemorrhage is suspected. Once healing has commenced and swelling decreases, exercise can commence. Surgical repair of split muscle sheath will help speed up healing and reduce recurrence of injury. Consult a veterinary surgeon for further advice.
4	PAIN, SWELLING, HAEMORRHAGE, RUPTURE OF MULTIPLE FIBRES, LARGE TEARS, DROPPED (TORN AWAY) MUSCLES.	Careful and thorough examination will reveal squelchy (haemorrhage) areas, tears in the muscle sheath, and gaps in the muscle fibres. Pain and swelling will develop after a few hours. Muscles may be torn ("dropped") from their normal location.	**First Aid:** Do not allow dog to walk. Apply cold packs to injured area(s). Strap the muscle back in place where possible. Prompt treatment by a veterinary surgeon is absolutely essential.	Surgical repair of torn or severely damaged muscles may be necessary. Physiotherapy and controlled exercise at appropriate times, and exercise as directed by a veterinary surgeon will aid repair. Usually 1-2 months recovery time is necessary.

When racing, Greyhounds lean towards the running rail as they corner. With the lower limbs and joints subjected to centrifugal, gravitational and frictional forces, there is an increasing risk of sprains and strains of these structures at each footfall.

If a Greyhound has sustained a relatively minor injury, and continues to race without recognition of the injury or treatment, then more serious types of muscle injury can develop. However, most of the more serious types of muscle injury are due to accidental falls or over-exertion, particularly in a keen chaser accelerating rapidly in an attempt to make up lost ground from a check or fall.

Although the relative degree or severity of muscle injuries can be roughly classified, it must be realised that more than one type of injury may be present at one time. Not all injuries – even the more severe ones – are detectable by signs of discomfort or lameness immediately after a race. However, careful observation of the way the Greyhound gallops, negotiates corners, or finishes in the home straight during a race, combined with replay of a race video or even timing a Greyhound over each sectional division in a race, will often help the trainer or vet pinpoint the type and likely location of a muscle injury.

If the initial examination after the race cannot detect sore spots in the major muscle groups, or a change in consistency in the individual muscles, then the Greyhound should be thoroughly checked again on the morning after a race. In most cases, a check by a vet at trackside, when a Greyhound is hot and still excited after a race, may fail to detect soreness or even more serious injuries, including haemorrhage within a torn muscle. In these cases, it takes from three to eight hours for the muscles to bleed internally, or to develop sufficient inflammation, pain and bruising to be detected. Only the more severe forms – where a separation occurs within a muscle, or when a muscle tears from its anchorage point, to become a 'dropped muscle' – will be detected.

Any Greyhound that shows a loss in performance in a race, caused by a noticeable change in direction or speed, or is interfered with during a race, should be thoroughly examined after the race. Certain characteristic changes in gait, or the way the Greyhound tracks around the corner, will give vital clues as to where the Greyhound could be injured. For instance, if a good railing Greyhound starts to run wide when cornering, then the animal should be examined in the upper-right hindlimb hip support area, and also in the spare rib area for soreness due to injury.

Certain 'stress pathways' of the front and back limbs on each side are the areas that are most commonly affected in most Greyhounds. These include the deltoid and triceps group on the front leg, and the whip and vastus area of the hip support area of the left hind, which are the major sore spots in straight line deviations. The stress pathways in the right side shoulder and right hind leg should be checked in a Greyhound that runs wide on the bends. Male dogs with a retained testicle should also be examined for soreness in the testicle canal area in this case. It is important to be particularly observant for changes in the way the Greyhound jumps from the traps, enters and leaves the first bend, gallops up the straights, and pulls up at the end of the race.

MUSCLE AND LIMB EXAMINATION

Greyhounds are easy animals to examine for race injuries. They have little hair and subcutaneous fat when in racing condition, and their muscles are usually well-developed. The animal, however, must be adequately restrained, with a muzzle in place, to stop it biting or pulling away. Generally, Greyhounds do not bite unless aggravated to fight with other dogs, or excessive squeezing of sore areas during examination causing discomfort.

It is important to use a set examination routine to check a Greyhound. Simple checking routine involves carefully feeling along, or palpating the length of each muscle, using the thumb and forefinger. There is no need to press excessively hard as this may cause further bruising and pain. Sufficient pressure can be gauged when blood colouring appears under the fingernail when pressed over the muscle. It is best to feel for thickening, swellings and gaps, as well as knotty, hard or spongy areas, in muscles. These changes can indicate bruising, cramps or strains, or blood-vessel rupture in and around a damaged muscle. It is important to press more firmly on the anchorage points of the major muscles to test for pain reaction.

Most Greyhounds show pain by responses such as yelping, moving the eyes, growling, apprehensive looks, limb withdrawal, or curling or quivering the lips. It is not necessary to cause sufficient discomfort to result in a 'yelp' reaction. A gentle feel of each muscle is more useful in detecting minor injuries. It is important to watch the animal's expression while the muscle groups

A veterinary surgeon should carry out regular muscle checks on a Greyhound after racing in order to locate minor injuries before they develop into serious injuries.

are being checked. Although severe pain normally causes a yelp, or an attempt to bite or pull away, it may not always be a sign that a muscle is injured, as some Greyhounds will yelp from pressure on nerve areas or if the general checking technique is rough or the animal is frightened.

Generally, the checking is best carried out with the Greyhound standing on a raised platform, although some prefer to lay the Greyhound in a relaxed position on its side with the left side uppermost initially. However, Greyhounds are not bearing weight on the limbs when lying down, and tensing of muscles is often less obvious than when a Greyhound is standing and bearing weight. Alternatively, standing the Greyhound on a stepped raised platform helps keep more tension on the hind limb muscles and this may make it convenient and more likely to elicit a response to a sore area when being checked.

Often more than one area of soreness can be detected in a muscle check. It is a good idea to mark the spots as they are found to enable these to be treated by massage or other treatment, after the checking procedure has been finished. Not only should the upper main muscles of the limbs be checked, but also the limbs themselves should be thoroughly examined on both the fore and hindlegs. Each joint should be flexed and pressed, and each toe joint manipulated for signs of soreness and any evidence of sideways movement compared with the adjacent toes.

The toes of Greyhounds are prone to injury when racing on grass, or uneven track surfaces, where the grip from stride to stride can change. This increases the risk of deviating the toes excessively or spreading them out so as to tear the webbing during acceleration or cornering. The incidence of toe injuries on grass tracks is higher than on sand tracks, as the toe nail can be snagged in the turf surface at the completion of each stride. Therefore, in Greyhounds racing on grassed surfaces, the toenails should be kept as short as possible so that they do not touch the ground when the Greyhound is standing on a flat surface. This is contrary to a sand track surface, where it is better to have the toenails slightly longer for improved traction during acceleration and cornering.

The foot pads and webbing should be checked for cuts, lacerations or torn areas. Unfortunately, some synthetic grass tracks lacerate the webbing area when the track surface is dry. This can be overcome by dampening the surface prior to galloping. On sand tracks, the coronary band area at the toenail-skin junction (cuticle) can become packed with sand, particularly in Greyhounds with white toes on the back limbs. The cuticles should be checked for signs of inflammation and embedded sand after each gallop, particularly on the outside toes of the left hind limb.

Once the muscles on each side have been carefully examined, the limbs should be flexed forward and backward to check for any restriction in the limb movement, or tensioning of the limb due to pain in an injured leg. After checking all the muscles, it is best to stand directly behind the Greyhound and check for the symmetry on each side. This is very important, as swelling on one side of a hind limb can be easily seen by checking the line of symmetry from the midline to the top of the back. It is also a good idea to compare the bodyline of the forelegs in a similar way, by standing in front of the animal. A change in contour on either side of the inside of the hind limbs could indicate a torn away or 'dropped' muscle.

In many cases, the Greyhound may not necessarily be lame after a race as haemorrhage and inflammation around the torn muscle can take from twelve to twenty-four hours to develop. A follow-up examination the day after a hard race is advised, particularly in a Greyhound that failed to perform or deviated to one side when galloping.

FIRST-AID
It is most important to apply appropriate first aid to muscle injuries. In the more serious forms of injury, particularly where haemorrhage of the torn muscles is present, quick and expert first-aid to

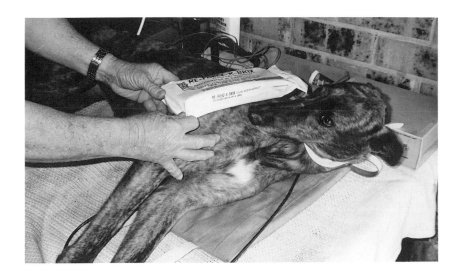

Prompt application of an ice-pack immediately after racing is an important first-aid measure following a track fall, or a tear in a major muscle group.

stem the seepage of blood will enhance repair and healing. In most cases, simple first-aid, such as application of a cold pack on to a limb or the body under a pressure bandage, will help minimise the minor bruising and inflammation that develops in strained or injured muscles.

The healing rate and long-term outcome for many muscle injuries is improved when a cold pack is applied following falls, bruising, muscle tears, sprains of joints or strains of ligaments and tendons. Cold and pressure help to confine the injury, constrict broken blood vessels, control swelling and inflammation and comfort the pain of injury. The benefit of cold therapy as an initial first-aid measure for treating musculo-skeletal injuries cannot be over-emphasised.

Cold therapy should be applied for about three minutes on the limbs, and for up to seven minutes on the body areas over major muscle groups. Cold therapy, ideally, should be applied for these short times on a frequent basis, rather than for extended times. Prolonged ice cooling of tissue can cause 'frost bite' type skin damage, and further discomfort to the animal. It is best to apply cold therapy at regular intervals of four to six hours during the twenty-four to forty-eight hour period following a severe muscle injury in order to stem blood seepage, control swelling, and minimise pain and discomfort. It is unwise to massage or ultrasound an area of muscle injury during the first forty-eight hours until the risk of internal bleeding has been eliminated. This should give sufficient time for the damaged blood vessels to heal, and the cold therapy to reduce swelling and pain.

TREATMENT OF INJURIES
Following the application of appropriate first-aid, various forms of physiotherapy can be used to aid repair of injured muscle tissue. The specific applications and comparative benefits of physiotherapy alternatives are summarised in the table on page 198.

Rest is also an important factor in the treatment of more severe muscle injuries in racing Greyhounds. An adequate period for healing should be allowed, depending on the seriousness of an injury and the advice given by a veterinary surgeon. A stepwise programme of initial walking and short handslips to reintroduce the Greyhound to galloping will help rehabilitate the animal back to the racetrack. Physiotherapy and controlled exercise will help in recovery from muscle wastage and loss of fitness.

FIRST AID – PHYSIOTHERAPY

In cases of minor muscle and ligament injuries, physiotherapy to increase blood flow and tissue healing can be started within 6–12 hours. In more serious injuries involving tearing and swelling, apply cold therapy for the initial 24–48 hours, then follow up with warming treatments and physiotherapy.

	Mode of Action	Benefits	Method of Use	Types of Injury	Risks
FINGER MASSAGE	Helps increase blood flow to injured area, warms skin and tissue, relaxes muscle spasms, increases muscle pliability.	Increases circulation by light pressure and warmth of massage friction.	Use lubricating medium such as paraffin oil, or MR Iodised Oil for added warming effect. Use a gentle circular action, 5-10 minutes twice daily.	Sprains of joints. Strains of ligaments. Minor muscle sprains. Soreness after racing. Cramping.	Do not massage over fresh bruises or tears, abscesses or infected areas. Do not use a pain killing liniment unless supervised by your vet.
VIBRATOR MASSAGE	As above.	As above. Saves time over hand massage.	Use lubricating oils. Start on low setting. Use gentle massaging action, 3-5 minutes twice daily.	Suitable for body muscle areas.	Lack of "feel" when massaging. Some animals resist vibrator initially. Do not vibrate over joints. May cause reddening of skin - discontinue.
HYDROBATH MASSAGE	Pulsed jets of water. As above.	Warming and relaxing tissues. Helps remove soreness after galloping.	Use only luke-warm water and hydrobath salts etc. Limit to 5-7 minutes twice daily.	General muscle injuries and relaxation after hard racing. Useful follow-up to massage and ultrasound therapy.	Do not hydrobath under hot humid, poorly ventilated conditions. Avoid hydrobathing within 24 hours prior to racing. Do not use strong smelling liniments. Do not use on animals with moist skin disease.
ULTRASONIC THERAPY	High frequency sound waves penetrate tissue up to 30mm, with mechanical vibration, warming and relaxing effect. Deep heating effect.	Most popular form of general therapy. Helps reduce adhesions and scar tissue. Use of oily liniments such as MR Iodised Oil reduces therapy time by 50%	Do not ultrasound over bony areas. Use low power 0.5-1.0 watts/sq.cm for 3-5 minutes twice daily. Use coupling mediums-Vetsearch Ultrasound gel, or MR Iodised Oil.	Keep machine head on tissue at all times, moving continuously. Do not ultrasound over or near to spinal column.	Do not use lanolin based oils or creams as a coupling. Do not apply within 72-96 hours of severe muscle injury - apply COLD therapy for initial 48 hours.
MUSCLE CONTRACTOR	Supplies low voltage electrical impulse to contract muscle. Regulate impulses to give controlled muscle contraction.	Makes muscle contract without load - helps strengthen weakened muscle.	Apply electrode pads over area and increase power until muscle group contracts. 10-15 contractions per session adequate.	Ideal for limb injuries involving muscle wastage to enhance strength and rebuilding. Can be used to diagnose muscle injuries.	Must start on low settings to accustom animal to forceful contractions. Discontinue if animal objects to therapy.
MAGNETIC FIELD THERAPY	The strength of the magnetic field and pulse rate have possible effects in increasing blood flow, rate of healing of muscle and bones.	Reduces swellings, discomfort of bone and joint injuries. Medium pulse settings beneficial to warm up greyhounds prior to racing without tiring muscles.	<u>Low Pulse</u> (2-6 pulses/sec) -reduces minor discomfort, restricts bleeding and swelling. First aid "cooling" like application. <u>Medium Pulse</u> (10-15 pulses/sec) - reduces pain, increases circulation and relaxes muscle. <u>High Pulse</u> (20-50 pulses/sec) -used to enhance bone healing in toes, shins and other fractures.	Popular for bone fracture repair and deep muscle injuries where other therapy not beneficial. Long treatment times of 15-30 minutes twice daily must be applied regularly over 2-3 weeks for best results.	Do not apply in presence of acute infection. Do not use in pregnant bitches. Do not apply high pulse settings to newly bruised or injured tissue.
LASER THERAPY	Various types of "cold" and "low power" lasers. May act by increasing blood vessel numbers and size and repair tissue. May be used to stimulate acupuncture points for pain reduction.	Increase tissue metabolism and healing. Save time on acupuncture needle treatments - 10-20 secs per point instead of 20 minutes.	632nm short wavelength machines for surface injuries. 904nm long wavelength machines for deep injuries and pain relief.	<u>Tendon injuries and wounds.</u> 5mw output for 5-10mins twice daily. <u>Deep muscle tears. Painful muscle injuries.</u> 5mw output for 4-5mins twice daily.	Do not look into beam exit window. Do not use over broken skin, in conjunction with liniments, or very hairy skin areas. Consult manual prior to use.
ACUPUNCTURE	Considered to stimulate release of chemical activating substances to relieve pain and increase healing.	Has been used for bone, tendon and many internal conditions.	Specific "formulae" developed for a wide variety of injuries. 10-20 minutes each treatment - time consuming.	Shoulder muscles, spinal problems, sprung toes, wounds, muscle wastage.	Experience needed to locate acupuncture points. Clean sterile needles - experienced operator only.
MICROWAVE	Microtizing therapy has a heating action on tissue to increase circulation and metabolism/healing.	Benefit for general muscle soreness or focused onto particular area.	Power settings of 70mw for 5-7 minutes once daily.	Back and cramping soreness, toes and wrists.	Risk of surface burns, overheating of tissue. Do not use over limb bones.
CHIROPRACTIC MANIPULATIONS	Relax muscles and realign spinal column?	Provides pain relief and reduces spasms, nerve pinching?	Skilled manipulation of relaxed greyhound - often under anaesthetic - consult your vet.	Chronic back and bone related problems.	Inexperienced operators may cause greater injury. Chronic injuries often recur in 4-6 weeks.

MINIMISING MUSCLE INJURIES

The risk of musculo-skeletal injuries in racing Greyhounds can be minimised by adopting the following management procedures.

1. Feed a well-balanced diet containing essential vitamins, minerals, and particularly adequate calcium, on high meat-based diets.
2. Check the Greyhound before and after each trial or race for sore spots. It is essential to detect minor injuries early, before more serious injuries develop in a trial or race. If in doubt, consult a veterinary surgeon for advice.
3. Warm up the Greyhound by walking or jogging for two to three minutes, or massaging the shoulder, back and hind limbs prior to racing.
4. Ensure a dog is healthy, fit and prepared for the distance. This includes adequate preparation by walking and jogging to build up strength and tone in the muscles, prior to galloping. It also includes a regular programme of galloping work once a Greyhound is conditioned. Most Greyhounds will maintain their fitness and keenness by racing at least once a week.

BONE STRESS SYNDROMES

Although muscle strains, tears and ruptures are the major form of musculo-skeletal injury in racing Greyhounds, bone stress syndromes and joint sprains develop as a result of concussion on hard tracks, shear forces of galloping around corners, and acceleration and braking stress on the skeletal structure. Bone stress syndromes include metacarpal soreness (often called shin soreness) in fast, young, immature Greyhounds that are raced on tight end circle tracks.

Depending on the training programme, the type of surface cushion, and the circle radius and crossfall or banking on the corners of the trial or racetrack, stress fractures of the outside two metacarpal (shin) bones of the left foreleg and inside two bones of the right foreleg can develop as early as sixteen months of age in pups during their introduction to lure circle track racing. The highest incidence occurs between sixteen and twenty-two months, once the young animal starts regular racing.

Low-level metacarpal stress can be slight inflammation of the bone (periosteal) surface tissue cover, which results in the young animal shortening in stride and losing speed on approach to corners, with lifting of the head and tail. More severe forms can develop as microfractures in the surface of the bones, with extreme lameness and discomfort when the thumb and forefinger are run down the top surface of the metacarpal bones (shin bones). With repeated racing, ridges or thickenings develop on the 'railing' metacarpals as they remodel to withstand the stress of galloping on circle tracks. Acute overload on an already stressed bone often results in fracture, and extreme lameness.

Other relatively common injuries prevalent on certain tracks include

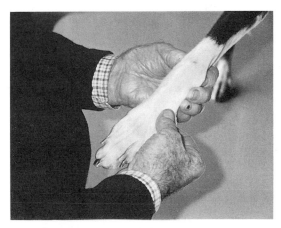

Young puppies galloping around circle tracks often develop soreness over the metacarpal (shin) bones on the two inside toes, closest to the rail, on both front limbs.

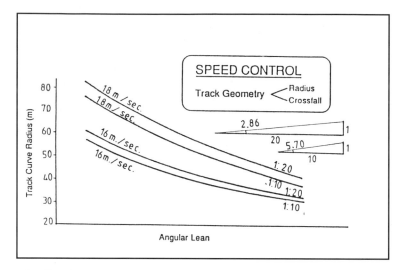

This graph illustrates the speed potential in relation to angular lean and track curve radius on banked tracks.

Courtesy of B. Ireland, 1989.

Ideally, the track geometry should match crossfall, or banking slope on the turns, to the end circle radius in a smooth transition to enable a Greyhound to maintain maximum speed with minimal centrifugal stress forces. The galloping Greyhound will naturally lean towards the rail when cornering, and ideally the angle of lean to the track slope should remain almost perpendicular for maximum speed. However, in practice a compromise between crossfall and radius – to minimise surface material wash-down and drift movement down the slope as Greyhounds gallop – is often necessary to reduce track maintenance procedures.

dislocation ('popping') or fracture of the central tarsal bone in the hock, and collateral ligament injuries in the toes (sprung toes). Indeed, individual tracks have a high incidence of specific types of musculo-skeletal injuries, which are related to geometry and surface conditions. One example is the development of fatigue stress microfractures (called radial stress fractures) on the inside of the radius, or forearm bone, on the right front limb in older, heavier male Greyhounds racing on highly-banked circle tracks.

Affected Greyhounds exhibit signs of lameness in the right forelimb for two to three days after four or five successive races on a particularly highly cambered track, with a small radius and short acceleration distance to the first corner. It is considered that the mature bone in older Greyhounds cannot bend or flex as much when subjected to high 'G' force stress on highly cambered tracks, resulting in metal-fatigue-like microfractures, about one-third of the way down the inside of the right forearm area. Diagnosis can be confirmed by radiograph (X-rays) in more severe cases, although nuclear medicine bone scanning techniques have been used to locate the stress fracture area.

METABOLIC PROBLEMS

Problems of metabolic origin often result from the extreme stress of sprint racing or excitable behaviour in many Greyhounds, when racing on a repeated basis.

The skin pinch test is a simple method of assessing the degree of dehydration during hot weather, or following transport, in excitable Greyhounds.

DEHYDRATION

Dehydration, or loss of water from blood and tissue fluids, is a common problem in the racing Greyhound. Dehydration can be caused by insufficient water intake, lengthy periods of panting, excessive barking, eating large amounts of dry food, and gut problems such as diarrhoea. Electrolyte imbalances, particularly due to the excessive loss of potassium salt in 'hard walking', nervous types of Greyhounds, also leads to dehydration, and a high risk of cramping.

Signs of dehydration are well known to most Greyhound owners. They include a rough, dull coat, tucking up in the belly, a dried out appearance, and reduced elasticity of the skin. When pinched up along the back line the skin returns slowly over two to three seconds. Loss of bodyweight, and the passing of small amounts of dark concentrated urine is a sign of more chronic dehydration, usually associated with extreme stress or very hot weather. Blood tests will show increased packed cell volume (PCV) and plasma protein concentration.

There are commonly two forms of dehydration seen in the racing Greyhound – simple and chronic.

SIMPLE DEHYDRATION

Because dogs are unable to sweat to lose heat, their main heat-loss mechanism is by panting. Panting creates airflow in and out of the respiratory tract, with evaporation of water vapour from the respiratory tract. During this air exchange, the cool, inhaled air and the heat transfer by evaporation of moisture cool the blood. Panting results in a net loss of fluid from the body, which in turn increases the electrolyte or body salt concentration in the blood. This stimulates the thirst response and the animal seeks and drinks water. A panting Greyhound will normally drink every thirty to sixty minutes during hot weather to replace fluids lost by panting, if water is available. Greyhounds are often thirsty after a race, and they should be given immediate access to water to replenish their fluid loss and cool themselves. It is most important to provide Greyhounds with an adequate supply of cool clean water at all times.

Although it is common practice in many countries to withdraw water from Greyhounds for six hours leading up to a race, it is unwise to do this during hot, humid weather or when a Greyhound is prone to dehydration prior to racing. Excitable, nervous, Greyhounds that pant and bark during

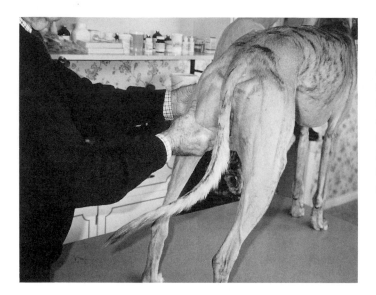

Minor cramping of the major driving muscles on the left hind limb is a common cause of reduced performance in the final stages of a race.

travelling and while waiting in the kennels prior to racing, often benefit from fluid replenishment immediately prior to race kennelling. Volumes of 1/2 to 1 cupful of electrolyte rehydration drink after travelling, just prior to kennelling, will assist in replacing fluids and electrolytes lost during hot weather, or when panting during the journey to the racetrack.

CHRONIC DEHYDRATION

Many Greyhounds become chronically dehydrated, particularly during hot weather or when raced on a regular basis. The actual mechanism by which chronic dehydration develops is not fully understood. However, Greyhounds that are excitable, 'hard walking', and those that bark a lot in kennels – particularly in the race kennels whilst waiting to race – are more likely to develop a complex form of dehydration.

It is thought that barking and panting Greyhounds pant more forcibly, losing water vapour from the lungs in heat exchange, with forced exhalation of carbon dioxide. This in turn is thought to increase electrolyte excretion by the kidneys to maintain ionic balance within the blood. Greyhounds therefore lose both water from panting, and electrolytes from the kidneys, but the thirst response is not triggered. Because the Greyhound does not feel thirsty, it declines a drink to replace fluid, even when dehydrated. Chronically dehydrated Greyhounds often do not drink much water even during hot weather, despite it being freely available. Many of these Greyhounds also pass darker, more concentrated urine, increasing the risk of urinary tract problems.

The desire to drink can be improved by adding body salt mixtures to the diet (preferably with a low sodium chloride content but a higher potassium content which suits the specific needs of dogs) to replace electrolytes lost during exercise, particularly in panting, 'hard walking' nervous types of Greyhounds. Studies indicate that this type of Greyhound cannot conserve potassium adequately, and this is aggravated by adding extra salt (sodium chloride) on top of that contained in a normal amount of dry food. The preferred form of potassium supplement is a slow release, coated tablet which gives sustained release of potassium for absorption from the small bowel. If electrolytes are not replaced in the feed the normal thirst response will not be stimulated as efficiently.

The Greyhound will remain dehydrated, especially if it is already in a chronic state of dehydration that has developed due to hot weather, excitement, or repeated racing. Extra fluid can be added to the diet by soaking all dry foods in water for fifteen to twenty minutes prior to feeding, so as to retain their form with a soft moist consistency. In chronically dehydrated Greyhounds, a supplement of electrolytes and up to 60-90 grams of fat such as lard, suet or fresh meat trimming fat, is recommended. It is also useful to add a flavouring to water to tempt the animal to drink. A small amount of honey, or soup mix, can be added to the water to flavour it and increase acceptance.

TRAINING

In cases where Greyhounds are nervous and described as 'hard walking', it is wise to reduce the amount of walking to five to seven minutes twice daily. It is preferable to exercise in the cool of the early morning or evening, and ensure that these animals receive adequate fluids and electrolytes in their diets. Excessive distances of road or lead walking perpetuates the problem, tires the Greyhound, and can cause a Greyhound to 'train off' more quickly. Greyhounds are best kept fresh by providing regular short gallops and handslips, and racing on a regular basis.

DEHYDRATION AND HOUSING

It is important to provide well-ventilated kennels during hot weather. Adequate cool airflow, as provided with a high ventilated roof structure or insulation, is useful in hot weather or warmer countries. As Greyhounds rely primarily on panting to cool themselves, with a small loss of heat from the skin, the efficiency of heat exchange is decreased in hot humid environments. Evaporative-type air conditioners generally increase humidity during hot weather and can reduce the cooling efficiency of a panting Greyhound. Therefore, refrigerated air conditioners are preferred during the hotter part of the day, but should be switched off in the cool of the night to prevent excessive drying out of the respiratory tract by dehumidifying the air, which can increase the risk of respiratory complications.

CRAMPING

Cramping of the major back and upper hind limb muscles is a relatively common problem in the racing Greyhound. Cramping affects excitable, dehydrated, unfit Greyhounds that are not warmed up adequately or prepared for the distance or speed of a race. Certainly, Greyhounds that are fit to race are less prone to cramping. The underlying metabolic changes that occur during the onset of cramping are not fully understood. However, while rapid muscle activity will accumulate acids in the muscles and cause fatigue and soreness, cramping itself may not always be related to an increase in lactic acid retention. Observations have shown that an imbalance of electrolytes, or a lack of potassium or calcium in the diet may increase the risk, particularly in dehydrated animals.

   Diets containing high levels of carbohydrates, such as three or more slices of bread, or large amounts of cereal-based dry food, appear to increase the risk of cramping in certain animals. Young, lightly-built bitches racing under cold conditions appear to be more prone to cramping, particularly in the later races in an evening meeting. Greyhounds that have been resting due to muscle or other injury and are given a long handslip or gallop without adequate preparation and conditioning, are also more likely to cramp.

SYMPTOMS

Symptoms of cramping vary, depending on the severity. Mild cramping in one leg may result in a Greyhound running on three legs and in severe cases, stopping in a race and even collapsing. The back and upper hind leg muscles will usually feel knotted and sore when pressed, and in severe

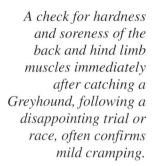

A check for hardness and soreness of the back and hind limb muscles immediately after catching a Greyhound, following a disappointing trial or race, often confirms mild cramping.

cases, become swollen after a hard gallop. However, many Greyhounds that slow up towards the end of a race, but do not show obvious signs of cramping, may have developed a subclinical form of cramping.

This is best diagnosed by catching the Greyhound immediately after a race, and examining the back and hind leg muscles for hardness and soreness. In many cases, by the time the Greyhound walks back to the kennel room, the symptoms of mild cramping will not be apparent, and this particular cause of loss of speed will not be recognised.

MANAGEMENT

Greyhounds that cramp severely and are in pain must be treated and managed under veterinary supervision. In severe cases, fluids into the vein and other medications may be required.

Because the underlying causes of cramping are not fully understood, there are a myriad of treatments that are popular for preventing cramping in the racing Greyhound. However, consideration should be given to reducing the level of carbohydrates if a lower protein, high carbohydrate dry food or bread constitutes more than 60 per cent of the ration. It is wise to cut this back to about 40 per cent, and make up the energy shortfall with 2-3 tablespoons of fat. It is also important to provide adequate levels of electrolytes, particularly potassium and calcium, in the diet. Supplementary forms of slow release potassium are recommended for excitable dehydrated Greyhounds that have a history of regular cramping. In severe cases, supplements of Vitamin E, and controlled doses of selenium as prescribed by a veterinary surgeon, may also be beneficial.

It is also essential to adopt additional management techniques in Greyhounds that cramp. Providing a rug to keep these animals warm when kennelled prior to racing, and if possible, vigorous massage of the back and hind limb muscles for up to a minute before the animal is taken to the starting area, will help to reduce the risk of cramping in nervier types of Greyhounds racing in the later races in an evening meeting. Any Greyhound that fails to finish strongly should be checked for signs of subclinical cramping in the catching area after racing.

HEAT STRESS

Greyhounds that are confined to hot poorly ventilated kennels, or accidentally left unattended in enclosed trailers or cars during hot weather, especially after a hard run or trial on a warm day, may become overheated, and in severe cases, collapse and die within ten minutes, due to heat stress. Hydrobathing a Greyhound with warm water during hot, humid weather in a confined kennel area can lead to heat stress and death within five minutes. Dehydrated Greyhounds are also prone to heat stress under hot or humid conditions. Larger male Greyhounds, and nervous, excitable, or 'over achiever' types of animal are prone to heat stress under hot conditions.

In hot, humid weather, the efficiency of cooling from panting is decreased, so it is essential that Greyhounds are given adequate fluids and electrolytes to prevent dehydration, and some form of air circulation to aid cooling. Signs of heat stress are very obvious and include rapid panting, increased heart rate and warm dry skin. A Greyhound can collapse and die if its body temperature rises above 42-43 degrees centigrade for only a few minutes.

FIRST-AID

Heat stress is an emergency situation. It is essential that the Greyhound be cooled as quickly as possible. Ideally, the Greyhound should be immersed in a tub or bath of cold water for twenty to thirty seconds at a time, or, alternatively, stand the animal and hose it down or pour cold water over the body for thirty to forty seconds at a time. Do not leave the coat saturated with water, as the animal will retain body heat. It is important to wipe off excess water and slowly massage the skin for fifteen to twenty seconds to promote circulation and cooling, then rub lightly with a dry towel. Repeat cold water hosing or immersion every two to three minutes, drying off between cooling, until the animal shows signs of responding by reducing its panting and its degree of stress.

It is very important to observe an affected animal for some time after the heat stress episode, as in many cases the reservoir of blood trapped in the gut area will raise the temperature again if the initial cooling is not adequate. It is advisable to offer cool water to drink, about a cupful every ten to fifteen minutes until the Greyhound recovers. Walking a Greyhound will also aid heat loss in between cold water immersion or hosing, and removing water trapped in the coat. In the following 24-48 hours, offer light meals with plenty of fluids, such as a thin stew, and give adequate electrolytes in the post-recovery period.

COURSING OR RACING THIRST

An insatiable thirst can develop in Greyhounds that are raced hard under hot humid conditions, especially in animals that over-exert themselves due to keenness or length of the chase or course, or are unable to be caught quickly after a race or long coursing gallop. The condition is called 'water diabetes' is some countries. This term describes the intense thirst developed by an affected Greyhound following extreme physical stress. The most common sign that alerts the owner is an empty water bowl, and urinary flood in the kennel.

Within twelve hours an affected Greyhound may drink 4-8 litres of fluids, if available, and urinate large amounts of weak diluted urine. If water is not available, or if the kidney outflow exceeds that available to replace fluids, the animal will rapidly dehydrate and lose body weight over a twelve to twenty-four hour period. In most cases this type of stress syndrome is best managed under veterinary supervision. However, limiting the amount of water to one cupful every hour for about six hours from the time symptoms are recognised, will help reverse the problem in mild cases. If the Greyhound becomes weak, loses weight and is severely dehydrated, then veterinary treatment is advised.

ACIDOSIS OR RHABDOMYOLYSIS

Although severe acidosis, or rhabdomyolysis, is not a common problem, it can have a devastating effect on a Greyhound's future racing career. Symptoms include depression, inability to walk or stand, muscle seizure with pain and swelling along the back and hind limbs, and extreme dehydration with weight loss of up to 1-2kg in twenty-four hours. It is considered to be a form of severe cramping, occurring most commonly in unfit, highly-stressed, excitable animals, or those that over-exert themselves following a collision or fall in an effort to catch the rest of the field.

Affected animals pass small volumes of urine, which is extremely dark due to muscle breakdown, and this should alert trainers to the severity of the condition. Although electrolytes and fluids, with supplements of potassium are useful in mild cases, in all cases it is best to seek veterinary advice. Dehydrated and collapsed animals must be given intravenous fluids, vitamins and metabolic aids, and be monitored over a twenty-four to thirty-six hour period. If not treated quickly, the affected Greyhound can dehydrate severely and will die within two to three days due to kidney and liver shutdown.

However, while fluid therapy under veterinary supervision is helpful in overcoming the immediate life-threatening problem, many Greyhounds are left with extreme muscle wastage along the back, which hampers return to their future racing career. Physiotherapy and exercise to rebuild wasted muscle, including measured doses of anabolic steroids and an adequate protein diet, are useful. But recovery from the more serious forms of the disease can take two to six months, and the Greyhound is unlikely to regain its previous speed or class of racing.

BEHAVIOURAL PROBLEMS

Racing Greyhounds can develop a number of behavioural problems due to their highly alert and intelligent nature. The most common is a hyperactive or excitable temperament that leads to dehydration and risk of premature fatigue when racing.

Younger bitches, in particular, can be timid in nature and 'crowd shy' at the racetrack, and lack aggression for competitive racing. A timid nature can often be overcome by kennel companionship with another more mature Greyhound, or introducing these animals in a step-wise programme to raceday practices and noise, so that they become more settled and will perform to their potential. Some supplements, such as high doses of Vitamin E or Vitamin B1, are also useful in settling nervous temperaments in some Greyhounds. Veterinary surgeons may prescribe medications that have a calming effect on the Greyhound, but obviously in most countries these cannot be used in the pre-race period.

The other common behavioural problem that develops in Greyhounds is what is termed 'fighting' or 'turning their head'. It is considered that nine out of ten male dogs may become 'fighters' due to aggression, failure to chase, muscle soreness, or simply playing during a race. Many trainers believe that nine out of ten bitches that appear to 'turn the head' when racing are actually not aggressive, but simply failing to chase properly or playing during the race. As fighting can be caused by muscle injury or other soreness, a thorough musculo-skeletal examination should be carried out. Where Greyhounds have a history of fighting, hormone therapy (male hormones for bitches, female hormones or oestrogens for male dogs) may be beneficial when given under strict veterinary supervision. However, in some cases, aggressive Greyhounds will continue to fight, and the only longterm cure is retirement.

Greyhounds can develop other habits due to boredom brought on by long hours of confinement, combined with a highly intelligent and excitable nature. These behavioural problems include tearing up their bedding, tail-wagging, barking, paw-licking, urinating in their beds, and eating their stools. A programme of regular exercise, a balanced diet, regular turnouts to urinate and empty out, and in some cases provision of kennel toys, or a companion Greyhound, are helpful. A change of bedding material, or protecting the walls with hessian or burlap bag, etc. is also useful to discourage bed destruction, or mutilation of the tail-end by compulsive tail-wagging.

The common 'bald thigh' syndrome, where Greyhounds develop areas of bare skin on the buttocks, the sides of the upper rear legs and the chest, is often caused by bedding down on hessian or burlap bags or similar material. Each time the animal gets up and down, hairs sticking through the weave in the bag are shaved off by rubbing on the bedding, or other abrasive floor surface. Although bald thighs are often considered to be stress-related, and may respond to thyroxine hormone medication, the type of bedding should be considered as an underlying cause of hair loss on the tail butt and thigh areas.

A FINAL TRIBUTE

The Greyhound is a remarkable breed of canine. Selection for speed and strength has developed a highly competitive racing animal that appears to enjoy racing to the limits of its physical capabilities. It is prone to the same musculo-skeletal and metabolic problems as other sprint athletes, due to the extreme physical stresses of racing.

However, the racing Greyhound is an intelligent animal, forming a strong bond and empathy with caring and considerate trainers and owners, in keeping with the dog as 'man's best friend'.

Greyhounds can be timid and gentle in the kennels, excited to see their owner or trainer, but out on the racetrack they become focused racing athletes. On retirement, racing Greyhounds make excellent and faithful pets. Their clean habits, short hair coats and intelligence make them excellent companion animals to have around the home. They are affectionate and are generally safe with children, although some will chase cats and small dogs as part of their race-bred instinct. The Greyhound is adaptable and obedient, and with understanding and training, a retired Greyhound can become an ideal family pet.

Chapter Sixteen

THE COURSING GREYHOUND

THE ULTIMATE TEST

Coursing is the ultimate test of a Greyhound. In fact, many people would argue that open coursing across natural country is the only legitimate way to assess the true qualities of this extraordinary breed, and that everything else – track racing, enclosed or 'park' coursing, and the show ring are all artificial abominations. Where else can you see that thrilling explosion of sprinter's pace from slips to first turn over three hundred yards in a dead-straight line? With the cramped circumference of some modern tracks, the runners would have negotiated almost three bends in that distance.

In coursing, the Greyhound's elastic agility and innate sense of balance is used to control and dominate the movement of its natural quarry, not to try to avoid the multiple first bend pile-ups, which do nothing for track racing except produce acceptable betting margins. And what else could test the courage of these amazing dogs to the point where it almost breaks your heart to see them running a two-minute trial to the bitter end, over the boundless Lincolnshire fens? This is not just the mindless slog of two laps round the track. In a course, a Greyhound stops, starts, checks, and accelerates again behind a balletic opponent over ditch and plough. As for the show ring, I pass. After a lifetime spent with dogs, I could no more tell you the 'points' of a Greyhound than whistle my way through Beethoven's Ninth Symphony; but let him run up the Withins and you can judge his looks well enough.

COMPETITIVE COURSING

A course is a match between two Greyhounds in which points are given for superior speed to the first turn made by the hare, and subsequently to the dog which forces the hare to turn, as it uses its agility to evade her pursuers. The means of deciding competitive courses were regulated by the end of the sixteenth century, and by the early 1800s the modern pattern of coursing events was established. The Swaffham Cup, still run today, was probably the first modern Greyhound stake, where sixteen Greyhounds ran in a knock-out competition in which the winners of the matches between two dogs progressed in order to the next round, until there was a final between the last two survivors. Previously Greyhounds had simply run a succession of aimless matches. Anyone familiar with modern tennis, snooker, or match-play golf tournaments knows the system. As the nineteenth century progressed, the major stakes grew from 16, to 32, and to the classic 64-dog format of the Waterloo Cup, and even to the monster 128-runner Scarisbrick or Gosforth Gold Cups.

Sports which are not decided by a first-past-the-post system always court danger and disagreement. Prize fighting was never the same again after the Marquess of Queensberry's points system replaced the scratch line. It may have been brutal but no one could quarrel with the winner,

Coursing over Epsom Downs: The sport has always attracted an enthusiastic band of followers from the time when it was first introduced to Britain.

if bleeding but unbowed, he alone after the "count" could "come to scratch" while his opponent remained senseless on the ground. Courses, however, were always decided by a complicated points system. That initial burst of speed to the first turn always received the lion's share of the marks, but then the dog with the most heart and skill had his chance as he received the points for forcing the subsequent turns from the hare.

THE JUDGE
Thomas Thacker was coursing's first celebrated judge, and drew up a code of rules which remains the basis of the modern code. He also published two invaluable books on the Greyhound as well as his Courser's Annual Remembrancer and Stud Book. Thacker was ideally suited to draw up a set of rules as he had had a lifetime's experience as a coursing judge, and it was said too that he was a natural for his profession, "having eyes like a hawk, being deaf as a post, and riding like the devil."

As in the mid 1800s coursing became more popular, and the stakes more valuable and the bets bigger, the integrity of its judges became central to the success of the sport. Will Nightingale was the first of the great professional coursing judges, and he was known with good reason as the "Chief Justice". Nightingale judged the Waterloo Cup from 1839 until 1857, except in the years when the classic meeting clashed with the Roman Camp fixture at Dalkeith outside Edinburgh, where the club dinners and the scenery were too good for him to miss. Nightingale, like all the best judges, was not only a great judge of a course but also of a Greyhound. 1850 was one of the years when he forsook Altcar for the pleasures of Dalkeith. When the Waterloo draw was known in Scotland, it was shown to Nightingale who, apart from one course where he refused to give an opinion, went straight through the card tipping every winner and finished up by saying: "The ground should suit Cerito and Neville best," – and they turned out to be winner and runner-up respectively.

Nightingale came from Gisburn in the Yorkshire Dales above Skipton, and when he was laid to rest there, it was in a coffin with a Greyhound carved on the lid. His rather grand tomb, although it has seen better days, still dominates the churchyard. The rigours of his profession took their toll – he once drove himself alone clean over the Pennines in a downpour one night, from one meeting to the next, and judged the following day without having slept. He attended meetings as a spectator towards the end of his life, driving himself in a gig as his legs had gone and he could no longer sit a horse.

When coursing became a national sport and a major betting medium with the Waterloo Cups and enclosed coursing grounds of the 1880s, a man of iron was needed to resist the temptation of the

The Judge: Ron Mills on horseback.

bribes and the baying of the mob when a favourite went down. George Warwick, who had replaced Nightingale and officiated at all Master M'grath's victories, never judged again after he had been surrounded during the 1873 Waterloo Cup final by the vast crowd, who had held him by his stirrup leathers until he pulled for Muriel. The crowd wrongly believed that Warwick had accepted £500 to "pull through" her opponent, Peasant Boy.

Warwick was replaced by James Hedley. Hedley took up judging in the late 1860s, and in his career judged some 70,000 courses. Born in Newcastleton just over the border in Scotland, Hedley followed in the footsteps of his father, who had been a considerable tenant farmer of the Duke of Northumberland, until hard times encouraged him to take up judging as a full-time profession. Previously, James Hedley had been a coursing owner, breeder, trainer, and slipper, and so he knew the game backwards. In 1859 he had taken Selby and Clive to Altcar to divide the Waterloo Cup for John Jardine.

With his career bestriding the days of the enclosed 'park' meetings with their heavy gambles and huge prize money, Hedley's inflexible honesty and commanding presence were just what was required in a judge. He was once offered £2,000 to pull a dog through the Waterloo Cup, and on another occasion, when he was approached at a Coquetdale meeting to favour a runner, Hedley was overheard to thunder: "Ye damned scoondrel; I've a good mind to cut yer heed off wi' the whip." When he retired, a testimonial of £2,500 was raised (still considerably less than the bribes he had refused in his time) to support him in his old age, which he spent playing golf, until rheumatism, brought on no doubt by the rigours of his life, crippled him.

In two hundred years of coursing, judging has been dominated by just six men: Will Nightingale, George Warwick, James Hedley, Bob Brice and his son Arthur, and Jack Chadwick. When Bob Brice retired in 1911 because of ill health, he had judged 54,326 public courses and once had judged in every month of the year by judging not only in Britain and Ireland, but in France and Russia as well. Brice, like his Waterloo predecessor, Hedley, was a man of unflinching integrity. A Russian noblewoman once exclaimed as he gave a decision on the Steppes: "Mr Brice must be a good judge. He dared to put the Emperor out!"

His sense of honour also forced him eventually to give up judging in Ireland. 'Boxed-hare meetings' were a scandal in Ireland at the turn of the century, and Brice once arrived at a meeting to find everything ready, dogs, owners, and all. There followed an inexplicable delay until Brice asked the little man standing next to him what the problem was. "I'm sorry, your honour," came the reply, "but the hares have not yet arrived." Brice immediately left the field and never went back to Ireland again. He judged thirteen Waterloo Cups between 1898 and 1910, and was the first southerner allowed to do so.

THE SLIPPER

Apart from the judge, the other key official on any coursing field is the slipper. A bad judge can disappoint a few people, but a bad slipper can ruin your dog as well as the course. Slipping at enclosed meetings is simple enough as the hare comes close to the slipper's shy, or hide, and there is no problem in releasing the dogs on the line of the hare. His only problem is to judge the strength of the hares and ensure an even length of run-up.

In open coursing, however, the hares can come in at all angles and often wide of the shy, so that the slipper has to be able to move laterally and run forward with up to 180lbs of straining dogs under control, to release them right behind the line of the hare. These problems are multiplied if the coursing is 'walked-up', where, instead of the hares being driven to the slipper by beaters, the slipper walks in the middle of a line of spectators so that the hares jump up in front of them.

At first the landowner's gamekeeper was a favourite choice as slipper, but as coursing

The Slipper: Bob Blatch waiting with a pair of Greyhounds in the slips at Newmarket.

developed, professional slippers were hired in the same way as judges. Tom Raper, the first slipper to be hired to slip as much in the South as at home, came from the little village of Gilling near Scotch Corner. If you go to Gilling today, although the last member of the Raper family to live there died some thirty years ago, opposite the pub you will find the family home, called to this day 'Waterloo House' after the event that brought Tom Raper fame and some fortune.

When the Waterloo Cup was upgraded to a 64 in 1857, Raper was sent for to slip the Blue Riband for the first time. Previously old Will Warner, Lord Sefton's volatile keeper, had done the job along with everything else. Warner had two plankmen in close attendance to help him and the dogs over the ditches, and he slipped in the 'traditional' style. He dug his heels in, held on to the dogs until the hare had her law, and then let them go. Raper was a considerable athlete, who could walk and run all day to get his dogs properly on line behind the hare.

Warner, piqued by Raper's appointment, told the plankmen to hang back to make things as difficult as possible. It made no difference to Raper, who showed he could not only clear the ditches himself with the dogs, but deliver them in mid-air if necessary. As one of the keeper's cronies was heard to say in amazement: "It won't do, Mr Warner, it won't do. Bugger goes over 'em like a pair of compasses." "His delivery is as smooth as oil," said 'Stonehenge' of Raper; and another correspondent, 'Skiddaw', called him "as fleet of foot as a cinder-path sprinter."

THE WATERLOO CUP

There is no more famous coursing event than the Waterloo Cup, and no more famous coursing grounds than the Withins and Lydiate on which the classic is held. The Waterloo Cup was created by William Lynn, the owner of the Waterloo Hotel in Liverpool, which acted as the headquarters for the Altcar Club. After a trial run for just eight dogs in 1836, the Waterloo Cup quickly grew into the championship of coursing. Lynn originally used it as part of a three-day sporting package. On the first and third days there was coursing, and on the intervening day he staged a great steeplechase at the racecourse which he had set up just down the road from Altcar at Aintree. The local press called his steeplechase 'The Grand National', and the name stuck. The Waterloo and the Grand National were run in tandem until 1857 when the coursing meeting became a three-day affair. The field with which Altcar and the Waterloo Cup is most commonly associated is the Withins. People spell its name in all sorts of ways these days, but 'Withins' it was when the first edition of the *Ordnance Survey* was published in the last century. On this reclaimed marshland it is a corruption of Withies, of course. The Withins is the masterplan of all great coursing grounds. The field itself is a tapering funnel of old turf which the hares enter by the broader end and then run past the shy towards a bank at the apex. This bank is bordered by rough grass and reeds and is topped by rhododendron bushes. Around it there are any number of 'soughs', refuges for the hares to dive into.

One of the fascinating things revealed by old newsreels of the Waterloo in the 1920s was that the bank was bare, and it was not until the 1930s that the undergrowth was planted. Like its sister field at Lydiate, the Withins is permanent pasture over peat, significantly the only grass for miles. It has been ploughed once in living memory, and that was during the War to "dig for victory".

The field is bordered on the southern side by another steep bank, the 'Popular Side' of Waterloo meetings, and on the other by a raised causeway. Behind the field there is another lane, and then the holding ground for the hares. Fenland coursing has always made good use of the inevitable watercourses, and the Withins holding ground is backed by the steep bank of the River Alt itself. The other two sides are closed off by flankers and beaters, and the beat in its last stages is slowly compressed to push the hares through a screen of artichokes, across the road and on to the back of the Withins itself.

The hares are brought towards the river bank and swung into the holding ground in a huge U-turn. This means, of course, that when they are flushed on to the running ground, theoretically with the prevailing wind behind them, they are going home and they pelt hell for leather towards the welcome refuge of the bank at the foot of the field, where the keepers feed the hares in the weeks before the meetings as a further encouragement. The net result is long, straight run-ups and the racing hares behind which a fast Greyhound can look his best.

The Withins and its companion field at Lydiate are the last of the old grounds created specially for coursing. It may seem to be a contradiction in terms to have a prepared field for "open" coursing, but all the hares live in complete freedom and the running grounds are not enclosed. The Withins, apart from having a ditch filled in and the bushes planted at the far end, has remained unchanged since Master M'Grath ran his finals there a hundred and twenty years ago. In the palmy days, great landowners competed to set up similar grounds such as Lord Lonsdale's Whinfell, J.V. Rank's Druids Lodge, and Edwin Baxter's Isle of Thanet grounds, but now open coursing must take the countryside as it finds it.

ENCLOSED COURSING

In 1876 a Sussex farmer, Tom Case, revolutionised coursing when he bought an estate at Plumpton, a little village nestling in the lee of the downs above Brighton. The whole farm ran to 1200 acres, but Case had a third of it wired, into which he introduced stocks of hares to run a coursing meeting. Hares were often moved to bolster the numbers and act as a breeding outcross on coursing estates, but Case's project was novel in two ways. Firstly, he intended to make money out of it, and secondly, he introduced a revolutionary form of coursing ground.

The use of special holding grounds for hares was nothing new. Years before at Ashdown, Compton Bottom was netted round to make sure that the hares ran out on to the down in the correct direction. Case not only fenced in the covert where the hares were held before coursing, but he fenced in the running grounds as well. Unlike the modern enclosed coursing meetings in Ireland where the whole meeting is run on one field, Case, in the beginning, used three fields at Plumpton. Each was about fifty to sixty acres in size, and nearly half a mile in length.

Case constructed two 'coverts' at either end from wire and canvas, the first to hold the hares and the second to act as an escape. The hares lived wild on the estate and were only driven into the coverts on the morning of the coursing. Beaters, trailing a long strip of canvas between them, moved across the farm at 9.00 a.m. Their job was to push the hares into the holding ground, which was about an acre in extent, where they settled until the coursing started at midday.

It soon became obvious to everyone that the success of enclosed coursing depended entirely on one factor, the strength of the hares. Case showed himself an expert in hare management right from the start, and his system had a decided advantage over the methods used in Ireland today. Case, as he owned the farm, could enjoy the luxury of preserving the hares in an entirely natural manner, with a significant proportion of them bred on the ground itself. The hares lived alongside the other 'stock' on the farm and in its usual crops. For the September meeting of 1880 the potato haulm was still so luxuriant Case mowed it before the meeting to make it easier to drive the hares out of it. With so much space to roam in, the hares were proof against sickness and, of course, enjoyed a natural knowledge of the ground, although there is no doubt that they were 'trained' up the field as well, in the same way as they are in Ireland today.

All this entailed a substantial investment, and it was Case's intention right from the start to make coursing a paying public spectacle. It was no accident that the farm stood next door to the station, and soon the 'specials' from Brighton and London were bringing down spectators by the carriage-load, who otherwise would have never thought of going coursing. A field ticket cost three shillings, and a sit-down lunch in the barn was another half-crown, similar in value to the prices you would pay to watch a day's racing today.

For the third meeting, held in March 1877, 1400 people paid to see the coursing on the first day and 600 of them sat down to the lunch, provided by a Brighton caterer with the appropriate name of Mr Mutton. His mockturtle soup was a great stand-by on a cold and wet Plumpton day. Case's coursing meant that there was no hanging about on a windswept moor waiting for a slip. Large programmes were guaranteed a finish, and courses were run at an average rate of 16 an hour.

Soon even Plumpton itself was to appear crude and primitive compared with the wonders of enclosures like Gosforth and Haydock. In 1875 the opening of Sandown Park as an enclosed racecourse – as opposed to the old open heath meetings in the style of Newmarket and Epsom where the public were tolerated rather than encouraged – signalled the beginning of a new era in making sport a commercial paying venture, and in the 1880s there was a gold-rush for the leisure money of the children of the industrial revolution.

The coursing men found it more difficult to stomach the behaviour of the crowds. Even Mr Dunn, who played a major role in the organising of Gosforth, was scathing:

"In these degenerate days it (coursing) appears to be a business, and the sporting element has been almost entirely eliminated from it. The spectators, who in former times arrived in scores, come now in their thousands. And who are they? Go to the plains of Altcar on the first day of the Waterloo meeting for the answer. The residuum, the welchers, the ruffians, the betting men with their flags and ladders and stools, their umbrellas rivalling the rainbow in their varied hues, their coats of as many colours as Joseph's, and hats which even the hatter in Wonderland would have been ashamed to have worn. Let us hope against hope that in this modern Sodom ten righteous men might have been found, whilst the clamour, and turmoil, and screaming of the odds at the top of hoarse voices in our ears created a Babel of sounds..."

Although the parks seemed at first an ideal medium for mass betting, it was not long before the shine went off it for the bookmakers. By late 1883 the *Coursing Calendar* noted little betting at Gosforth and could describe gambling at enclosed meetings as an "exact science". "Out of the thousands of Greyhounds now running, one could almost count on his fingers those that could beat the remaining lot at an inclosed meeting, where speed is always too much of a sine qua non." The death warrant for park coursing in England had been signed, not because of indifference on the part of the owners nor because of any fears about its effect on the Greyhound breed, but because the crowds dwindled and it did not pay.

IRELAND

The country most closely identified with park coursing, of course, is Ireland. The first Irish park meeting was at Mourne Park outside Belfast and started in 1879. It failed eleven years later, but the system so suited Irish conditions that park coursing had come to stay at Trobolgan, Ards Racecourse, and Purdysburn where in 1894 they ran 103 courses in a day between 11.00 am and 5.00 in the afternoon.

The Irish Cup at Clounanna for most of this century has been the definitive park meeting, and it probably gave as good an impression of what coursing might have been like at Haydock and Gosforth as anywhere. At the early meetings there the coursing was open, but sometime during the latter part of the First War it went over to the enclosed system that you see now. Even so, the trials on that massive Charity Meadow involved plenty of work after the turn and the lead could be beaten.

At Powerstown Park, Clonmel, where the National Meeting has been run since the 1920s, the lead has probably not been beaten in living memory. As well as the massive slips, the hares at Clonmel have the advantage of a ridged hill above the first turn which throws the dogs out at the turns, and so it is virtually impossible for the lead to be beaten. The first meeting was held here in 1913. The style of coursing has changed since Adair Dighton, the English Greyhound journalist who paid Clonmel a visit in the 1920s, wrote: "To be absolutely honest, I have never witnessed more work or better contested courses."

UNITED STATES OF AMERICA

Coursing is still legal in several states of America, although it lost its major role in American Greyhound sport at the end of the 1970s. Originally coursing was popular throughout the Mid and Far West as they were being settled by English and Irish farmers, although the biggest meetings were held in Kansas and Texas. Much of it was open coursing, although enclosures were often used for major fixtures. In the 1920s the National Meeting was held in a different Kansas town each year. In 1925 at Oswego the meeting went on for ten days and there were 800 entries, including some from Jack Dempsey, the world heavyweight champion. At Garnett in 1926, the mayor, city officers and 125 Greyhounds paraded behind the city band to open the meeting.

Finally, the National Coursing Association and the National Meeting settled in the old cattle town of Abilene, explaining why the American Stud Book is based there although track racing was non-existent in Kansas until very recently. The NCA ran two meetings a year in its own enclosure, including the American Waterloo Cup at its Spring Meet. The ground was on the small size, 466 yards by 200 yards, and if the course went on too long, a 'relief dog' was slipped to hurry things up. There were three judges who gave their decision by ballot.

Opposition to its coursing meetings within the NCA grew throughout the 1970s. New members were often only interested in track racing, and track races for puppies on a newly-built schooling track, adjacent to the coursing park, began to take precedence at NCA meets. With its eye on gaining new pari-mutuel betting laws in states like Wisconsin, Kansas, and Texas, the NCA changed its name to the National Greyhound Association and coursing was finally dropped by 1978.

Coursing still continues in states like California, Colorado, New Mexico and Wyoming, but it is very different from classic Greyhound coursing. American-style 'field coursing' meetings include all sight-hound breeds from Salukis to Whippets and, although the jack rabbit is usually the quarry, they will have a go at coyotes as well. Three dogs are released at a time, and the dogs are assessed by a judge on foot, who gives a total of points for each dog, which is often carried on to another meeting. The points are awarded subjectively for speed, agility, endurance, and something intriguingly termed 'desire'. Barbed wire and razor-sharp sage brush are natural hazards, although the going is best at Merced in California where major Greyhound meetings were held in the last century. It's all a long, long way from Altcar.

AUSTRALIA

The first Australian club was founded in 1867 at Narracoorte where the dogs coursed wallabies, but hares were specially introduced in 1873. In the same year Miss Heller won the first Victoria Waterloo Cup, and coursing soon spread throughout New South Wales and South Australia. At first all the coursing was on the open system, often over some pretty rough going, but the first enclosed meeting was the Victoria Cup of 1881. Enclosed coursing quickly gained the upper hand, and 'plumpton coursing', as it was known in Australia after Tom Case's original ground, continued until finally banned in all states by the 1970s.

The Australians probably brought enclosed coursing to a perfection at grounds like Geelong, Werribee, and Rooty Hill, not matched even at Haydock and Gosforth. The Victoria Coursing Club insisted that the grounds should be 650-1000 yards long and 300-400 yards wide. In 1948 at the Derby meeting at Donald there were 149 courses in which only three hares were killed, a remarkable record over such big fields.

Australian coursing was on the grand scale from the very start. In the 1880s grounds boasted a telegraph, a refreshment bar opposite the first turn, a lunch marquee, and an elevated covered box for the Press. In 1882 a Mr. Cooper imported Capri from England together with his trainer, McDougal, and lifted £40,000 in bets, worth possibly two million today.

Although live hare coursing is illegal, Australians still retain a form of "plumpton coursing", straight 350 yard sprints behind a drag hare run from slips in a coursing stake format.

PORTUGAL

Apart from Ireland and Britain, only Portugal has coursing on a significant competitive basis. There were major open meetings in the 1950s and 1960s with the Taca Fundacao as the climax of the season. The Revolution in the 1970s put an end to coursing – and every scrap of game in the Portuguese countryside – but in the past three years there has been an enthusiastic revival. Coursing is on the enclosed model but over very large grounds.

THE FUTURE

Coursing in the 1990s, therefore, is practised only in Ireland and Britain to any degree. It is probably true to say that the Irish have the best coursing Greyhounds, but the English have the best coursing. There are ninety-two coursing clubs affiliated to the Irish Coursing Club and twenty-three to the National Coursing Club, although the English clubs normally run several meetings in a season and the Irish only one. The vast majority of the Irish meetings are enclosed or 'park', while all the English fixtures are open coursing.

The future of coursing is uncertain to say the least. In Ireland, which until very recently seemed the impregnable citadel of the sport, muzzling has been introduced in enclosed coursing. The effect of muzzling appears to have been beneficial since it was extended after New Year 1994 to all enclosed courses in Ireland. Long slips and 'straight runs' became the bane of Irish park coursing in the 1980s, although it helped the hares to reach the escape unscathed. With the dogs muzzled, slippers have regained their confidence, and there was more actual coursing on Irish fields towards the end of the 1993-1994 season than had been seen for many years. On the debit side, political correctness has demanded that the Irish Cup field be shortened considerably, and the coursing at Clounanna is now a dim shadow of its former self.

In England, Wales and Scotland, where there is no enclosed coursing, muzzling is probably the one thing on which both supporters and opponents of the sport agree. 'Antis' claim that it is irrelevant, as the hare is still terrorized by the experience of being chased, while 'pros' maintain that muzzling in open coursing exposes the dogs to injury in hedges and fences and the hares to being mauled rather than quickly despatched. On average, seven out of eight hares coursed escape unharmed. There are no straight runs or courses with just one turn possible in open coursing. The sentiment appears to be that if coursing is to die, it will do so with its boots on – or at least with the muzzles off.

Chapter Seventeen

SPORTING HEROES

Greyhounds have always had a tremendous public following, with enthusiasts delighting in their speed, their elegance, and often their courage. The sports of coursing and track racing have brought certain Greyhounds to the fore for their remarkable achievements.

BRITAIN AND IRELAND

MASTER M'GRATH

Master M'Grath (Dervock – Lady Sarah) was the first Greyhound to become a national star when he won coursing's premier event, the Waterloo Cup, a record three times. During his illustrious career he met Queen Victoria, and was even depicted on the Irish sixpence.

But this brilliant creature was such a scrawny-looking sapling that he was nearly put down before he ever reached the coursing fields. The black and white dog was whelped in Waterloo Cup week, 1866, bred by Lord Lurgan's partner, James Galway, who reared Greyhounds in County Waterford, Eire. Apparently, Galway was so unimpressed by the 54lb pup that he believed he had no future. But the dog's life was spared following pleas by an orphan boy who walked him – Master M'Grath.

In 1868 Master M'Grath lined up for his first Waterloo Cup, and he won the sport's blue riband at just two years old. Competing against the very best in training, the Irish dog beat Loelia in the semi-finals and coasted to an easy victory in the final. The next year a record crowd of 12,000 gathered at Altcar to see if Master M'Grath could pull off the double. He was drawn against the great Bab-at-the-Bowster in the final, and in one of the greatest courses of all time, Master M'Grath drew away to record his second victory.

In 1870 he suffered the only defeat of his career when attempting to win the Waterloo Cup for the third time. The event was staged amid controversy, with many people saying the frosty ground was unfit for running and would produce fluke results. This proved to be the case, for not only did Master M'Grath get beaten, he was almost killed into the bargain. Racing after his quarry he plunged into the River Alt and was caught beneath the ice. As he struggled to get free, an Irish slipper, named Wilson, burst through the crowd, jumped into the river and saved the dog.

Lord Lurgan swore that Master M'Grath would never race again. But the next year his wonder-dog was as fit as ever, and he could not resist the challenge of going for a third Waterloo Cup victory. Reputedly backed to win £150,000 for his owner, Master M'Grath showed all his star quality to win coursing's premier event for an amazing third time. The dog was in his fourth season and had been defeated only once in thirty-nine courses.

*Master M'Grath:
Winner of the
Waterloo Cup on
three occasions.*

MASTER MYLES

Nobody loves a good coursing dog more than the Irish, and during his short career Master Myles enjoyed the following of a pop star. Other Greyhounds may have won more trophies, but this was the dog that all coursing fans took to their hearts. In one perfect season he was never beaten, and his last victory was in Ireland's premier event – the Mulvaney Derby at Clonmel.

Master Myles was immaculately bred. His sire, Flying Merry, had produced 1976 Derby and Irish Cup winner, Quarrymount Riki, and his dam, Better Get One, was the mother of the 1977 Derby winner, Boston Pont. Great things were expected from the hefty 95lb dog – and he did not disappoint. The Big Dog, as he became known, made his first public appearance in the 1977 Desmond Cup, and he disposed of the opposition without much trouble.

Master Myles obviously had pace, but it was not until the Listowel Cup that Jerry O' Carroll's puppy showed what he was made of. Competing against the best in running, he looked in a different class as he ran unbeaten to the final. Rumours about The Big Dog were now widespread, and a record crowd saw him dispose of the great Cisco Wood, leaving five lengths to spare.

Offers for the dog poured in, and O'Carroll turned down over £10,000, preferring to take his chance in the Corn na Feile at Abbeyfeale. Literally thousands of supporters invaded the little town on the Limerick-Kerry border, and there were mass celebrations when Master Myles retained his unbeaten record. In fact, strong men had to link arms to prevent the crowd trampling O'Carroll and his dog into the mud.

All attention focused on the 1978 Mulvaney Derby, and Master Myles gave a faultless display to win all the way through, finishing by beating Coxcomb in the final. The competition was watched by record crowds, and unprecedented scenes followed the dog's triumph.

Then news came that The Big Dog had been sold to Captain Tim Rogers and was to be trained by Dick Ryan in his second season. But tragically, Master Myles, who was unbeaten on every outing, was never to run again. In March 1978 he suffered fatal injuries during an exercise gallop, and died some ten hours later.

MICK THE MILLER

In the late 1920s Greyhound racing was catching on in Britain, but it took an exceptional Greyhound – the legendary Mick The Miller – to take the sport by storm and capture the public's imagination. Mick The Miller was bred by Father Brophy, a parish priest in Killieigh, Eire. Mick,

Mick The Miller pictured with his owner Mrs Arundel H. Kempton and two of his puppies – Mick the Mighty and Mick the Maiden – from a litter out of Toftwood Misery, whelped in June 1933.

sired by Glorious Event out of Na Boc Lei, was named after the village odd-jobs man, and he was reared for the race track. However, when he was twelve months old Mick The Miller caught distemper – often a killer disease in those days before inoculations. The youngster's life was saved thanks to the efforts of Arthur 'Doc' Callanan, manager of Shelbourne Park, Dublin, and a qualified vet.

Mick took some time to recover from this ordeal, and he did not make his racing debut until he was twenty-two months old. He won first time out at Shelbourne, in April 1928, and went on to record a run of fifteen wins in twenty outings. Father Brophy was anxious to try his speedster in the English Derby, and so the unknown Irish Greyhound set sail for England. In his first solo trial at White City, he blazed round in a record time, and soon Mick The Miller was headline news in the sporting papers. Offers for the dog poured in, and Father Brophy had to decide whether or not to part with his protégé. Finally he agreed to the sale, and an auction was held on the terraces of White City. Mick The Miller was sold for the princely sum of 800 guineas – the successful bid was made by trainer Stan Biss who was acting on behalf of London bookmaker A.H. Williams.

Mick The Miller soon started to reward his new owner. He won his opening heat in a recordbreaking 29.82 – the first time a Greyhound had ever run the 525-yard course in under 30 seconds. He continued through the competition undefeated, reaching the final as the clear odds-on favourite. Then disaster struck. Three dogs collided at the first bend and Mick The Miller trailed home. However, the race was declared void, and in the re-run thirty minutes later, he quickly made amends and took the race by three lengths in 29.96.

After the Derby, Williams cashed in on his investment and sold Mick The Miller for 2,000 guineas – the first Greyhound to exchange hands for more than £1,000. The new owner, Arundel Kempton, bought the Greyhound as a gift for his wife. Now trained by Sidney Orton, Mick The Miller went from strength to strength. He became the first Greyhound to win the English Derby in successive years, and he also triumphed in the Welsh Derby and the Cesarewitch.

In 1931, at the grand old age of five, Mick The Miller contested his third English Derby – and he very nearly pulled off the hat-trick. He reached the final and crossed the line in front. But the Greyhound Ryland R was judged to have fought and a re-run was called. This time, age took its toll and Mick The Miller could not cope with another big race. He trailed in last. However, he recovered to end his racing career on a high note, winning the St Leger.

Mick The Miller had proved exceptional as a Greyhound, and he was adopted as a national hero by the British public. He starred in a feature film called *Wild Boy,* and when he died, his body was preserved. It now stands in a place of honour in the Natural History Museum, London. Interestingly, it was discovered that this great competitor had an abnormally large heart – it weighed a phenomenal 14.5 ounces – and many believe that this was the secret of Mick The Miller's tremendous pace and stamina.

SPANISH BATTLESHIP

The astonishing achievement of winning three Irish Derbys has never been equalled, and so Spanish Battleship has earned a special place in Greyhound racing history. Sired by the dual Laurels winner Spanish Chestnut, the fawn brindle was the weakest of a litter of seven whelped in August 1951. Kerryman Tim O'Connor, the owner of a pub in Kilorglin, nursed him along, reputedly feeding him with milk and Guinness from a baby's bottle. The dog remained on the small side – his racing weight was 60-62lbs – but this did not affect his pace. He won on his debut in April 1953, and following a crack at the St Leger at Limerick, he was taken on by trainer Tom Lynch.

O'Connor thought the dog's future lay in sprinting, but it soon became clear that his early pace could be used to better advantage. At Harolds Cross he consistently set up an early lead and so the Derby was a natural target. Showing disdain for the opposition, Spanish Battleship won his first round heat, his semi-final, and then went on to beat Smokey Glen by three-quarters of length in 29.78, recording his first Derby triumph.

Despite reaching the final of the Laurels, the McCalmont Cup and the McAlinden Cup, Spanish Battleship had to wait until after his winter break for his next success, but he came back in great heart, showing the stamina and consistency that set him a class apart. He contested the Corn Tostal at Harolds cross and the Easter Cup at Shelbourne – events which ran concurrently – and both finals within seven days.

He needed a month's lay-off to recover from an injury sustained in the Callanan Cup at Harolds Cross, but he was back to his best for the 1954 Derby. In the opening heat Spanish Battleship clocked a new track record with a lightning 29.50. He was only nine spots slower in the second round, and in the semis he repeated his 29.50 run. However, Spanish Battleship's relentless progress looked like coming to an abrupt halt in the final when he missed his break. There was a stunned silence from the enormous crowd when Jimmy Dunne's Dignity was the first to show. But showing his remarkable pace, Spanish Battleship stormed ahead to win by three lengths in 29.64.

Despite his huge public following, many people thought O'Connor and Lynch were mad to attempt the treble in 1955. Spanish Battleship was four years old, and few believed he could survive against top-class opposition for four rounds. In the opening round, it seemed as though the doubters would be proved right when he was beaten by Crosty's Bell in 29.94. By the semi-finals Spanish Battleship looked more like his old self, winning in 29.74. But Crosty's Bell put this time in perspective when he won his semi in 29.53.

On the night, the crowd was behind the great Spanish Battleship, and he was backed down to 5-4 favourite, with Crosty's Bell on offer at 7-4. As the traps rose, Spanish Battleship shot out and reached the first bend two lengths ahead of Dancing Jester. Crosty's Bell was bumped and then set off in game pusuit. But this time there was no catching the flying Battleship, and he coasted home four lengths clear to win his third successive Derby.

SCURLOGUE CHAMP

When Greyhound racing was most in need of a tonic, it was provided, remarkably, by two sensational Greyhounds, running during the same glorious twelve-month period. Ballyregan Bob proved unbeatable over six bends, and Scurlogue Champ, dubbed the People's Champion, made the marathon distance his own.

Scurlogue Champ (Sand Man – Old Rip) was a real crowd-pleaser. This brilliant, but erratic Greyhound would canter for the first circuit of the track, trailing by as much as twenty lengths. Then suddenly he would move into another gear, and power through the field. From a seemingly impossible position, the Champ would surge across the winning line, often smashing the track record in the process. Trainer Ken Peckham had no explanation for his dog's extraordinary style of running – it really seemed as though Scurlogue Champ knew where the winning line was, and timed his late, late run to perfection.

At the start of 1985 he had four track records to his name, but it was when he competed in the Greyhound TV Trophy, televised by the BBC, that he became adopted as the People's Champion. Attendances soared when Scurlogue Champ was on the card, and before long he had notched up a sequence of sixteen consecutive wins. The British record stood at twenty straight wins, and the Champ looked poised to take the new title. However, controversy was never far away from the big black dog, and his title-tilt ended in disaster.

The race took place at Peterborough. Scurlogue Champ strolled out of the traps, and, following the other runners to the first bend, he stumbled – turned round and headed back to the traps. He was swiftly removed from the track – but this was not the end of the bizarre race. A spectator leapt on the track, trying to stop the leader, Sneaky Liberty. The Greyhound swerved past the trouble and went on to win. The result stood.

The People's Champion may have failed in his record-breaking attempt, but he was still a great crowd-puller. He triumphed in the Cesarewitch at Belle Vue, and seemed to be back to his best form. London bookmaker John Power saw the potential in a meeting of the two great stars of the time: Ballyregan Bob, who was proving to be supreme over six bends and Scurlogue Champ, the brilliant marathon performer. His expectations were not disappointed as crowds flocked to Wembley Stadium in December 1985 to see the John Power Showdown. Spectators wore rosettes supporting their chosen dog, and according to George Curtis, trainer of Ballyregan Bob, six out off every eight rosettes were for the People's Champion.

The distance was 710 metres, and two other fine stayers, Glenowen Queen and Track Man, made up the numbers in the four-dog race. The atmosphere was electric as traps went up. Ballyregan Bob stormed ahead, with Glenowen Queen and Track Man in hot pursuit. Scurlogue Champ walked out of the traps, trailed the field for two bends and then stopped chasing. Ballyregan Bob went on to win by 11 3/4 lengths, with Glenowen Queen and Track Man dead-heating for second place.

After the race, Scurlogue Champ's trainer, Ken Peckham, declared that his dog was lame. But George Curtis had another theory. Looking back on the race he said:

"Ken Peckham said his dog was lame, and I'm not disputing that. But in the Showdown he came out walking, like he always did. Bobby (Ballyregan Bob) shot out, and by the home straight first time round, Scurlogue Champ was thirty yards adrift. The crowd was going crazy and the hare was thirty yards in front. Scurlogue couldn't hear the hare and he couldn't see it, and I think he just packed it in. He was such a brainy dog he was almost human. This time he didn't understand what was happening, so he simply gave up. I think that Scurlogue Champ was just too intelligent."

Despite the controversies, Scurlogue notched up some notable wins in his career, and he returned in 1986 to take the TV Trophy for the second year. His final race tally was fifty-one wins from sixty-three races, but his impact on Greyhound racing can never be measured.

BALLYREGAN BOB

Some Greyhounds make their name because of their phenomenal pace, others show great consistency, notching up a spectacular series of wins. Ballyregan Bob was blessed with both these qualities – and the result was the best six-bend racer in the history of the sport with a run of thirty-two successive wins – a world record that has yet to be broken.

Ballyregan Bob, a son of Ballyheigue Moon out of Evening Daisy, had wonderful natural ability, but he had another ace card up his sleeve – he was trained by George Curtis, one of Britain's finest and most experienced Greyhound trainers. Curtis has the gift of understanding his charges, and it was his preparation of Bobby, coupled with his immaculate sense of timing, that sowed the seeds of success. Ballyregan Bob was owned by Cliff Kevern, a longtime devotee of the sport, and Cliff, accompanied by his wife, Jessie, was there to see every race Bobby ran in.

Ballyregan Bob was shipped over from Ireland when he was thirteen months of age and went straight to Curtis's Brighton-based kennel. Following some spectacular trial times, Curtis soon realised he was looking after something a bit special. Yet, even at this stage, there were problems. Bobby recorded some very fast times over four bends – he broke the track record at Hackney in the first round of the William Hill Lead, and then smashed his own record by sixteen spots in the final. But Bobby often ran into trouble at the first bend, and despite a run of eight successive wins,

Old rivals: World recordbreaker Ballyregan Bob (pictured with Jess Kevern) and Scurlogue Champ – the People's Champion – (pictured with Pat Peckham).

Curtis feared that his star runner could end up seriously injured. At Harringay, when contesting the Pall Mall, disaster struck. Ballyregan Bob hit trouble at the first and was brought down. He picked himself up, and despite being twelve lengths adrift, he took up the chase and was four lengths ahead at the trip.

George was far from down-hearted despite Ballyregan Bob's elimination from the Pall Mall. But there was something niggling in the back of his mind, which made him uneasy. This nagging doubt came to the fore following another first-bend melee, this time at Wembley. "Bobby simply did not have the pace of a classic dog to the the corner," said George. "He always stood the chance of getting into trouble – and I thought we stood a very real risk of ruining a brilliant dog."

To Curtis, the dog had the unmistakable look of a six-bend specialist – but this would mean missing the English Derby. Cliff Kevern had already backed his dog ante-post to win £7,000 for the kennel, but to his credit he backed Curtis's judgement and scrubbed the bet. "I tried not to worry about the criticisms for withdrawing Bobby from the Derby," said Curtis. My concern was with the dog, first and foremost."

Bobby's first attempt at a six-bend competition was at Walthamstow, and it was as if he knew the Curtis reputation was riding on him. He won all three rounds of the competition, and broke the track record into the bargain. From then onwards, Bobby simply went from strength to strength, notching up a succession of spectacular victories. On Derby final night there were no regrets as the sport's greatest stayer stormed to a record-breaking win in a supporting open race.

Soon Bobby had built up a run of ten successive wins. The British record, set by Westpark Mustard was twenty successive wins, but Curtis claimed he was not interested in breaking the record. His sights were set on the St Leger, the stayers' classic, a competition that Curtis had always longed to win. Bobby was in tremendous form for the competition, breaking the track record in the second round. But there was an appalling first-bend pile-up in the semi-final which was to have disastrous results. The courageous Bobby managed to jump over a fallen dog, and powered his way through to win by one length. But he had landed awkwardly, and after the race he was found to be lame with a tendon injury in his wrist.

"The most amazing thing was that he managed to carry on and win the race with an injury like that," said Curtis. "You could see the poor dog was suffering, but he wouldn't give in. He was

Ballyregan Bob in action: This superb six-bend specialist still holds the record of thirty-two consecutive victories.

determined to win." The dream of winning the St Leger – so tantalizing close – was not to be. Bobby was withdrawn from the final, and faced a long period of convalescence. Eventually, rest worked a cure, and Curtis timed his dog's comeback to perfection. Bobby stormed round the Brighton track, notching up his fourteenth victory, and following Scurlogue Champ's failure to break the British record when he reached Race 17, Bobby was now officially on course for a tilt at the record.

Bobby never looked better than in his next races. In an incredible run, he broke five track records in seven runs, and was one race away from beating Westpark Mustard's record. The venue for the Bobby's attempt on the British record was Wembley, and the opposition included brilliant marathon runner Scurlogue Champ. This was the match that everyone had been waiting for. It ended in disappointment for the connections of Scurlogue Champ – but Bobby was hailed as the new British record holder. Ballyregan Bob was now the undisputed king of British stayers, but there was another goal, which now seemed attainable. The American dog, Joe Dump, held the world record of thirty-one consecutive wins, and Curtis and Cliff Kevern decided that this was a prize that Bobby could win.

Bobby's progress towards the world title was relentless, and as he closed in on his target, his public following grew. Soon there was not a household in Britain that had not heard of Ballyregan Bob, and as an American dog held the world title, there was growing interest in Bobby's challenge from across the Atlantic. However, the demands of a Greyhound competing in top-class company for an extended period of time are very high, and when Bobby notched up victory number 27 he was found to have aggravated his old wrist injury. It seemed as though the dream was shattered. Very few greyhounds return to the track following such an injury.

"The only hope lay in rest and patience," said Curtis. "We knew it would be fatal if we tried to force the pace." Even so, few could have envisaged that it would take five and a half months before Bobby was back on the track. However, Bobby's comeback was again timed to perfection, and on a cold December night in 1986 in front of a packed stadium, he raced to victory on his home track, Brighton, to take the world title. It was a fairytale ending for Curtis and Cliff Kevern, and all the agonising months of nursing Bobby back to fitness were forgotten on that night of glory. "It was the most wonderful thing for all of us," said Curtis. "But what pleased me most was when I saw the newspapers the next day, all with Bobby making headline news. I felt we had really done something for the sport."

AMERICA

THE GREYHOUND HALL OF FAME
The Hall of Fame was established in Abilene, Kansas in 1963 to honour Greyhounds and individuals who make significant and lasting contributions to the sport. Currently forty-three Greyhounds and fourteen people have been inducted. There is an international section, and Mick The Miller (England), Mutton Cutlet, one of the foundation sires of track racing (Ireland), and Chief Havoc (Australia) have been honoured with inductions.

Tim Horan, Managing Editor of *The National Greyhound Review*, has selected four of America's great Greyhounds who have earned their place in the Hall of Fame.

FLASHY SIR
Racing from 1944 to 1947, Flashy Sir earned the reputation of being the world's greatest Greyhound. Many will make the same claim to fame for him today. So well respected was Flashy Sir that when the Greyhound Hall of Fame came about, Flashy Sir joined legends Real Huntsman

ABOVE: The Greyhound Hall of Fame in Abilene, Kansas.

LEFT: A lasting memorial is made to those great Greyhounds who have made an outstanding contribution to the sport of Greyhound racing.

and Rural Rube as the first three inductees. The National Greyhound Association also honoured his name in calling its prize for America's best distance Greyhound, the Flashy Sir Award.

Racing pioneer and Hall of Fame inductee Merrill Blair saw something special in a young pup by Lucky Sir and Flashy Harmony at a coursing meet in Abilene, Kansas, in 1944. He purchased the pup for $800 from Hazel Morrison. It was reported that Blair and his partner, Cal Ohlinger, had the opportunity to sell Flashy Sir for $1,500. They even had the cash in hand when they decided to back out of the deal.

It proved to be a wise move. In his first year and half of racing for the Ohlinger-Blair kennel, Flashy Sir won twenty-five of his first thirty-two races, including a streak of eighteen straight. His stake victories included the West Flagler Inaugural and the Taunton Derby. Flashy Sir set the 5/16 mile track records at Taunton and Raynham, and equalled the 5/16 mile and futurity records at West Flagler. His prize money totalled $10,000.

By this time, Flashy Sir had earned such a reputation that tracks paid Blair not to race the Greyhound. "At many a track this dog has been paid to stay in his kennel because he was so sure to win that the bettors placed large sums on him to collect the short price," it was reported in *The*

Coursing News. Later in 1946 Flashy Sir moved to Biscayne and the longer Biscayne Course. There he won the All-Florida Derby, setting a new track record, running 34.2 seconds. From Biscayne, Flashy Sir went to Raynham winning the Inaugural, and to Taunton for the Inaugural at those two Massachusetts tracks.

His biggest test, however, came in the American Cup Challenge at Taunton and Revere race tracks. Racing over three different distances, Flashy Sir raced against Lucky Pilot, another Hall of Famer. Flashy Sir beat Lucky Pilot in the first race over the futurity course but ran second to Pilot at the second meeting. At 5/16, twice Flashy Sir ran second to Lucky Pilot. But Flashy Sir scored two wins over the 3/8 course, and Lucky Pilot ran second and third. The third place finish in the last of the Challenge series proved to be the winning point for Flashy Sir.

Flashy Sir rested in late 1946 due to a split web in his right foot. After a recovery, Flashy Sir won the Orange Bowl Salute at Biscayne in a track-tying time of over 34 seconds over the long Biscayne Course. He also won the Raynham Inaugural, the West Flagler Inaugural and a special three-dog match race at Raynham.

"He could go around dogs in a race if the rail was blocked, and had exceptional high early foot which carried him into a long lead," wrote Joe Brown in the *Course News*. "Few Greyhounds have been able to overcome him once he got to the front."

One of his greatest triumphs came again over arch-rival Lucky Pilot in the $10,000 World's Championship Greyhound Match race series. Held at West Flagler and St. Petersburg, Flashy Sir won the event 4-1.

MISS WHIRL

If ever a Greyhound deserved the honour of Dog of the Decade for the 1960s, it would be Miss Whirl.

"Like everybody else who saw her run, I felt she was the smartest Greyhound of that time," said her owner Ralph Ryan at the time she was inducted into the Greyhound Hall of Fame in 1982. "They would go watch the re-runs the next day, and it looked like she could see trouble in front of her and dodge it. Even as a pup she was smart. On a hot day we would go out and find her sitting in a tub of water."

Miss Whirl was whelped on February 13th 1963, a brindle daughter of Ed's Silver Putty and Meanwhile. Her dam was by Saddler and Little Rosey, who was tightly linebred to the English import, Glenbawn Lass. She was raised by Ryan on his Longwood, Florida farm, leased to Larry Hughes, and trained by Larry's brother, Jerry.

Miss Whirl started at Sarasota in June 1974. Even though it was mid-season, schooling races indicated that a new star was about to shine on the racing scene. On July 1st she made her official debut, and though almost knocked down at the first turn, Miss Whirl recovered and won. She won again on July 4th, and when it was time for the Sarasota Sapling Stake, Miss Whirl's home-stretch drive earned her the trophy and a win purse of $1,250. She finished the Sarasota meet with six wins and three seconds in ten official starts. Her next stop was Colorado, where a slight injury kept her sidelined part of the season. Still she managed to finish with a 2-3-4 record in thirteen starts. For 1964, Miss Whirl received an Honorable Mention on the All-America Team.

The next year turned out to be a record-breaker for Miss Whirl. She earned $75,000 and was national champion with a record of 45-9-7 in sixty-seven starts, racing at five different tracks. She set track records at three tracks. By year's end she was the leading all-time money winner in the sport. At Orlando that year she finished 16-5-3 in twenty-eight starts, including her first of three Central Florida Derby victories. She was also the winner of a match race series against the best from Jacksonville. At Sarasota she finished with a record of 8-2 in ten starts.

That summer she raced against the heavyweights on the South Florida circuit. Her victory in the Flagler International Classic, by a margin of 8 1/2 lengths, gave her a record of 7-3-1 in eleven starts. To prove her claim as Greyhound racing's new queen, she took on the winner of the Wonderland Derby, L.L.'s Bilko, in a $10,000 winner-take-all match race series. The event lasted two races as Miss Whirl took the home opener at Flagler, then completed the job at Massachusetts. To top off the victory, she set the Wonderland track record, running 38.73. After the match race win she went back to Sarasota and had two starts, both victories and one a record-setting 37.45 performance.

Flagler followed its summer meeting with a fall meeting, and Miss Whirl was back to defend her Classic title. She did just that, finishing her ten stake starts with eight wins and a second. In the semi-finals she set a record of 36.9 for the Flagler Course. She then made an unsuccessful bid for the Biscayne Irish-American title, running only third in two starts. It was obvious Miss Whirl preferred the 3/8 course. She finished up the year in Orlando, winning her first three starts to wrap up national win honours with forty-five victories. That great year was capped when Miss Whirl was named captain of the All-America Team.

She won eleven more races at Orlando that winter, including her second Central Florida Derby crown. At Raynham she qualified for the finals of the Derby, but took a hard spill. After a brief rest she returned to the track at Sarasota, compiling a 6-2-1 record in thirteen starts, which included a win in the Sarasota Derby. At Tampa she won the Inaugural and finished the season with a 9-4-4 record in twenty-four starts. On December 6th at Tampa, she set her fourth distance record, a 37.15 mark, recognised as a world record at the time.

She finished the year the second leading vote earner to Westy Whizzer on the All-America Team. Still her racing career was far from over. In 1967 she won ten more races at Orlando including her third Central Florida Derby title. After she lost three straight 3/8 races to Irish Tray, rumours that she was washed up began circulating around the track. What followed was one of the most amazing parts of her career. She posed a twelve-race win streak.

At Tampa that autumn she won three of her first four starts, the last two by 11 lengths. On November 11th she won her last race, career win number 115, and came off the track with a hip injury. For the third straight year she was named to the All-America Team, and for the second time she was named captain.

Her career record was 115-40-29 in 232 starts. It was the most wins by any Greyhound in the United States at the time. She also became the sport's all-time money-winner with earnings of $108,000. That record stood for nearly a decade. Miss Whirl continued to win races through her offspring. One of her sons, Axe Maker, broke many of his mother's win records in Central Florida.

DOWNING

It is doubtful that any Greyhound has enjoyed as much success in a single year as did Downing in 1977. Before Downing (a son of Big Whizzer and Hookers Flower) had enough starts to win a Grade A race, his owners entered him in the $115,000 Hollywood World Classic. Downing met the challenge impressively with a win. The 1977 World Classic was being promoted as the Super Bowl of racing at that time. Downing's victory not only made national TV news, in which millions saw the replay, but internationally known magazine *Sports Illustrated* carried an in-depth feature.

Downing followed that stake victory with a win in the 15,000 dollar Hollywood Futurity. After Hollywood, Downing went to Biscayne and won the $71,500 Biscayne Irish-American. What followed many still consider today the greatest match-race series in the sport's history – Downing and the great Rooster Cogburn. Downing won both legs of the event, at Biscayne and Wonderland. He also stayed at Wonderland to capture the Battle of the Ages Stake. That summer, Downing

Downing: A big winner on the track, and a highly influential sire of the eighties. Inducted into the Hall of Fame in 1984.

travelled out west to the Black Hills where he won a match, lowering the track record by nearly half a second. Downing's final stake victory came in the prestigious American Derby at Taunton.

He finished the Hollywood meet as track champ with a record of 16-0-1 in twenty starts. At Wonderland his record was 8-0-2 in ten starts. His short career record included thirty-five wins, one second and five thirds in forty-eight starts. He established new single-year and career earning records for the spurs, having collected 124,471.57 dollars in purses. He won the Rural Rube Award (the NGA's award for the fastest sprinter) and was named captain of the All-America Team.

"He had a real temper, but it was short-lived," said Keith Dillon, who stood him at stud. "He would get mad at another dog and he would just go over and knock him down."

"He became an adopted son of mine," said trainer Don Cuddy. "I hope everyone has a Greyhound half as wonderful as he was."

An injury forced his retirement in 1978 where he was syndicated as a stud dog. Downing was owned by Jim Frey and raced for the White Shadows Kennel co-owned by Willis Lawson. As a sire he became one of the sport's most influential sires of the 1980s. He appeared in the Top 10 of the Sire Standings from 1982 through 1986, capturing national titles in 1983, 1984 and 1985 (overall standings and sprint). He was placed third in 1982, and was third and fifth on the Distance Sire Standings in 1984 and 1985, respectively.

"No sire of the eighties gave the sport more impact-sons to carry on the family's name than Downing," said Gary Guccione, in 'Great Names' in *Pedigrees Vol. II*. "Leading the way was Perceive (out of Lucky Carmell), who would join his dad in the Hall of Fame." Perceive was a three-time All-American and sire of All-Americans Blendway and Keefer.

Downing's cross with Irish bloodlines became legendary. Some of Downing's offspring that became great track stars or producers are: Swift Kick (by grandsire Single Solution), Fallon (by dam Curryhills Jem), Havencroft (by grandsire Rocktown Darkie), For Real (by dam Moss Drain), Bold Footprint (by dam All Heart), Understood (by grandsire Dillard), Nicky Finn (by grandam Countess Gazette), and Barry Lyndon (by grandsire Top Speed).

DUTCH BAHAMA

"What made Dutch Bahama such a good Greyhound was his intelligence," said owner Herb 'Dutch' Koerner. "His mother and his grandmother were both intelligent Greyhounds," Koerner said. "They just knew how to race. Those are your good ones. And this is the reason Bahama was such a good stud dog – he was so intelligent."

Dutch Bahama was whelped in January of 1982 out of Hairless Joe and Dutch Debit. Dutch Bahama's intelligent racing earned All-America status two straight years. He captained the 1984 team, and a year later came as close as any Greyhound in winning both the NGA Flashy Sir Award, presented to the America's best distance, and the Rural Rube Award, honouring the best sprinter. Bahama won the Flashy Sir Award and placed second in Rural Rube balloting. It was inevitable Dutch Bahama be inducted into the Hall of Fame.

"He's the best dog I have ever been around," Koerner said at the time of his induction. "I have had a lot of fast dogs and I have had intelligent dogs, but he knows how to run a race. He never was a breaker, but he knew how to win."

Just how smart was Dutch Bahama? Koerner used an incident at the American Derby to illustrate. He was in the kennel compound and noted Bahama was standing up in his crate leaning against the side. "I asked the trainer what was wrong," Koerner said. "I walked over to let him out. The scale was across the room and Bahama walked over and got on the scale. The trainer said: "Oh, heck, I forgot to weigh him this morning." I went over and weighed him and he went back to his crate and laid down. He knew he hadn't been weighed, so he wouldn't relax until he was weighed."

Bahama's sire, Hairless Joe, was track champ at Lincoln Park in Rhode Island in 1979. He won twenty-five races that meet. Hairless Joe (Trap Rock – Kahana) was purchased by Koerner in 1981. Koerner stood him at stud on his farm in Hays, Kansas. Dutch Debit came from a good litter that won over 250 races for Koerner. Out of Woodward and Dutch Discreet, she is also the dam of All-America Dutch Delusion.

Dutch Bahama started his career in Colorado where he won the Pueblo Puppy Stake. He also ran third in the Cloverleaf Classic in 1984. He so impressed his owner that Koerner sent him to the East Coast to compete in stake races. At Biscayne, racing over the longer Biscayne Course, he captured the Irish-American – a stake race which challenges Irish Greyhounds and their descendants with American-born champions. Next on his list of stake victories was the American Derby at Raynham-Taunton near Boston, Mass. Here Dutch Bahama showed his ability to win over the longer 3/8 course. It was a great year for Dutch Bahama, who was rewarded when he was named captain of the All-American team, an award presented by the American Track Operators Association.

But 1985 proved to be a greater year. Dutch Bahama repeated as American Derby champion. He also finished second in the $100,000 Greyhound Race of Champions and the $150,000 Wonderland Derby. A third place finish in the Rhode Island Derby gave Bahama not only a second spot on the All-America Team but the coveted Flashy Sir Award. Named after one of America's greatest racers, Flashy Sir, the award is voted on by National Greyhound Association members for the best distance.

Dutch Bahama's career did not end upon retirement. He went on to become one of this country's most sought-after sires. He has produced more litters than any other sire in America, probably in the world. One of his daughters, Swedish Episode, went on to become an All-American. Her entire litter included top-grade and stake winners. Jamaican Episode won the Southland Derby. A son, Allegis, runner-up in the Greyhound Race of Champions, was also an All-American in 1989.

In 1991 Dutch Bahama was the second ranked sire overall, the number three ranked sire for sprinters, and the top ranked sire for distance dogs in the *Greyhound Review* Sire Standings. A year later he was the top ranked sire overall, runner-up sire among sprinters and top-ranked distance producers. He is expected to lead all three categories when the 1993 standings are published. Some of his stake-winning sons and daughters are Solution, Dutch Shannon, Dutch Dugan, Coastal Sunset, Flying Missille, Buzz Around, Elect Bush, Market Tipster, Noble Cause and Flying Riflelady.

AUSTRALIA

CHIEF HAVOC

In Australia during the latter half of the 1940s there emerged in Greyhound racing a wonder dog who would eventually become a household name throughout the country. His name? – Chief Havoc. With Australian sport making its unrestrained emancipation from the Second World War, Chief Havoc became Greyhound racing's knight in shining armour, a canine salvation who, in 1947, was acclaimed to be the world's fastest Greyhound.

A wonder of his time, Chief Havoc astonished Greyhound's racing fanatics with his record-breaking performances. He smashed track records over distances ranging from 345 yards to 800 yards and is arguably the most versatile Greyhound to have graced a racetrack. The Chief Havoc story originated in 1944, at a time when all Sydney greyhound meetings were transferred to Harold Park. (Wentworth Park was utilised as a temporary base for the Allied troops.)

Two predominant figures in the creation of a canine legend were Rus Westerweller, a public trainer of Gunnedah, Northern New South Wales and Ernie Swan of Manilla. Westermeller raced Naw's Own on lease from Swan and trained Trion which was bred by Mrs Swan. Their clash in the 1944 NCA Trophy was to be the catalyst of a breeding venture that would ultimately produce a Greyhound immortal – Chief Havoc.

Whether it was design or sheer luck, Westerweller and Swan decided upon a mating between Trion and Thelma's Mate – a litter sister to Naw's Own. It was to produce an impeccable pedigree that crossed back to Sterling and imported sire, Great Limes. This 'union' was the first for Trion, who boasted imposing racetrack credentials. He was a winner of forty races on fifteen different tracks throughout New South Wales.

Thelma's Mate whelped her first litter, comprising six dogs and two bitches. Enter another prominent figure in the Chief Havoc story, Jack Millerd of Werris Creek, who sent a letter requesting a pup from the litter. The wheel of fortune certainly turned favourably for Millerd, who purchased a five-week-old white and fawn dog for the princely sum of eight guineas in October 1944. Chief Havoc or Patches as he was affectionately called, became a mollycoddled member of the Millerd family. He was reared in the backyard and if it rained, he sought sanctuary on the verandah.

Chief Havoc commenced his career in a blaze of glory. At the tender age of nineteen months, he won his heat and final of the Grafton Easter Maiden. He was backed off the map in his heat, firming from 4/1 to 2/1 favourite. Chief Havoc would never start at such "liberal odds" for the remainder of his highlight-studded racing career. The tag – World's Fastest Greyhound   was justifiably bestowed upon Chief Havoc following a dazzling track record performance over 520 yards at Casino. Chief Havoc took almost ten lengths off the previous mark, and immediately he was the subject of some substantial offers from syndicates and sportsmen wanting the most valuable piece of 'canine flesh' in the country. However, Millerd refused the temptation of selling his Champion, knowing full well Chief Havoc's stud potential on retirement from the racetrack.

At Casino's next meeting, Chief Havoc had patrons and respected judges of greyhound ability

Chief Havoc: This dog raced in the 1940s and was acclaimed as the world's fastest Greyhound.

spellbound with an electrifying effort to smash the 440 yards record. The price of greatness was the refusal of owners and trainers to nominate their greyhounds against The Chief. As a consequence, small invitation class fields and a match race were organised. Chief Havoc was pitted against Park's track specialist, Beau Magee, over the short-course of 325 yards in a spine-tingling match race. Backing their judgment, the connections of Beau Magee accepted a £250 side-wager, believing the distance was unsuitable for Chief Havoc. They were right, but only just. Chief Havoc failed by a head to overhaul Beau Magee in course record equalling time.

Late in 1946 Jack Millerd relocated from Werris Creek to Carroll, where he operated a general store (Carroll is situated 12 miles from Gunnedah). Chief Havoc faced his 'litmus test' in November 1946 – his metropolitan debut. He was graded against a top-quality field at Harold Park over 500 yards, including track record holder, Blonde Glen. The legend was in the making! Chief Havoc demolished the field, winning by six lengths, and registered the time of 27 seconds, only 2/10ths of a second outside the track record!

At Wentworth Park the following month, Chief Havoc clocked a stunning 30.20 over 500 yards in the sprint championship. Chief Havoc only raced at Wentworth Park on two occasions for the perfect score. Maitland was the venue for Chief Havoc's first distance attempt in January 1947. And what a staying debut it was! Chief Havoc battered his rivals into submission, winning by twelve lengths in 40.70 over 740 yards. The time was six lengths under the previous record. At Harold Park nine days later, he equalled the 800 yards record held by his grandsire, Robert Kent.

Chief Havoc's most publicised run was on May 24th 1947, when he made a solo attack on all existing Harold Park records. A near capacity crowd of 17,000 Greyhound fans witnessed his amazing attempt. Chief Havoc broke the 440 yards record, equalled the 500 yards record and broke the 660, 700, 750 and 800 yards records. His performance was even more phenomenal considering the track was not rated fast, and there were reports that Chief Havoc had blisters on his hindquarters and between his toes. Chief Havoc's solo attempt also proved financially rewarding for Millerd. He earned £250 plus £100 appearance money and £25 for each record.

Following the solo run, Millerd dropped a bombshell to the large media contingent, announcing Chief Havoc's retirement to stud duties. Chief Havoc's introductory service fee was the highest ever for a sire in Australia. The Champion commanded a £25 fee, compared with the average stud fee of £5-£10 in 1947. Millerd was ultra-conservative with the usage of Chief Havoc as a sire. As a result, Chief Havoc only covered approximately forty-five matrons in his first season – an unbelievably low figure for a Greyhound of his calibre by today's standards.

Ironically, Chief Havoc never raced on his home track (Gunnedah). But after trialling nearly one second under the Gunnedah track's 450 yard record, Chief Havoc made a successful comeback. His reappearance on the Greyhound stage took him first to Dubbo, where he played a cameo role in a match race. Starting at the prohibitive odds of 1/5, Chief Havoc set new figures over the 345 yards short-course. Chief Havoc competed in only another seven starts, securing four wins and two placings, including a metropolitan record-breaking Harold Park distance championship victory. The Greyhound megastar contested a total of thirty-six starts for the sensational record of twenty-six wins, five seconds and two thirds. In the process, Chief Havoc established ten track records and equalled six, on fourteen different New South Wales tracks.

His exploits as a sire are also legendary. Chief Havoc's stud earnings were estimated at £14,000, which was big money in the late 1940s, early 1950s. The National Coursing Association records reveal that Chief Havoc has 453 registered litters in the Australian and New Zealand Greyhound Stud Book. The Chief received recognition as a sire of top-quality brood bitches. A select list includes: Macareena (dam of Rocket Jet), Gorgeous Babe (dam of Magic Babe), Lady Janellen (dam of Sunview), Kay Havoc (dam of Dasher's Bow), Maggie Moss (dam of Elsie Moss), and Another Havoc (dam of Havoc Rise – this produced the foundation dam line of Tivoli Chief, sire of Temlee).

Chief Havoc also produced outstanding sires such as Plunkett's Pride, Oakleigh Chief and Gogadalla. Gogadalla sired Classy Jane, the dam of Black Top. Many Champion Greyhounds of the 1950s and 1960s were line-bred to Chief Havoc. Zoom Top – unquestionably the greatest bitch ever to grace Australian tracks – had The Chief's blood coursing through her veins. Benjamin John and Shan's View, both leading sires in New South Wales and Victoria in the 1960s and 1970s, passed on to their offspring the white and fawn Champion's attributes.

Millerd and Chief Havoc had an extraordinary affinity. Gunnedah locals recall Millerd walking down the main street with Patches, minus collar and lead, beside him. Chief Havoc passed away peacefully in his sleep in 1957 at the age of thirteen. Possibly his greatest honour was his induction in April 1963 to the American Hall of Fame in a ceremony held at Abilene, Kansas.

A tragic chapter in the Chief Havoc story was the death of Jack Millerd in a road accident. Millerd lived for Greyhound racing, but ironically it was this love of the sport which was responsible for his death. Millerd was leading descendants of his former Champion to trials at Gunnedah in March 1966 when fate struck him a cruel and tragic blow. In a fitting tribute, the Gunnedah Greyhound Club and the Owners, Breeders Association erected a life-size monument of Chief Havoc at the track's entrance, not far from his resting place.

ZOOM TOP

Australia's First Lady of Greyhound racing during 1968/69 is the undisputed Champion of Champions, Zoom Top. Whelped in August 1966, Zoom Top (Black Top – Busy Beaver) was bred and raced by Hec and Leah Watt. The superstar commenced her racing career at just under fourteen months of age and made the meteoric progression to canine immortal. Her distinguished racing career spanned two and a half years in which she established fifteen track records and won on twenty-four tracks in four States. Amazingly, Zoom Top raced on 136 occasions for the superb record of sixty-eight wins, twenty-five seconds, and fourteen thirds, netting an Australian stakes record of A$59,032. Considering the spiralling prize money levels in the modern era, Zoom Top's stakes figure is phenomenal and would easily match the earnings of current top winners.

Zoom Top inherited classical bloodlines which made her a true aristocrat. Her sire was the

Zoom Top took the Australian racing scene by storm, winning all the major competitions during her outstanding racing career.

legendary sprinter and stud supremo, Black Top, and her dam was the prolific producer, Busy Beaver. Zoom Top was the top gun in a litter which won a cumulative total of 146 races (Zoom Top: sixty-eight; Busy's Charm: fifty; Top Bomber: fourteen; Busy's Gem: twelve; and Busy's Ace: two). Unplaced only twenty-nine times in 136 starts, Zoom Top started favourite on ninety-five occasions. She established track records at Wentworth Park, Beenleigh, Richmond, Dapto, Temora, Newcastle, Cessnock, Bulli, Gosford, Mossvale, Taree and Wangaratta. Zoom Top's record on New South Wales metropolitan tracks is fantastic: Harold Park – forty-four starts for twenty wins; Wentworth Park – twenty-eight starts for eleven wins. Zoom Top's superlative performances earned her dual New South Wales Greyhound of the Year honours (1968, 1969).

'Sweetie', as she was affectionately known, took the Greyhound world by storm, winning the Wentworth Park Gold Cup, Association Cup, Beenleigh Championship, New South Wales St. Leger, Sydney Cup, Dapto Silver Collar, Summer Cup and Richmond Oaks during that year. And in 1969, Zoom Top virtually repeated the dose, making it successive Wentworth Park Gold Cups, Association Cups and Beenleigh Championships. The Iron Lady also added the NCA Cup (Sandown Park), Olympic Park Distance Championship and the Hobart Thousand (2nd) for good measure.

The Rossmore Rocket retired on April 11th 1970. Unfortunately, Zoom Top did not achieve the same distinction as a brood matron. Her maiden litter (November 1973) to Thunder Lane produced nine pups, her second and final litter to Benjamin John (January 1976) were whelped when she was at the ripe old age of nine and a half years. The resultant litter comprised three bitches, with two being registered and trained by Hec Watt (Zoom's Wealth and Madam Zoom). Zoom Top died on November 23rd 1978, aged twelve years and three months. The hallmark of her greatness can be measured by the gold and silver trophies which fill a complete room. Zoom Top was the prima donna. Unquestionably, she is the greatest race bitch in Australian greyhound history.

TEMLEE

Temlee was the all-conquering canine monarch of the mid-seventies and early eighties and is synonymous with immortality. A brindle dog, Temlee was whelped in March 1972 by Tivoli Chief out of Temora Lee. His sire, Tivoli Chief, was bred and raced in New South Wales, but commenced stud duties at Tony Marion's Diamond Creek property in Victoria. Tivoli Chief was an unproven sire when mated with Temora Lee. He later became leading metropolitan sire in Victoria and South Australia during the 1976 and 1977 seasons. Temlee's dam, Temora Lee, was bred by astute New South Wales breeder Tony Duke and was eventually purchased by Victorian trainer Tom Davidson for A$800. Tragically, due to severe wrist problems, Temora Lee never raced in Victoria.

Prior to his death, Tom Davidson made a verbal request that all his Greyhound stock should be humanely destroyed. However, in a strange, but fortunate, quirk of fate, his wife, Mary, decided against her late husband's request and gave Temora Lee to Barry Bailey for breeding purposes. Temora Lee whelped her first litter in March 1972, comprising four dogs and four bitches. The litter was registered in Mary Davidson's name, although Barry Bailey paid the stud fee, cared for Temora Lee during her pregnancy, and whelped and reared the litter. Later, he purchased Temora Lee for A$250.

When the litter was eight weeks old, Barry Bailey and a family friend, Frank Cray, produced the entire litter outside local publican Ray Hocken's Maffra Hotel for his

Temlee: The all-conquering hero of the mid-seventies and early eighties.

inspection. Ray Hocken was impressed, and he purchased a brindle dog pup for a meagre A$135. He then commissioned Frank Cray to rear and train the brindle pup, which they christened 'Tiger'.

Frank Cray relates: "At eleven weeks of age Tiger was diagnosed by veterinarian Dr Phillip Kidd as having a severe bout of hepatitis and distemper. He was given the biggest injection I have ever seen." For the next eight weeks, Tiger received around-the-clock attention inside the Cray's family home. The medication and tender loving care were successful and he made a complete recovery. Bailey had offered a replacement for the ill pup, but Cray and Hocken decided to take the chance with Tiger. Tiger, alias Temlee, had his first race at seventeen months. Amazingly, his racing career only spanned fifteen months. Trained by Frank Cray, Temlee contested thirty-seven races for twenty-five wins and three placings. He amassed stake earnings totalling A$26,000, plus a motor vehicle. On March 25th 1974, in the Autumn Trophy final (511m) at Olympic Park, Temlee established a track record of 29.67. Temlee held the sensational mark for over ten years until enigmatic sprinter, Super Max, finally eclipsed the record on August 6th 1984, registering 29.66. During 1974 Temlee recorded the second fastest time for the year at Wentworth Park, He clocked a scintillating 30.78 in the New South Wales Derby heats (530m), defeating Early Copy by eight lengths.

Without doubt, Olympic Park was Temlee's favourite track. He won thirteen races over the sprint at 'headquarters': 29.67 rec., 29.71, 29.91, 29.96, 30.05, 30.11, 30.15, 30.20, 30.25, 30.71, 30.90 and two handicap wins, 29.08 (10 metres) and 29.44 (9 metres). Temlee raced for the last time at Olympic Park on November 25th 1974. He was severely injured during the race and was found to have a cracked bone in his left hind leg. He was retired to stud at the age of two years and eight months, leaving behind a magnificent list of racetrack accomplishments. His career highlights were: Won 1974 National Sprint Championship (Olympic Park). Won 1974 Maturity Stake (Olympic Park). Won 1974 Lord Mayor's Trophy (Olympic Park). Finalist 1974 NSW Derby (Wentworth Park). Finalist 1974 Melbourne Cup (Sandown Park).

Temlee was transferred to Tony Marino's Diamond Creek property to stand at stud alongside his sire, Tivoli Chief. Temlee's introductory stud fee was A$300 in 1975 and progressively spiralled to 1,000 dollars by October 1979 – an Australian record. National Coursing Association records reveal that Temlee has 735 litters registered in the Australian Stud Book. His progeny totalled a staggering 4410 and his earnings were 500,000 dollars. Temlee's progeny won 1800 races on five metropolitan tracks in three States (Olympic Park, Sandown Park, Harold Park, Wentworth Park and Gabba) between 1976 and 1985. Temlee headed the Victorian Metropolitan Sires List for five consecutive years (1978-1982) and won the Gabba Sires Premiership (1980/81 and 1981/82). He was also runner-up behind Waverly Supreme for two years in the Sydney Sires Premiership. Temlee reached his pinnacle as a sire in 1979 when his progeny won 220 metropolitan races on Victoria's two major tracks, Olympic Park and Sandown Park – another Australian record.

His progeny, who held twenty-eight race records at one time throughout Australia, have won virtually every Classic on the Australian greyhound racing calendar. Thirty-five of his stock are/were registered stud dogs, including Satan's Legend, Tempix, Tangaloa, Chief Dingaan, Roy Trease, World Acclaim and Little Blad. An abbreviated list detailing highlights of his progeny includes:

Satan's Legend: Broke the world record at Harold Park (457 metres), registering 25.95 in winning the 1978 Bi-Annual Classic. He also won the 1977 Silver Chief and 1978 Maturity Stake.

Tangaloa: Won the 1978 Melbourne Cup; 1980 Australian Cup and runner-up 1979 Australian Cup.

Winifred Bale: Dual New South Wales Greyhound of the Year (1982-83) and first Australian Greyhound to earn more than 100,000 dollars in prize money.

Tempix: Won 1978 Silver Chief Classic; runner-up 1980 Australian Cup; Victorian Greyhound of the Year (1979-80) and leading Victorian Metropolitan Sire in 1984.

Chief Dingaan: Leading Victoria Metropolitan Sire 1985-86 inclusive.

World Acclaim: Leading Sydney Sire 1985-86 inclusive.

Flat Flyer: 1982 Victorian Greyhound of the Year.

Temlee has sired the winners of virtually every feature event on the Australian Greyhound racing calendar. These time-honoured Classics include: New South Wales St Leger (1981, 1982, 1983); New South Wales Bi-Annual Classic (1978, 1982, 1982); Adelaide Cup (1977, 1978, 1979); Futurity (1980, 1982, 1983); Sandown Cup (1979, 1980, 1981); Australian Cup (1980, 1983); Silver Chief (1977, 1978); Maturity (1978, 1981); Sandown Laurels (1977, 1982); National Sprint

Championship (1981, 1983); Association Cup (1977, 1982); Vic Peters Memorial (1981); Sydney Cup (1983); Ladies Bracelet (1983); National Distance Championship (1983); Melbourne Cup (1978); Hobart Thousand (1982); Darwin Cup (1982); Sapphire Classic (1979). In addition Temlee has sired three Victorian Greyhounds of the Year (1979/80, 1982, 1983), South Australian Greyhound of the Year (1981) and New South Wales Greyhound of the Year (1982, 1983).

Temlee died on November 18th 1984 after suffering a stroke. He was twelve years and eight months old. The demand for Temlee as a sire was so great that Tony Marino had to refuse at least sixty bitches per month while he was at his peak. During his last two years, Temlee served only a handful of bitches. He had been partially blind during the last seven years of his life. Following his death, saddened stud master Tony Marino could not provide enough superlatives to describe the legend.

"He was the greatest sire in the world and the first Greyhound to command a A$1,000 stud fee," Marino said. "I feel as though a part of me has gone. I have always said that the day Temlee dies, I will retire from the sport."

Temlee has created his own dynasty as a sire. He received the sport's ultimate accolade when he was awarded the 1974 Victorian Greyhound of the Year honours. Given the flamboyant words of boxing great Muhammed Ali, Temlee could lay justifiable claims to Ali's well-worn statement: "I am the greatest." And a fitting epitaph? The King is dead, but his legend lives on!